THE RIGHT PLACE AT THE RIGHT TIME

Finding A Job in the New Economy

Robert Wegmann, Ph.D.
University of Houston-Clear Lake

Robert Chapman, Ph.D.
King, Chapman & Broussard, Inc.

1○ TEN SPEED PRESS

1☉ TEN SPEED PRESS
P.O. Box 7123
Berkeley, California 94707

Book Design by Fifth Street Design, Berkeley, CA
Cover Design by Fifth Street Design, Berkeley, CA

Library of Congress Cataloging-in-Publication Data

Wegmann, Robert.
The Right Place At The Right Time.

Includes index.
1. Job hunting—United States.
2. United States—Occupations.   I. Title.
HF5382.75.U6W45 1986   650.1′4   86-6047
ISBN 0-89815-175-9 (pbk.)

Printed in the United States of America

 2 3 4 5—91 90 89 88 87

Acknowledgments

A great many creative pioneers have discovered and refined the methods used in this book. I have tried to cite specific works when dealing with their major contributions. In addition to these specific citations, I would like to recognize my overall debt to their efforts.

While a listing of each individual name would go on for pages, I cannot avoid mentioning Richard Bolles and Miriam Johnson. Both have done ground-breaking work without which this book could not have been written. Each has made a major contribution to my understanding of how the job choice/job search process works. Both have an overwhelming concern for the plight of the unemployed person. They also share a special feeling for those who do not understand how the employment system works, and who therefore feel they are always on the outside looking in.

If this book has the feel of reality, a major debt of gratitude is owed to my students, and to the unemployed with whom I have worked over the years. I have watched them struggle to sort out their priorities and find potential employers. I have seen them suffer through nail-biting periods when everything looked good but no definite offer had been received. This has shown me, better than any research could, how stressful unemployment can be, and how important it is to know how to handle it.

Bob Chapman's work on this book was made possible through the generosity and patience of his partners, since the time devoted to writing meant doing less corporate work. Bob, too, acknowledges his gratitude to the unemployed with whom he has worked, and their openness during the often painful time spent moving from one position to another.

Howard Eisner, Helen Heyder, Elizabeth Neeld and Kim Soltero read drafts of this book as it evolved, and made thoughtful and critical comments. Their assistance is gratefully acknowledged. George Young acted as editor, and also contributed to the book you are now reading. The support and help of everyone at Ten Speed Press is much appreciated.

Anna Mae Bozsin and Tami Leger at the University of Houston-Clear Lake, and Debbie Kelsoe at King, Chapman and Broussard, Inc., typed parts of this book, putting sections on computer disk. From then on, my Compaq Deskpro performed beautifully as I made multiple revisions. The text was sent, on disk, to Fifth Street Design in Berkeley, where type was set electronically.

The information in this book has been gathered from a wide variety of sources. Despite all my efforts to be accurate, and despite the many excellent suggestions made by those who read the book in its initial drafts, there are no doubt still some errors, as well as much that is incomplete. These imperfections are, of course, my responsibility.

R.G.W.

Table of Contents

Foreword

It has been said often, but it needs to be said again: the job hunt is essentially a search for information. Information about where "the jobs" are. Information about who is hiring, and....like that.

So, let's not call your search for a job "a job hunt." Let's call it what it is: "your information hunt." The better you are at hunting for information, the better you will be at finding that job. The more information you have at your fingertips, the faster your job hunt will proceed to a happy conclusion.

In that process this book should be a great help. Here is gathered information that otherwise you would have to dig up from many different sources. One cannot say that "here is all the information you will need, for your job hunt." But one can say, "here is much of the information that you will need."

That information, of course, is only as reliable as the person who gathered it. So, let me say a word about the author. I have known Bob Wegmann for a number of years now. He has worked with me often in workshops I have run. He is aware of every study, set of statistics and latest research finding about the subject of the job hunt or career change that you could possibly want to know. He stays up-to-date, rather than resting on his laurels. He speaks and writes well.

But beyond all this, he has kept a sense of wisdom and balance about him. He knows how to use statistics, when to trust them and when to distrust them and how to make them serve the thoughtful job hunter.

He also knows that the most valuable information a job hunter can have is not information about what's available "out there," but some sure and certain information about what's going on "in here" — within the job hunter — in terms of what kind of work you really want to do. And, in his courses at the University of Houston-Clear Lake, he has tested and mastered effective techniques for helping the job hunter to find that most valuable information.

This book exhibits, of course, all the characteristics of Bob Wegmann that I have just alluded to. It contains the most up-to-date facts and figures, but beyond that, it uses them with wisdom and balance, and sets them within the larger context that many books on job hunting overlook: how do you figure out what you most want to do. The book has many effective exercises for getting at that. So, it should help you to have a more effective information hunt, wherever you live and whatever you want.

Happy Information Hunting!

Richard N. Bolles

Preface

Knowing how to find a desirable, appropriate job in a reasonable amount of time is an essential adult survival skill. Yet this skill is rarely discussed, and even more rarely taught. Everyone is somehow supposed to learn all they need to know on their own. In today's highly competitive job market, that puts many people in a very difficult and frustrating situation.

This book is written in the belief that occupational choice and job search skills can and should be consciously learned and taught. A body of both research findings and practical experience has been built up on these topics. The purpose of this book is to share this information with you. Our hope is that your job choice and job search efforts will be more effective as a result.

This book contains a synthesis of information from a wide variety of sources. The stimulus which led to my interest in these topics occurred one summer a decade ago when I first came upon a book with the odd title, What Color Is Your Parachute? In it I found the results of an extensive, two year search by the author, Richard Bolles, to discover an effective approach to employment problems.

My reaction to Bolles' book was two-fold. First, my sociological training suggested that the book's stress on informally approaching employers was sound. This is how the world works. Second, I was struck by the fact that, despite many years of education (including three graduate degrees), I had never before come across this essential information.

I began to read everything I could find on this topic. References, footnotes and suggestions from friends and colleagues led me from one book and article to another. Ideas and research findings began to fall into place, like the pieces of a puzzle. Within a year there was enough material to introduce an undergraduate course on career development at the University of Houston-Clear Lake, where I teach. A graduate course, Life/Work Planning, was added two years later. I began to produce materials to use in these classes. Eventually there was enough for a book, How To Find A Job In Houston, published by Ten Speed Press in 1983.

My students at the University of Houston-Clear Lake have taught me a great deal about making occupational choices and changes. UH-CL is an upper level school. We have no freshmen or sophomores. About half the students are graduate students. The average age is somewhere around 32. These men and women have shared their efforts, concerns and frustrations with each other and with me while working through the materials in this book.

My work with group job search programs funded by the government, and also those run privately, added another dimension to my experience. Studying these programs made me aware of how many people now assist the unemployed without benefit of university training. This can cause serious problems. Much of the research about the labor market and its operations is published in obscure sources. It is not easy for most people to locate the information they need.

This realization led to a second book, Looking For Work In The New Economy, written with Miriam Johnson and Robert Chapman. It was published in 1985 by Olympus Publishing of Salt Lake City. Here we attempted a synthesis of essential information on America's changing labor market. The most important findings from studies of how people seek employment, and what typically happens to them, are summarized in this book.

The book you are now reading is a revision of the original How To Find A Job In Houston. It also draws on the research reported in Looking For Work In The New Economy, and adds new insights which have come from working with the unemployed in the years since How To Find A Job In Houston was written. And, of course, it is no longer oriented toward just one city.

Robert Chapman is a founding partner of King, Chapman and Broussard, Inc. This Houston consulting firm does a great deal of outplacement work. I have worked with them as a consultant for some years. Bob, too, was deeply influenced by a reading of What Color Is Your Parachute? several years ago. Bolles' ideas and methods first helped him to move from social service work to the private sector, and then later into outplacement work.

As each chapter was written, Bob reviewed it carefully. He helped to reorient what was not clear, rewriting sections that needed improvement. Above all, his extensive experience with the unemployed helped assure that the book was practical and realistic.

The purpose of this book is, then, to prepare you to take on today's highly competitive job market. Meeting this challenge will involve a good deal of time and hard work. Genius is still only 2% inspiration and 98% perspiration. But, as in other fields, preparation pays off. The alternative to adequate preparation, after all, is to risk being caught by surprise, with all the potential for panic and bad decision-making this can hold.

Using This Book

Section I gives an overview of the major changes in the American labor market during the last decade. The information in these chapters will show you where to expect growth and decline, and why there is so much more competition for employment than there used to be.

Section II discusses the first step in making a wise occupational choice: a thorough review of your skills, personality traits and interests, and how they blend together. The exercises in these chapters should prepare you to handle the request which is so often made during employment interviews: tell me about yourself.

Section III reviews the second area which must be explored to make an intelligent occupational choice: what employers are seeking, and what particular jobs are really like on a day to day basis. You need to find out how much competition you can expect for a specific job, who typically makes the hiring decisions and the outlook for the future. Section III shows you how to gather this labor market information, so you can choose an occupation which is both appropriate to your talents and available in today's job market.

Once you decide what you want, you still have to get it. Section IV therefore moves on to the job search process. To find the position you want, you must be able to obtain one or more employment interviews. The three chapters in this section review a variety of ways to do that. How you go about seeking interviews is more important than you might think. Your job search methods will influence both how quickly you find work and the quality of job you obtain.

Section V considers the final, crucial stage of the search process: doing well in the employment interview, and negotiating a good job offer. This section also presents some ideas on handling the first few months on a new job. It is important to act in such a way that your next search will be easier, whenever it may come. This whole process is, we are convinced, a lifetime adult survival skill.

In an effort to improve readability, footnotes have been omitted from the body of the text. Sources for quotations, suggestions for further reading and acknowledgments will be found in the notes on each chapter. These are located at the end of the book, just before the Index.

This book was written to be used either by an individual working alone, or in a group format. Instructors or group leaders who are interested in suggestions on how to handle these topics in a group setting should request an Instructor's Manual from Ten Speed Press.

Robert G. Wegmann

THE CHANGING LABOR MARKET

Introduction to Section I

Shortly after a major airline declared bankruptcy, one of us (Wegmann) ran into a former student who had been a flight attendant with the now defunct airline. She had taken the Life/Work Planning course for which an earlier version of this book was written. Using the methods outlined in Section III, she had explored commercial real estate, a field to which she was much attracted. Her non-flying hours in the months that followed the course were spent in a self-created apprenticeship. By the time her job disappeared she was able to move into a full-time real estate position.

Many of her colleagues, however, were caught by surprise when their jobs suddenly disappeared. They were, she reported, depressed and panic-stricken. Many had no idea how to get a new position. There was no obvious "next step," and they did not even know where to start. Some had gone to employment agencies, with painful results. They had been told they were unemployable. The agencies said that stewardesses had no professional experience, having really been only waitresses.

Like most Americans, these newly unemployed workers had never explicitly studied the labor market and how it operates. Finding themselves unexpectedly unemployed, they were lost. They had no idea what to do next. They were, in fact, a carefully selected group of talented, energetic, well-trained and responsible people with much to offer an employer. Their problem was not lack of ability. It was lack of understanding of how the labor market works and how to set new and realistic career goals.

Not knowing how to define an appropriate job or how to locate an opening would have made the situation difficult under any circumstances. The timing of their job loss made things worse. They were going into a much more competitive labor market than most had faced the last time they looked for work. Some had joined the airline immediately after college graduation, and had never worked for anyone else. They were discovering that jobs are harder to find now, having a college degree no longer guarantees a professional position and major corporations are as likely to be laying off as hiring.

What they were learning through painful personal experience was that the American labor market has undergone fundamental changes. These changes are both economic and social. More married women are working outside the home. Many people are delaying marriage and focusing on their careers. Families are smaller. Many men are earning lower salaries (after inflation) than they used to. We have moved, not only into a new and different labor market, but into a new and different society.

As is always true when such a complex set of changes occurs, what has happened to the job market has created both problems and opportunities. Some people find themselves in the wrong place at the wrong time, and stay there. They experience long stretches of unemployment, frequent job changes, limited career satisfaction and a marked decline in income. Others are in the right place at the right time, or move there. They enjoy increasing income as they meet new challenges and accept new responsibilities.

Change, in other words, presents problems, but change also presents opportunities. The same upheavals that have thrown many people out of work have made others rich. The essential question is: can you understand what's going on, adapt to it and find opportunities?

A Fish Story

One of our favorite stories is about the man who wants both big and little fish in his fish tank. When he first tries to put the fish together, however, he finds that the big fish eat the little fish.

So he puts a pane of glass in the middle of the tank. He then puts the big fish on one side of this pane, and the little fish on the other. The big fish swim toward the little fish, but before they can get to them they bump into the glass. They soon learn it is impossible to get to the little fish.

At this point the pane of glass is removed. The big fish will now swim peacefully around with the little fish, not bothering them in the least.

What we like about this story is how clearly it highlights the pitfalls of making assumptions. It is natural, but dangerous, to think that things are the same today as they were in the past. Although the glass is gone, the big fish go hungry because they don't notice that things have changed. At the same time, think of being the first big fish who realizes that the glass isn't there anymore, and the opportunities for good eating this realization opens up.

Today, many people are unemployed. Others, although employed, are unhappy with their jobs. Some of both groups are like the big fish. They learned over many years what kinds of jobs are available, and how one goes about getting them. They do what once worked, or what they think they're supposed to do. They are surprised when no job offers come. They don't understand how much has changed. They don't know that some pieces of glass have been removed and others put in place. They don't realize that some things which were true when they learned them are not true today. So some pass up great eating and others swim straight into thick glass walls.

Like all images and analogies, this one isn't perfect, but it does convey a sense of both the frustration and opportunity generated by labor market evolution. The point is this: the set of jobs for which you can apply has changed. Pay scales are often very different from what they were in the recent past. Jobs are now found in different parts of the country, in different industries and in smaller firms. There is often significantly increased competition for the available openings. There are also new jobs being created, new firms being founded and new opportunities opening up. The three chapters in this section are designed to show you where the problems are, and also some areas of opportunity being generated by these changes.

The Currents of Change

One painful side effect of any social and economic change is the degree to which it devalues experience. Old approaches don't work. Old habits get us into trouble. The natural order of things is reversed. The young, unburdened by experience and thus assuming less, sometimes do better than those who are older.

Survival during a period of rapid change requires that you, like the fish in the tank, look carefully to see what's really going on. You cannot simply assume that what's happening now is the same as what happened in the past. Not too long ago there was a surplus of elementary school teachers, and a booming market for personal computers. Today computer stores are closing, and a shortage of elementary teachers is developing. Demand changes, and both people and businesses must be flexible enough to adjust to these changes.

So that's what this first section is all about: taking a careful look at today's job market, and how it differs from the recent past. Once you understand how the market has changed, you can go with the current instead of against it. You can set a realistic goal, and use the most effective means to reach that goal.

This is not a one-time exercise. These labor market changes are continuing. What is true today may be false in five or ten years when you next seek new employment. This book is about lifetime survival skills.

On a camping trip one time, a group one of us was with decided to canoe up a rapids. The experience was a great image of what happens when you ignore the force of social and economic change. Going against the current was great fun, and a marvelous way to build up the arm muscles, but not at all effective as a way to get anywhere. The canoe moved, but at about a foot per hour.

If you really want to get somewhere, you need a good idea of where the current is moving. The choice of goals is yours to make. You can choose to go against the current. To do this effectively, though, you'll have to know when to hug the shore and hike around the rapids.

Again, images are imperfect. The point is that any occupational choice you make has to fit both you and the labor market. Just because there is a growing demand for computer programmers doesn't mean you have to be one. Despite declining demand, you can decide to be a high school history teacher, steel worker or petroleum geologist. But you had better give careful thought to how you will handle a situation where the number of openings is low, while the number of qualified applicants is high. It is not impossible to get a job offer, but it will be difficult. You will definitely feel you are paddling upstream, and you had better have a "Plan B" to fall back on if you can't get your first choice.

Where Do We Start?

Section I, then, will review the last decade's labor market changes. What you are facing will come through clearly in the facts and figures gathered by various divisions of the federal government. Armed with this data, you will be better able to set realistic career goals.

In Chapter One, we will look primarily at supply. How many people are looking for work? In what ways has the set of available workers changed? Who, in other words, are your competitors? When you finish this chapter you should understand why so many more people are looking for work, why they are a more highly educated group than ever before and what this implies for you in setting career goals.

Then, in Chapter Two, we will focus on demand. What changes have there been in the set of jobs which are available for you to obtain? What jobs are disappearing? What jobs are being created? This chapter will show you where employment growth is concentrated, and why.

Chapter Three, which concludes the section, reviews how today's increased pool of job applicants relates to this new set of job opportunities. This supply/demand relationship is the key to understanding today's labor market. You will take a look at how frequently men and women are changing both employers and occupations. You will note some of the downward pressures being put on wages and salaries. You will see how all of the changes we have discussed add up to a much more competitive job market, and why this means you have to undertake a more careful, better organized search for employment. You will then be ready for Section II, which will guide you through a detailed review of what you have to offer employers.

One. It's Off to Work We go — All of Us

How hard or easy it is to find employment is primarily governed by two factors: how many employers are hiring, and how many people are looking for work. In the job market, as in any market, both supply and demand have to be considered.

In this chapter we will take a look at the supply side of the American job market. What we will essentially be asking is: how many people are trying to find employment, and what are they like? Or, to put it another way, how many competitors are you facing, and who are they? You will need this information as you decide what position to seek, and plot a strategy to get it.

As Chart 1 shows, the size of the American labor force has been increasing for many years, especially since 1965. The total number of people working or looking for work has about doubled over the past 40 years. There are several reasons for this rapid growth.

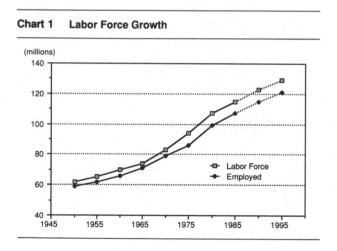

Chart 1   Labor Force Growth

The Baby Boomers

The entry into the labor market of the so-called "baby boomers" has been a major reason there are more people seeking employment. These individuals were born between 1946 and 1964. Birth rates during this period were much higher than they are now. In the words of one shrewd observer, during these years the country experienced the greatest barbarian invasion in history.

After years of placing heavy demands on parents and schools, the baby boomers entered the labor mar-

ket, seeking entry level positions. Most people get their first full-time jobs roughly around the age of 20. If you add 20 to 1946 and 1964, you get a period between 1966 and 1984. During this time unusually large numbers of young people began looking for their first full-time jobs. If you are part of this group, you noticed the same crowds looking for work that you experienced in school and on the playground.

The movement of this population bulge into the labor force had a major effect on the supply of applicants for entry level jobs. In the years ahead, this concentration of workers at certain age levels will continue to be important. It will play a significant role in determining the level of competition for promotions to more advanced positions as the years go on.

A high proportion of the baby boomers went to college. This large group of educated workers in their twenties and thirties has had a definite effect on the job security of experienced professionals. Although it is illegal to fire an older worker in order to hire someone younger, there is no doubt that this is done. In order to avoid lawsuits, it may be done in several steps. Under the guise of "restructuring," large numbers of older workers are asked to leave or take early retirement. Over time, younger workers are then brought into the organization with different job titles.

The baby boom group may also play a major part in the founding of new businesses in the years ahead. Today's young adults are more highly educated, more comfortable with computer technology and more focused on career success than previous generations. Many of them seem more able and willing to take the risks required to begin their own firms. This trend could be important in many ways, not the least of which is the potential for new job creation in these start-up companies.

Voting with Their Feet

A second contributor to rapid growth in the number of job applicants is immigration. In recent years, the United States has been admitting as many immigrants as the rest of the world combined. During the 1970s over 4.4 million legal immigrants, largely Asians and Hispanics, entered the United States. A large proportion of these new residents immediately sought work in their new homeland.

To complicate the situation, a large but unknown number of individuals have come into the United States illegally. Estimates of their numbers are inexact, but there is probably about one illegal immigrant for every two who enter legally.

Both legal and illegal immigration are increasing. One projection puts total legal immigration during the 1980s at 5.6 million, with several million more entering illegally.

Many of these immigrants work in family businesses. Mexican restaurants, Chinese computer stores and immigrant-operated gasoline and convenience stores dot the landscape. These immigrant families are often very hard-working. They will pool their earnings to purchase homes and stores, and to pay for the education of their children. This makes them very attractive as employees, and formidable competitors when they own or operate businesses.

Illegal immigrants are in a similar, but often more difficult situation. Vulnerable to deportation, they are often afraid to complain about mistreatment. This makes it easy for others to exploit them. They may work for wages below the legal minimum, being paid "off the books" by unscrupulous employers. Since no benefits are offered, they may cost an employer less than half what would be paid a citizen. Although this makes inexpensive products and services available to the consumer, it also helps to maintain a low-wage environment, particularly for unskilled labor.

We are a nation of immigrants, and we have been through these waves of ambitious newcomers before. They are contributing, and will continue to contribute, much to their new homeland. They do, however, swell the number of people seeking work in an increasingly competitive labor market.

When Is Mom Coming Home?

There is a third major labor market trend which, like immigration, is a continuing phenomenon. An increasing proportion of women have been seeking employment outside the home.

That more women are looking for jobs is really nothing new. The labor force participation rate of women (the proportion of adult women who either have jobs or are actively seeking them) has been growing steadily for many years, as Chart 2 shows.

Around 1978, however, for the first time in American history, the proportion of working women passed

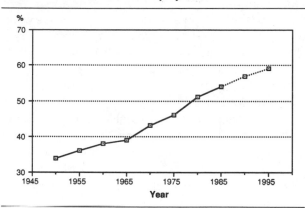

Chart 2   Women with Paid Employment

the 50% point. Around this time there was a change in social norms as well as in statistics. In the past, a minority of women had jobs outside the home, and a woman who had one might get a raised eyebrow. "Oh, you have a job?" Today working women are in the majority, and one might just as likely hear, "Oh, you don't have a job?"

Any of these sources of new workers, baby boomers, immigrants or women, would have individually had a significant effect on the job market. What is important is that they all sought employment at the same time. Absorbing them required the creation of millions of new job openings.

The baby boom group is now at work, moving out of entry level jobs and seeking promotions. The other two groups, women and immigrants, are still growing. The size of the American labor force therefore continues to increase, though somewhat more slowly than during the 1965-1984 period.

Where Have All the Openings Gone?

In addition to the rapid growth in the number of people seeking employment, Chart 1 also illustrates a second fact. Before 1975, the economy was able to generate jobs quickly enough to employ the growing numbers of people who wanted them. For thirty years, from 1945 to 1975, unemployment rarely went above 6%. After 1975, however, things changed radically. Since then unemployment has rarely gone below 6%. In the last decade we have had not only a great increase in those seeking work, but an even greater increase in those whose searches for employment are unsuccessful or greatly prolonged.

In a labor force with well over a hundred million participants, each percentage point of unemployment represents more than a million Americans out of work. Additional millions have given up in frustration, and others are working part-time because they cannot find full-time jobs. This increased unemployment represents significantly higher levels of pain and frustration for millions of people.

The impact of unemployment is lessened, though certainly not eliminated, when another member of the family is still employed. This often happens when there are two or more adults in the household. The one-parent family and the single individual are, of course, much more vulnerable.

It is striking how quickly we have come to tolerate these high levels of unemployment. Twenty years ago a president who faced an unemployment rate over 6% would have had little chance of reelection. In 1984, Ronald Reagan carried 49 of the 50 states in a year when unemployment averaged 7.5%. We have clearly gotten used to a new piece of glass in our fish tank.

It's the Women Who Did It

The change in those seeking employment is not just a matter of numbers, but also of quality. Today's workers are significantly better educated. The baby boom group has poured into (and out of) the country's colleges and universities. This has greatly increased the number of persons who have college degrees. There has also been a jump in the number of people who have at least some college education, but did not complete their degrees.

There's another factor which hasn't received much publicity, but is important in understanding why the competition for professional jobs is so intense. Men have only slightly higher labor force participation rates as their educational levels increase. Men, in other words, tend to have jobs (or to be seeking them) whether or not they have much education.

Chart 3 shows how different the situation is for women. Note how closely a woman's educational level relates to whether or not she is in the labor force. The likelihood that a woman will work outside the home increases markedly as her educational level goes up. Only half the women who dropped out of high school are in the labor force, compared to four-fifths of those with college degrees. This pattern may be even more significant in the years ahead, since more women than men are expected to receive college degrees during the 1985-1995 period.

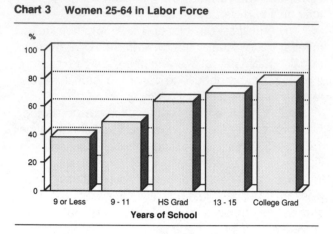

Chart 3   Women 25-64 in Labor Force

This pattern of educated women seeking employment, while less educated women do not, has produced a labor force which is much more highly educated than the general adult population. It has also ballooned the proportion of the labor force which is college-educated.

This situation has greatly increased the competition for middle management and staff positions in major corporations. Many of these positions are being eliminated as businesses try to become "lean and mean" in order to meet intense foreign competition. The computer allows a small number of people to prepare and process information which formerly took several staff professionals. At the same time, a large group of educated women are now seeking these positions, as are the educated men who have traditionally held them. The result of shrinking demand and growing supply is that many applicants do not get the

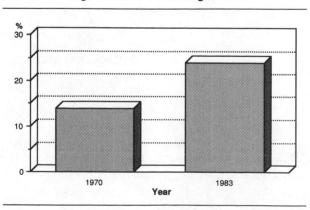

Chart 4   College Graduate Workers Aged 25-64

corporate jobs they expected, and others who lose one cannot find another.

In 1970, only one worker in seven had a college degree, as Chart 4 shows. If you applied for a job in 1970, and had a college education, you had something that six out of seven applicants lacked. Those were good odds when competing for a well-paid, professional position. Today, though, the proportion of adult workers with college degrees is one in four.

Having a degree is, as a result, no longer that special or unusual. The implicit question from employers with professional openings has become, "And what else besides a degree do you have to offer?" If you are a recent college graduate, you will need to focus on the qualifications you have in addition to your degree. If you do not have a degree, you will have to be unusually persuasive when presenting the experience and qualifications that offset your lack of formal education.

This surplus of college graduates produces some important side effects. For one thing, it allows corporations to lower the salary offers made to those just out of college. It also diminishes the economic value of having gone to college without completing the degree. The pattern of jobs taken by those who have not finished college degrees is now similar to the employment pattern of those with only high school educations. A typical employer has many applicants with completed degrees from whom to choose. As a result, those who didn't finish college usually aren't seriously considered, at least for the more demanding and highly-paid positions, unless they have outstanding skills.

Now What Do I Do?

Given the high level of competition for professional positions, some people with college degrees inevitably don't obtain the more attractive jobs they thought their diplomas would bring them. They then apply for less prestigious positions as waitresses, factory workers, cab drivers, office workers, and so on. This "bumping down" process, in turn, makes the competition that much tougher for those who have less education.

There is no evidence that these competitive pressures will lessen significantly in the years ahead. The number of college graduates entering the labor market will exceed the number of job openings requiring college degrees by more than 200,000 per year throughout the 1980s. There were already 3.8 million persons with college degrees in the 1980 labor force who were either unemployed or underemployed. There is there-

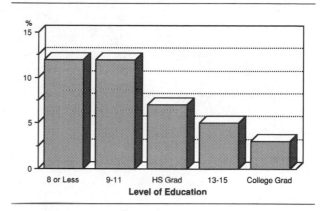

Chart 5   Unemployment Rate Among Persons Aged 25-64

fore little doubt that the United States will have a high rate of underemployment for many years. One college-educated worker in four can expect to hold a job which does not require a college degree.

A college education is essential for most challenging, well-paid professional positions. It is no longer enough, however. The degree gets you in the game. Without it you can hardly compete. But it does not guarantee success.

A degree *is* definitely helpful, however, in avoiding unemployment. As Chart 5 makes clear, it is the less educated who largely bear the unemployment burden. Those with more education may not always get the jobs they want, but they usually get something. The unemployment rate for those with college degrees is less than 3%. For high school dropouts, it's four times as high.

There's a Major Difference

The government recently followed a sample of college graduates to see how well they were doing a year after graduation. Most were employed, but many were underemployed. The likelihood of both unemployment and underemployment varied dramatically depending on the graduate's major.

There are two clear patterns in Table 1. First, those who majored in subjects that involved at least some mathematics got more professional, technical and managerial positions. Second, those whose degrees had an obvious relation to a job title were significantly less likely to be underemployed. That is, it is clear that an accounting degree prepares you for a job as an accountant, and a nursing degree for a nursing posi-

Table 1: May 1981 Status of 1979-1980 College Graduates

College Major	% Un-employed	% Under-employed
Computer/Information Sciences	0	3
Engineering	4	4
Nursing	0	6
Chemistry	2	7
Mathematics	3	7
Accounting	2	9
Education (except Phys.Ed.)	4	14
Home Economics	5	22
Physical Education	6	23
Biological Sciences	4	23
Business (except Accounting)	2	24
English	4	26
Economics	4	26
Agriculture & Nat'l Resources	3	28
Communications	9	33
Psychology	6	37
Art	7	39
History	6	42
Sociology	8	45
Political Science	4	46

Source: Bureau of Labor Statistics.

tion. It is not as clear what an English or history or sociology degree prepares you for. This ambiguity can create severe problems for many graduates when they must enter a crowded job market.

This is not to suggest that liberal arts and social science degrees do not have many humanizing values. People seek educations for many reasons other than preparation for employment. Furthermore, we are looking at the results only one year after graduation. The situation 20 years from now could be different. The broader training given in the liberal arts and social sciences could turn out, over time, to lead to more satisfying employment than the specialized training given in computer science, engineering or nursing.

In the short run, however, the more technical and focused the training, the more likely it is to lead to a professional position. To put it another way, the less your degree is focused on employment, the more your job search efforts will have to be carefully planned and vigorous.

Not every college student has seen these figures. There is no doubt that many students do, however, have a general awareness that things have changed. They know that just having a degree no longer guaran-

tees a professional position. As a result, there has been a significant shift in the majors college students are choosing. Some of these shifts make sense, and some don't.

Enrollment in business courses has gone up rapidly despite the fact that business majors have an underemployment rate which is about average. It is a reasonable assumption that many of these students believe majoring in an area such as business administration has solved their employment problems. Unfortunately, this is not true.

Education majors have dropped by half. This was understandable when the demand for teachers was low because of the low birth rates of recent years. It is unfortunate today, however, when the baby boom women are in their prime child-bearing years. Enrollment in elementary schools is rising. There are now more preschool children than there have been in 20 years. This will generate a strong demand for more elementary teachers in the years ahead.

The number of social science and humanities degrees being awarded has dropped significantly. The number of engineering, medical and computer-oriented degrees, on the other hand, has seen a major increase.

Does this mean you need to shift to a technical field? For some people, moving to a more employment-oriented degree might be a good idea. For others, however, such a move could be a serious mistake. What counts in any wise occupational choice is not only the needs of employers, but your own gifts and motivations. You will examine how best to match what you have to offer with the demands of the labor market as you proceed through the rest of this book.

So What?

This chapter began by looking at the expanding supply of people trying to find employment. Not only are there many more people looking for work, but they are much better educated. As a result, for the first time in American history we have a high level of underemployment among college graduates.

The practical implication of these facts is that you need to be more prepared for your job search efforts than if you were looking for work under less demanding conditions. Although the self-examination and labor market study outlined later in this book will require considerable time and effort, they will pay off. You will learn how to effectively communicate what you have to offer an employer. You will be able to explain clearly and convincingly why the job you want is right for you. You won't expect the employer to figure this out for you. You will realize that if you're not clear about what you're doing, there are other applicants who will be.

So Much for Supply — On to Demand

There have undoubtedly been important changes in both the numbers and qualifications of those seeking employment. Increased demand, however, is only half the story. What about the supply of openings? Until the mid-70s, jobs were available for almost everyone. At that point, however, the process of job creation faltered. What happened?

To answer these questions we need to take a closer look at the demand side of the labor market. How many and what kinds of jobs are being created, and why?

Two. Who's Hiring?

There are many people looking for work, and they are much better educated than ever before. This, however, is only part of the picture. The set of job openings available for them to fill has also changed significantly. The openings aren't where they used to be. Some kinds of jobs are being created in large numbers. Others are disappearing with equal rapidity. The purpose of this chapter is to show you where to look for growth, and where to expect decline.

To better understand what's been happening, let's first divide the country's nonagricultural jobs into four major groups:

- *Government positions*, such as police officer, public school teacher, prison guard or county tax collector.
- *Goods-producing jobs*, such as factory manager, miner, construction worker or oil field roughneck.
- *Work in wholesale or retail trade*, such as department store clerk, waiter, druggist or grocery store cashier.
- *Service jobs*, such as hotel manager, stockbroker, airline pilot, bank teller, nurse, university professor at a private college, real estate broker, accounting firm clerk or computer consultant.

Two of these sectors of the economy are offering employment to a declining share of the workforce, while opportunities in the other two have been rising steadily. This is making it easier to obtain some kinds of jobs, and harder to find others.

Chart 6 traces the decreasing proportion of the working population in the two sectors which have been declining, government and goods-producing employment.

Manufacturing firms employ most workers in the goods-producing sector. The proportion of the workforce employed in these jobs has been dropping steadily, as Chart 6 shows. These declines are expected to continue over the next decade.

For thirty years, however, from 1945 to 1975, the failure of manufacturing employment to keep up with the rest of the economy was at least partly offset by rapid growth in government jobs. As the population increased, more and better government services were demanded. State and local governments hired additional police officers, fire fighters, teachers, road repair

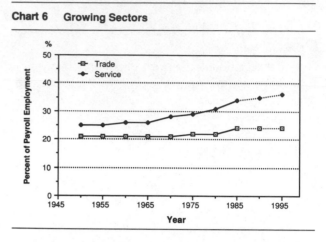

Chart 6   Growing Sectors

crews and so on. Most of these jobs were with state and local governments, since federal employment accounts for less than one in five government workers. This employment growth partly made up for the failure of manufacturing firms to create their share of the new jobs needed by the growing number of people looking for work.

About 1975, however, the proportion of the workforce in government jobs also began to decline, and this drop is projected to continue. Tight budgets, tax reductions, smaller high school and college enrollments, lower federal aid and other factors have resulted in lower government payrolls. Government jobs are therefore no longer absorbing an increasing percentage of those who are looking for work. In fact, government employment is not even keeping up its proportionate share. This trend reversal is one of several factors behind the high unemployment rates after 1975.

There are only two sectors of the economy left which can pick up the slack: trade and services.

Where's the Growth?

The proportion of workers employed in trade has been going up, though not dramatically. On closer examination, however, it turns out that this increase has been concentrated in only one type of retail business: bars and restaurants.

The United States today has more working women, more single individuals and more childless couples. Maybe these groups eat out more, or maybe the situation is just driving people to drink. At any rate, the rest of trade employment (in department stores, grocery stores, drugstores, wholesalers and so on) has been exceptionally stable as a proportion of total employment.

So, if you are looking for growth and don't want to tend bar or wait on tables, only one group of jobs is left. Here significant numbers of new openings *are* being created: in the service sector. Admittedly, this is a large set of exceptionally diverse jobs. Hospitals and other medical establishments, business consultants, real estate offices, banks and other financial institutions, public utilities, airlines, railroads and private schools are all part of the service sector. A world-famous brain surgeon has a service sector job; so does a parking garage attendant.

In 1950, service sector positions represented one job in four. Today they constitute one job in three, and this proportion is increasing. Again, 1975 was the key year. In 1975, for the first time, service employment equaled employment in the goods-producing sector. Today, of course, it is the service sector which is dominant.

Not Made in America

Although automation is certainly part of the explanation for declining manufacturing employment, foreign competition also played an important role. Chart 8 shows the extraordinary increase in foreign trade since 1975. Prior to that date, over 90% of all the goods America produced stayed in this country. After 1975, we began shipping far more of our production to other countries, and importing goods at an ever increasing rate.

Part of this increase was caused by the higher cost of imported oil. We weren't actually bringing more in, just paying more for it. The fundamental reason we are much more involved in foreign trade, however, lies in the benefits both sides believed they could gain. There was a strong demand for American goods in other countries. At the same time, foreign manufacturers were attracted by the vast potential of the United States as a place to sell their goods. These two forces created the potential for greatly increased trade.

Chart 7 Declining Sectors

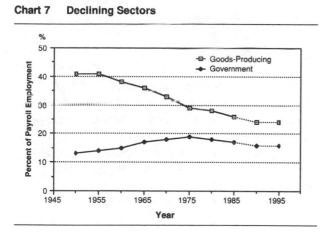

Chart 8 U. S. Merchandise Trade

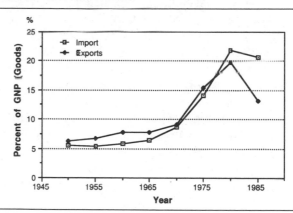

Productivity: Unemployment Spelled Backwards?

What slowed employment growth in manufacturing? Quite a number of things, actually. Increased energy and pollution control costs made some older plants unprofitable, and they were closed. More efficient machines and production methods made it possible to turn out an impressive quantity of goods with fewer workers. There is every indication that this latter trend is continuing. Indeed, by the 1990s robots should be

more widely used than they are today. The loss of manufacturing jobs may well accelerate.

In the last decade, this potential became a reality. Shipping merchandise long distances used to be expensive, dangerous and difficult. Even when foreign goods arrived in one piece they were often heavily taxed. Today this situation has changed radically. Greatly enlarged trade has become practical through a combination of mutual tariff reductions and much cheaper and more efficient means of transportation, such as supertankers and containerized cargo ships. As a result, world trade has grown rapidly.

We have now become part of an interdependent

world economy. American corporations are competing with businesses around the world. All of these firms are trying to obtain orders for similar products. To sell their goods they must maintain both quality and a competitive price.

Labor costs represent a large proportion of the expense of making most products. Wages are substantially lower in many other countries than they are in the United States. Since the other costs of producing goods (machinery, raw materials or transportation, for example) cannot be lowered easily, there is tremendous pressure to reduce the total cost of wages and benefits. This is the only way goods can be produced more cheaply. Hence corporations are shrinking employment whenever possible, adopting "two tier contracts" under which new workers are paid less than those already hired, and asking unions for "givebacks" (wage and benefit reductions).

One method of reducing employee costs is through "outsourcing." This new word refers to the purchase of goods and services from an outside source. A variety of parts used in the manufacturing process are no longer made in the corporation's factories. Instead, they are purchased at lower cost from other firms, some of which are located in foreign countries. Only final assembly takes place in the corporation's plant, and this requires fewer local workers. Services, too, are purchased whenever possible from smaller firms paying lower wages. All of these actions help an American corporation meet foreign competition. They also reduce the number of well-paid jobs available in this country.

Even aside from these wage pressures, there is another reduction in American job opportunities which comes from the consistent difference between our imports and exports. The goods sold by American producers are, on average, what economists call "capital-intensive." They are produced by efficient but expensive machinery. The products we buy from other countries, on the other hand, are more labor-intensive. They are produced using more workers and fewer machines. Consequently, we lose manufacturing jobs as a result of foreign trade even when we generate a trade surplus.

Much of the publicity about our foreign trading patterns has focused on the electronics products and automobiles we buy from Japan. However, our trade with Japan and all of Western Europe combined is roughly equal to our trade with the developing countries. These "third world" countries buy our computers and airplanes, and other things they cannot produce themselves. They sell us what they can produce, cancelling out their low productivity with even lower wages. On average, therefore, what we buy is significantly more labor-intensive than what we sell. As a result, we lose manufacturing jobs even when we come out ahead in dollars.

The basic pattern, in other words, is that we produce goods on our automated farms and in our automated factories, and sell these goods to other countries. We then buy from them products like shoes, clothing and leather goods which take many hours of a worker's time (and therefore more workers) to produce.

Our imports thus create more jobs in other countries than the openings created here by what we manufacture for export. With a slight trade surplus, such as we used to generate, we still lost four jobs for every three we gained.

To use a concrete example: when the Russians shot down a South Korean airliner some years back, they weren't shooting down an airliner built in South Korea. A modern airliner is far too complex for most countries to manufacture. So a country like South Korea, when it needs an airliner, turns to a firm such as Boeing Aircraft in the United States. They pay, say, $60 million for a plane that will meet their needs. We then turn around and use that money to buy $60 million worth of shirts from South Korea.

This transaction creates jobs in the United States: Boeing hires people to design and build the airliner. It also costs us jobs: American industry doesn't need to make as many shirts as before, since we're now importing them.

In dollars, it's an even trade. However, because it takes more people to make $60 million worth of shirts than it takes to make a $60 million airliner, we experience a net loss of American manufacturing jobs. Note, however, that goods made abroad are still shipped, advertised, sold and serviced in this country. Our expanded involvement in the world economy creates jobs in the service and trade sectors. They grow, even though manufacturing employment declines.

This situation is more difficult for the United States today because, in recent years, we've not produced our traditional trade surplus. In 1971, for the first time since 1888, we bought more goods from other countries than we sold them. Since 1976 we've run a merchandise trade deficit every year. We've been buying more but selling less. In 1984 and again in 1985, our merchandise trade balance ran well over $100 billion in the red. As a result, jobs are being lost two ways: in the industries that must compete with these foreign imports, and also in the industries which manufacture for export and now have reduced foreign sales. This double loss is one reason we have high unemployment despite an expanding economy.

Small is Beautiful

Rapid growth in foreign trade has generated major changes in both the size and type of employer who may hire you. More new jobs have been created in services than in the goods-producing sector. Related to this trend is the large proportion of new jobs being created in smaller businesses. Service sector corporations employ, on average, fewer workers per firm. The 500 largest manufacturing corporations, for example, employ over 14 million workers. The 500 largest service corporations employ fewer than 10 million.

You are more likely than in the past, therefore, to find your job with a small business. A sense of how employment is distributed throughout the spectrum of small, medium and large firms is important today when designing an effective job search strategy.

You need to be aware, though, that the available figures on employer size are somewhat ambiguous. The government gathers information on business "establishments." Many of these establishments are branch offices or subsidiaries owned by other corporations. They are not all independent businesses.

It takes many employers with only three or four workers to equal the number of people in even one firm with over 500. Although half the business establishments in the country have fewer than five workers, all those employees added together are only about 7% of the total workforce. Hence it is useful to look at

Chart 9   Proportion of Employees

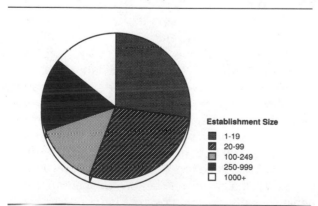

Establishment Size
- 1-19
- 20-99
- 100-249
- 250-999
- 1000+

Chart 10   Proportion of Employers

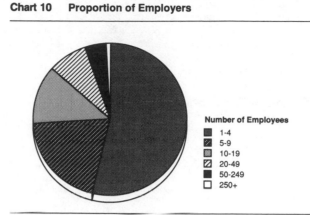

Number of Employees
- 1-4
- 5-9
- 10-19
- 20-49
- 50-249
- 250+

workplace size both by number of employers, and also by the proportion of workers they employ (Charts 9 and 10).

It is clear that the majority of Americans are employed by firms (or branch offices or subsidiaries) of relatively small size. Most employees have well under a hundred coworkers. When looking for work, it is therefore usually a bad strategy to approach only the largest firms. You need to identify small and medium-sized businesses also, and approach them in a way that fits their size and organizational structure.

My, How You're Growing

We've been looking primarily at the past and present. What about the future? Where are the jobs going to be in the next ten years?

The Bureau of Labor Statistics recently released projected changes in total employment expected during the 1984-1995 period. The first part of Table 2 gives the industries where the most new job openings are expected. As you can see, they are all in the trade and service sectors.

The second half of Table 2 gives the industries which will grow at the fastest *rate*. Note that there is some overlap between the figures on absolute growth (in the top part of the table) and those on proportionate growth (in the bottom part). Areas like business and medical services will be both growing rapidly and creating many new jobs.

Other areas, such as the production of materials handling equipment, are found only in the second half of Table 2. Although such industries will be growing rapidly, the total number of new jobs created will still be relatively small. This is because, in these industries, there is smaller initial employment on which this growth is based.

Table 2: Projected Changes in Total Employment, 1984-1995

Industries Creating the Most New Jobs	Employment Gain
Business Services	2,600,000
Retail Trade	1,700,000
Eating & Drinking Places	1,200,000
Wholesale Trade	1,100,000
Medical Services	1,100,000
Professional Services	1,000,000

Fastest Growing Industries	Annual Rate of Change (%)
Medical Services	4.3
Business Services	4.2
Computers & Peripherals	3.7
Materials Handling Equipment	3.7
Transportation Services	3.5
Professional Services	3.5

This may be confusing at first, but the key when looking at proportions is always to ask: *proportion of what?* It is better to get 1% of $1,000,000 than 40% of $100.

This same distinction is important when looking at Tables 3 and 4, which give Labor Department projections for the number of new jobs by *occupation*. (Note that an industry is the type of business where an individual works, such as an oil refinery. An occupation, on the other hand, is a job title, such as accountant.)

Table 3: Occupations with Largest Number of Net New Positions, 1984-1995

Occupation	Growth	Percent
Cashiers	560,000	30
Registered Nurses	450,000	33
Janitors & Cleaners	440,000	15
Truck Drivers	430,000	17
Waiters & Waitresses	420,000	26
Wholesale Trade Salesworkers	370,000	30
Nursing Aides & Orderlies	350,000	29
Retail Salespersons	340,000	13
Accountants & Auditors	310,000	35
K & Elementary Teachers	280,000	20
Secretaries	270,000	10
Computer Programmers	250,000	72
ALL EMPLOYMENT		15

Table 4: Occupations with Fastest Growth Rates, 1984-1995

Occupation	Growth	Percent
Paralegal Personnel	50,000	98
Computer Programmers	250,000	72
Computer Systems Analysts	210,000	69
Medical Assistants	80,000	62
Data Processing Repairers	30,000	56
Electrical Engineers	210,000	53
Electronics Technicians	200,000	51
Computer Operators	110,000	46
Peripheral Equip. Operators	30,000	45
Travel Agents	30,000	44
Physical Therapists	30,000	42
Physician Assistants	10,000	40
ALL EMPLOYMENT		15

Some occupations (retail salesperson, for example) will grow somewhat more slowly than average. Nonetheless, because so many people hold this job title, even below-average growth will generate a large number of new openings. Other occupations (physical therapist, for example) will grow almost three times as rapidly as average, yet generate relatively few new jobs. This is because only a small number of people are working as physical therapists to begin with, so even a big percentage increase doesn't involve many openings.

Today, rapidly growing occupations often involve the use of computers. These Labor Department projections clearly reflect the application of computer-based technology to a wide variety of tasks. Once installed, computers may increase or decrease the number of jobs in a given industry. In some cases the number of workers stays the same, but the nature of the job changes significantly.

Note that, for the first time, the Labor Department is projecting slower than average growth in the number of secretaries. Both office automation and corporate cost-cutting are at work here. A secretary with a computer or word processor can do more work than a secretary using only a typewriter. In addition, fewer managers now have their own secretaries, and more are sharing them with other executives.

Note also that computer programmers are now found not only on the fast growth list, but also on the list of jobs with the largest number of new openings. This, again, reflects the "computerization of everything."

These programmers will be working in almost every sector of the American economy.

The effect of demographic patterns is also noticeable. The "baby boom echo" is entering grade school, increasing the need for elementary school teachers. A growing population of older persons will need more medical care, creating a demand for nurses and nursing aides.

High Tech, Everyone?

Many communities, reacting to a decline in manufacturing jobs, are looking to "high tech" industries as a way to generate new employment. These industries employ technology-oriented workers in large numbers and spend above-average amounts for research and development.

For most cities, this search will be in vain. Although high tech employment will grow faster than average, the actual number of job openings will not be that large. High tech industries will increase from 6.1% to 7.0% of total employment over the next ten years. Because this is not nearly enough to replace employment lost in other sectors, the competition between cities for these new industries is fierce.

What will be important to the total economy is not so much new employment in these high tech firms, but how their products are used in every business and government agency. Most computer programmers, for example, will not be working for computer manufacturers. They will be writing programs for government offices, accounting firms and drugstore chains. In the years ahead, the demand will be great for people who can use technological products skillfully. Every industry will also need managers who can organize the workers using these important new tools to increase productivity.

Let's Get Moving

When discussing where jobs are to be found, we have looked at changes by industry, occupation and size of employer. We also need to take a look at geography. Just as there is more growth in some parts of the economy than others, there is also more growth in certain parts of the country.

Other things being equal, it is easier to find a job in a city which is growing rapidly. In addition, the larger a city becomes, the more specialized the stores and services it can support.

Table 5: Projected Employment Gains by State, 1983-1990

Highest Proportionate Growth	%
Arizona	32
Nevada	26
Florida	24
Alaska	24
Colorado	23
U.S. OVERALL	15

Highest Absolute Growth	Jobs
California	2,250,000
Texas	1,310,000
Florida	1,130,000
New York	920,000
Illinois	550,000
U.S. OVERALL	16,180,000
5-State Proportion	38%

Source: Bureau of Economic Analysis

Table 5 gives Commerce Department projections for expected growth by state through 1990. You need to interpret these figures cautiously. They were generated before the rapid fall in oil prices. The actual population changes in Texas and Alaska will vary considerably depending on what happens to the price of oil.

With cities as with jobs, one must distinguish between the actual numbers and the percentage growth. Cities with very rapid growth (over 20% during the 1980-1984 period, for example), were typically under 300,000 population, and often closer to 150,000. The 55 metropolitan areas with at least 10% growth during this period were concentrated in the South and West, and particularly in Florida (17), Texas (15) and California (7). The largest numbers of new jobs, on the other hand, will be found in large metropolitan areas. One projection is given in Table 6.

So What?

Two common errors are regularly made by people looking for work. First, they apply primarily at major corporations. These firms are visible and easy to find. Second, they zero in on large manufacturing firms. They know that the wages and salaries paid by these corporations tend to be higher than what they can earn at many other businesses. Since neither manufacturing nor large employers have been growing as rapidly

**Table 6: Metropolitan Areas
withLargest Job Growth, 1985-2000**

Area	Employment Growth
Los Angeles	1,000,000
Boston	760,000
Anaheim	700,000
San Jose	540,000
Phoenix	540,000
Washington	510,000
Houston	500,000
Chicago	490,000
Dallas	490,000
Atlanta	460,000

Source: National Planning Association

as the labor force, however, what often results is a report that "no one is hiring."

This isn't true, of course, but this is how it will seem if you concentrate your job search efforts in areas of little or no growth. Over the last decade, despite the increase in total employment, the number of workers employed by the 500 largest firms involved in manufacturing (the Fortune 500, as they are usually known) has gone down, not up. More generally, growth has been faster in firms under 250 employees, and slower in those above that size.

There are some important implications for you in these facts. Once you have selected one or more specific occupations you find attractive, you need to gather detailed information on the industries where openings are available. You will also want to take a close look at the proportion of those openings located in small, medium and large businesses.

One must be careful here. There is no reason you *have* to seek a job in a growth area. Most job openings do not occur because of growth. They occur because someone quits, or is fired, or retires, or when a business is reorganized. Further, as some businesses of a given type fail and others of the same type are started, job openings are available in the new firms even if there is a net decline in total employment.

However, other things being equal, the odds are better when there *is* growth. It is not only easier to get hired, but also easier to get promoted. You grow with the company. So feel free to look over all employment possibilities, but pay special attention to the parts of the country experiencing above-average growth, and to the high-growth occupations and industries.

To the extent that you will be looking for a job in a smaller firm, you need to adopt job search methods that fit smaller firms. Looking for work is always a personal process. It is especially so when you are dealing directly with the owner or manager, as you will be when seeking employment in a small business. Remember, over 90% of the businesses in this country do not have a personnel office. They are too small.

You will often need to use a split job search strategy, using one set of search methods for major corporations and another for smaller firms. We will discuss how to do this in Section IV. First, however, you need a clearer view of how the increased set of people seeking employment, and the equally changed set of available openings, relate to each other to produce today's labor market.

Three. What Am I Bid?

There are more people looking for work today, and they are better educated than ever before. There are a smaller proportion of jobs in manufacturing and government, and a larger proportion in trade and services. Much recent employment growth has been in small and medium-sized businesses, and little in the largest corporations.

The labor market is a *market*. Workers are selling their services, and employers are buying. How hard it will be to find work, and the salaries offered, are determined by how many employers are hiring and how many people are seeking employment. We come, therefore, to the question which most affects you: what happens when today's swollen group of job applicants tries to obtain America's new set of available openings?

The Pink Slip

For one thing, a lot of unemployment. It is clear from Chart 11 that the economy's ability to generate enough new openings to employ everyone declined significantly after 1975. For the 30 years before 1975, unemployment usually ranged between 4% and 6%, depending on the state of the economy. Since 1975, however, unemployment has only once gone *below* 6% (5.8% in 1979), and it was almost double that during several months of the 1981-1982 recession. As entire industries experience convulsive change (steel, auto, oil, chemicals), thousands of people lose jobs. Some cities and states where these industries are concentrated have experienced prolonged double-digit unemployment.

Chart 11   Unemployment Rate

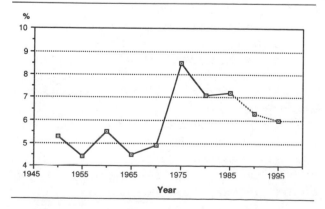

One effect of all this is that unemployment no longer bears the stigma it once did. Some very talented and productive people are unemployed because they were at the wrong place at the wrong time. Employers know this, and are therefore less likely to see a stretch of unemployment as evidence there is something wrong with an unemployed applicant.

The paradox is that this increased and chronic unemployment has occurred despite a high rate of job creation. There are now well over 100 million jobs in this country. There were less than 80 million in 1970.

The problem, then, is not that there are no new jobs being created. The problem is rather the *rate* of new job creation, which is not high enough to provide work for all those seeking it. Until 1975, the economy was able to handle the new workers pouring into the labor market. After that date, however, things changed. Increased energy costs, computer-based technology and intense foreign competition have all combined to hold down — but not to eliminate — the creation of new jobs.

People on the Move

With all this movement in the economy, workers have been changing both employers and occupations with great frequency. Who moves is closely related to age, as Charts 12 and 13 show. Fewer than one worker in ten over age 35 changes his or her occupation in any given year, compared to almost one in three teenagers. Similarly, those over age 45 are much more likely to have been with their present employers for 10 years or more. Younger workers, who move frequently, have shorter tenures. (Also, workers in their teens or early twenties aren't old enough to have worked long for *any* employer.)

Even taking age into account, however, there's a lot more movement from one employer to another in the United States than anywhere else in the developed world. The average West German will work for two employers over a lifetime. The equivalent number in the United States is over ten. In this country, a sound understanding of how the labor market works and changes is a necessary survival skill.

All this movement creates another paradox. On the one hand, there's a lot of unemployment. On the other hand, 30% of American workers have been with their

19

Chart 12   Occupational Mobility Per Year

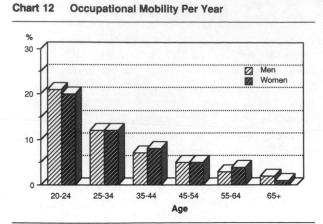

Chart 13   Years with Current Employer

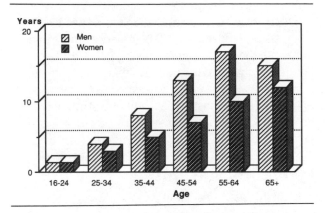

present employer for one year or less. This means that 30% of this country's jobs come open during a one year period. In round numbers, that's 30 million openings.

With 30 million jobs a year being filled, how can you miss?

More easily than you might think. These 30 million openings are not a random sample. The lower the pay, the more often a job comes open. Minimum wage jobs turn over rapidly. People are a lot more reluctant to leave higher-paying positions.

In addition, although 30 million is a big number, it's also a big country. We're talking about openings spread throughout the 50 states and the District of Columbia. And, of course, these 30 million openings aren't all available at the same time. Jobs open up throughout the year and are often quickly filled. The average position remains open for only two weeks. Despite the large number of job possibilities, therefore, you still have to be in the right place at the right time.

So it's a mixed picture. There is a lot of opportunity.

There are also many problems finding suitable employment. It's in the nature of things that there are many openings for undesirable jobs, since people leave these positions quickly. Under the pressures of foreign competition and domestic deregulation, many well-paid jobs have disappeared. Somewhere in those 30 million possibilities, of course, there must be many that would interest you. The key is to know how to find them, and what to do then to turn the opportunity into a job offer.

After the Pink Slip

It's one thing when workers decide to move on from one job to another because of greater opportunity. Usually they have a pretty good idea where they're going, and often they have another job lined up before leaving. For those who lose a job they would prefer to keep, however, the problem of finding new employment is often very challenging. The more unexpected the job loss, the more traumatic the situation can be.

This is especially true for employees who have worked for a major corporation for many years, and who assumed they would remain until retirement. Not having looked for work in many years, and with above-average salaries, they are often shocked at how few opportunities they can find in today's economy.

The government recently did a follow-up study of workers employed for at least three years at a job which was then lost because the firm either closed, or permanently reduced its workforce. These job losses occurred during the five-year period from January 1979 to January 1984. Chart 14 shows the employment status of these workers as of January 1984. Although the majority found new employment, a large proportion (26 percent) remained unemployed. Another 14 percent had either voluntarily retired, or given up because they were unable to find new jobs. All told, then, four out of ten were not yet back to work.

Chart 15 shows what happened to those who lost full-time jobs and then did find other work. Again, it is a mixed picture. Some were able to find employment at or above their old wages. Many, however, had to settle for part-time positions, or for jobs paying well below what they had been earning.

Another group did not return to working for someone else, but instead chose self-employment. This is an interesting and important trend, and we will look at it shortly. First, though, let's see what's happening to everyone's wages and salaries.

Chart 14   Workers Displaced 1/79 - 1/84

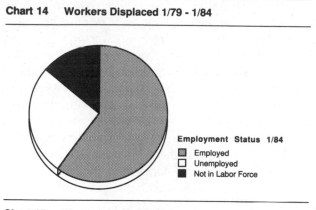

Employment Status 1/84
- ▨ Employed
- ☐ Unemployed
- ■ Not in Labor Force

Chart 15   Workers Losing Full-time Jobs

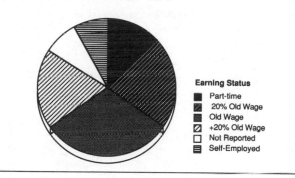

Earning Status
- ■ Part-time
- ▨ 20% Old Wage
- ■ Old Wage
- ▧ +20% Old Wage
- ☐ Not Reported
- ▤ Self-Employed

What Does It Pay?

Anytime you have a market with more supply than demand, you expect prices to fall. On average, that's pretty much what's been happening to wages and salaries, at least when you take inflation into account.

Historically, one result of unionization has been to keep wages within a somewhat limited range. Unions have been strongest within large government and manufacturing organizations. Union contracts have typically reduced the gap between white collar and blue collar pay. They have also kept the wages of skilled and unskilled workers at levels which are not too far apart.

In recent years, both manufacturing and government employment have either declined or grown very slowly. Many workers have moved into the trade and service sectors where unions are weak and incomes vary greatly.

The 1985 average hourly wage for nonsupervisory workers in manufacturing was $9.52, which works out to $19,800 a year if you assume a 40 hour week. In the services, however, it was $7.95 an hour, and in retail trade $5.97 an hour. Given these differences, you would expect lowered incomes when many people move from employment in manufacturing to working in the retail and service sectors. Workers in highly paid industries such as steel and auto have faced particularly steep income declines.

If you take total yearly income for both full- and part-time workers, you get an even wider income gap. The trade sector has many part-time employees. Workers in manufacturing, on the other hand, often put in overtime at time-and-a-half their normal earnings. Overtime is much less common in the service and trade sectors. Everything considered, the industry in which you work really does make a difference, as table 7 shows:

Table 7: Average Annual Pay,
Full- and Part-Time Workers, 1983

Industrial Sector	Average Annual Pay
Manufacturing	$ 21,469
Government	18,154
Services	15,351
Retail Trade	10,007

The industrial sector in which you are employed has a significant effect on employment stability as well as on pay. Many jobs in the service and trade sectors are held by women. As a result, an almost unprecedented situation occurred during the 1981-1982 recession. For the first time since such records were kept, men had a higher unemployment rate than women. The recession hit manufacturing, where many men are employed, much harder than the service sector, which hires a high proportion of women. As a result, the normal unemployment patterns temporarily reversed.

The Self-Employed

For much of the period after World War II, the proportion of self-employed individuals was decreasing. In recent years, however, this trend has reversed. As Chart 16 shows, the number of self-employed individuals is now growing more rapidly than the number of persons working for someone else.

Many observers see this as a healthy trend toward increased entrepreneurship. Perhaps it is. It is important to note, however, that if small employers lack economy of scale, and therefore usually pay less, this can also be true for the self-employed. The self-

21

Chart 16   Increase in Nonagricultural Employment, 1970-83

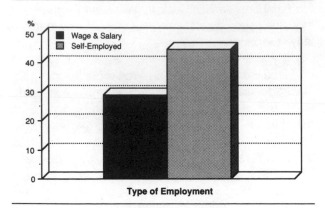

Chart 17   Average 1982 Earnings

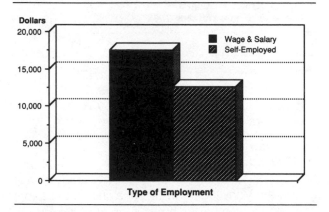

consequence, it is hard to measure the effect of each of these factors on changes in average income. Adjusted for inflation, incomes are definitely lower than they were a decade ago. Some observers, however, have attributed this decline to the large number of baby boomers and women returning to the labor market. It is natural, they argue, for those in entry level positions to receive lower wages.

Data from the Bureau of Labor Statistics, shown in Chart 18, suggest that there's more to it than this. By looking only at what has happened to adult males, we can set aside the lower average wages of women and young people.

Chart 18   Earnings of Full-Time Male Workers 25+

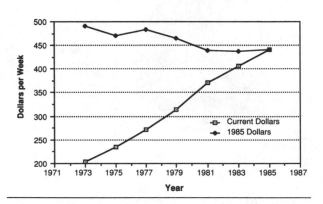

employed work more hours than those on someone else's payroll. Nevertheless, a glance at Chart 17 will show that they earn significantly less than those who work for someone else.

There are, of course, many individual exceptions, as is always true with averages. We all know about the statistician who drowned in a river with an average depth of three feet. Some self-employed individuals make a great deal of money. Furthermore, many self-employed persons deliberately take as little as possible in salary in order to build their businesses. They also pay for as many expenses as possible (health insurance, for example, or an automobile) through the business. The self-employed, therefore, end up balancing increased independence and fringe benefits against lower cash income.

Declining Incomes

The makeup of today's labor force is different from what it used to be. There are more women, more young workers, more immigrants, more self-employed. As a

It is clear that, in contrast to the income growth experienced during the 1950s and 1960s, men have been earning lower real incomes. Keep in mind, too, that these figures are only for men with full-time jobs. They do not take into account the increased number of men who are unemployed, or who have given up looking for work because they can't find suitable employment.

Of course the paychecks of most men (in current dollars, as the economists say) have increased. When the effect of inflation is removed, however, real incomes (actual buying power) went down by 10% over the 1973-1985 period. It wasn't a smooth decline; much of the reduction occurred during the high inflation of 1979-1980. It was, however, a painful drop.

What Does This All Mean?

To sum it up in one word, it means *competition*. There are far more people seeking jobs than there are openings, and this is true at every level of the labor market. We have already looked at the competition among college graduates for professional jobs, and the underemployment which this has produced. For high-paying jobs which do *not* require extensive education, the competition can be even more fierce.

The better the pay, the more applicants you can expect. According to government data, the average pay in industries generating large numbers of new openings is $210 per week. This is in sharp contrast to industries paying an average $310 a week, where few or no new openings are being created. With more people seeking a shrinking proportion of jobs that pay well, the competition is bound to be stiff.

One good index of the scarcity of such opportunities occurred a few years ago during a strike against Greyhound Bus Lines. Because of deregulation, Greyhound was facing lower-cost competitors. Management asked Greyhound employees to accept a pay cut. Understandably, the workers didn't react well to this proposal, and over 12,000 of them went out on strike. Management then threatened to replace the entire group unless they agreed to lower wages. Although this was only a threat, it was well publicized. As a result, the company received over 65,000 applications for employment. Greyhound could have replaced its entire striking workforce five times and still had applicants left over!

So What?

There is no indication that the level of competition for good jobs is going to lessen in the immediate future. You will, therefore, have to learn how to survive in this difficult labor market. Job search methods which might have worked well a few years ago will often not pay off today.

At the same time, this is a big country. In particular industries, for specific jobs, in some cities, opportunities are excellent. The competition, if you are at the right place at the right time, can be much less than average. What is important is being able to find these situations. How to do this will take the rest of this book to lay out in detail, but in essence you must:

1. Take seriously the necessity of setting aside enough time for a close look at both yourself and the labor market before you begin applying for positions. You want to choose an occupation which fits your talents. You want something satisfying. You also need to find something where the competition for available openings is within reason. It's not enough for

someone to tell you about a "hot" field: to whisper in your ear, "Plastics!" (or "Computers!"). You need to know how and where to get detailed information that will allow you to decide what makes sense for you. The exercises in Parts Two and Three of this book will help you with both self-analysis and labor market research. The goal of this work is to be sure you know what you're doing when you apply for a job.

2. Understand clearly how the labor market functions. There's a good deal of information available on how people typically find work. Studies have shown which jobs appear in the want ads and which don't, for example, or who is typically helped by an employment agency. Research on such matters is often published in obscure places, however, and these topics are rarely mentioned in high school or college courses. While there is media coverage of plant closings and unemployment problems, it is often superficial. One purpose of Part IV of this book is to give you detailed information on how the labor market really operates. Although studying these findings will take more time than a 30-second TV news report, it will also allow you to apply what you learn. Your goal is a well-conceived job search strategy that has a high likelihood of getting you what you want in a reasonable period of time.

3. Do what always has to be done when the competition gets rough: practice. You need to get a friend with whom to role-play talking to secretaries on the phone. You need to practice explaining to employers why it's worth their time to interview you. You need to become proficient at answering typical interview questions. You can expect questions like: "Tell me about yourself," or "What led you to apply here?" or "What are your salary requirements?" In a competitive market you have to handle such topics well so that you don't miss a good opportunity. Championship performances don't just happen. They are the result of practice, and that's as true during a job search as it is during a sports event.

4. Understand that looking for a job is a job. It's also a demanding one, and often requires six to eight hours of work a day, one day after another. In addition, it's a stressful job. Your ego is

on the line, and occasional curt treatment or cold nonresponse will hurt. Being rejected is part of the game, and a painful part. You need to blow off steam. Regular exercise is important. You also need contact with people whom you trust and with whom you can share what you're experiencing. Time with friends will let you vent your frustrations, and also just relax and forget the ambiguity of being "between positions."

As in any contest, there's always a luck factor. Even in a tough market some people get a good job offer at the first place they apply. Others take months just to obtain their first, unsuccessful interview. You can't control the luck factor and you shouldn't try. If you're acting intelligently, and working diligently, you're doing all you can.

More than anything else, a job search is an information search combined with a sales effort. The keys to success are knowledge and the ability to communicate. The chapters which follow will outline effi-cient methods for getting the information you need. You will develop a new understanding of your interests, skills and personality traits; learn what jobs require and what they pay; discover where job openings can be found and what employers are looking for; and seek information about specific companies and the people who will be interviewing you. Then, when you get an interview, you will have a chance to use what you've learned. Above all, you will strive to communicate in a way that motivates the employer to offer you the position.

None of this will guarantee you any specific job. There are, again, always chance factors. There's the uncertainty of personal chemistry, the need for approvals from top executives, the possibility that a more attractive candidate will show up at the last minute and so on.

Nonetheless, if you know what you're up against, and use the best strategies for handling the situation, you'll be in much better shape than you would be going in uninformed.

SECTION II.

TELL ME  ABOUT YOURSELF

Introduction to Section II

If you're going to be happy and successful at work, you need to be well matched to the job you do. The quality of that match will depend on the relationship between its two parts. Section II discusses the first part: you. Section III discusses the second part: the job.

You may already be clear about what job you want. This section is still important. In almost any job interview you're going to be asked to "Tell me about yourself," or to "Explain why you are applying for this job." This section is designed to help you give thorough and thoughtful answers to such questions. If there are several applicants for the job you want, and there typically will be, how clearly you explain who you are and what you want to do will be important in convincing the employer to select you for the job.

Let's look more closely at what is really involved in a good "match" between you and a job. The first and most obvious thing is that there are some results that you, the worker, have to produce. That is, each job is made up of a series of tasks. A cab driver has to find homes and offices, make change, respond to calls on the radio, deal with drunks and other difficult characters, keep the cab in good shape and figure out the best route to a given destination. He or she has to avoid getting tickets, find customers, pay for expenses and bring home enough money at the end of the day to make a living. If you're considering driving a cab, the question is: are you good at these things? Are these results you would enjoy producing?

Similarly, a college professor has to do research, write books and articles, prepare lectures, advise students, lead discussions, assign grades and work on faculty committees. A waiter or waitress has to record each customer's order, add the checks properly, balance a tray full of food on the way from the kitchen, remember who ordered what, serve the food cheerfully and deal diplomatically with any complaints.

There is no need to belabor the point. If you're attracted to a job, you first have to take a careful look at the tasks it involves, and the results you have to produce. Then you must ask yourself: do I have the skills to do these things? Am I confident of producing good results?

Chapter Four will show you how to inventory your skills in detail. An employer, after all, hires you to *do* something. When you have finished this chapter, you should be able to describe your strengths clearly to an employer.

There is more to being satisfied with a job than having the necessary skills, however. There are undoubtedly many jobs where you could do the work, but they would bore you, or frighten you, or embarrass you, or pressure you, or otherwise be a source of stress. Few highly accepting, warm-hearted individuals make good bill collectors, to take an extreme example. So another dimension you have to consider when looking for the *right* job is your personality. This will involve taking a close look at how you react emotionally to people and events, to pace and to pressure.

Chapter Five provides a series of exercises to help you review your dominant personality characteristics. Adults rarely leave jobs because they can't do them. They are much more likely to leave (or be fired) because of conflicts with others, or because the job "bugs them." On closer examination, what is usually involved is a serious mismatch between their personalities and the job's demands.

There is one final dimension to consider when looking at the person/job match. This is the issue of values and meaning. Here we look at a more subtle set of questions. Although sometimes hard to pin down, your values are of central importance in determining whether or not your work is meaningful to you.

Of course, a person's occupation may not be the major focus of his or her life. Paul the Apostle, for example, made tents for a living. It was not his major interest. For many, though, work *is* primary. They have dreamed since youth of being a doctor, or an airline pilot, or a legislator, or a baseball umpire. For other individuals it is not so much a particular occupational role that has a certain magic for them, but an entire area of life. *Any* job in a hospital, around an airport or train depot, in the Congress or in a sports stadium adds a certain sparkle to their lives.

Another group of people find meaning in their work primarily through the values advanced by their efforts. An accountant is an accountant, but the results of that accounting work will be different depending on whether the books being kept are those of the United Way, Megabucks Conglomerate, the Archdiocese or a local branch of organized crime.

In Chapter Six, then, we enter the domain of interests. Here we look at the personal context in which you see your work. Why do some people teach in an inner city school when they could work in a wealthy suburb, or sell a quality product for a modest commission rather than an overpriced product for a large commission? Their behavior makes sense in the light of their values and dreams, and the meaning they find in their work. We need to review, in Chapter Six, what you want to look back on when you come to die.

In the three chapters of this section, then, we will look at *skills*, which are the key to doing a job successfully; at *personality*, which determines whether you are comfortable with what you do; and at *values* and dreams, which give meaning to your efforts.

At the end of each chapter in this section you will find a series of case studies. They are not fiction. Each paper was written by an adult who had worked through this section's exercises.

As these case studies make clear, it is the *blend* of your skills, personality and interests that you bring to the labor market. It is how these personal characteristics relate to each other that determines the kinds of work you can do best. It is our hope that, as you share some of the process of self-discovery that others have experienced, you will understand more clearly how to deepen your own self-understanding.

FOUR. What are Your Skills?

Finding a job is often a surprisingly haphazard process. Even when unemployment is low, most people take the first position they're offered. This might work if employers were always on target when deciding who will do well at a job, but they're not. A job offer is evidence that an employer needs help and is willing to risk hiring someone. It is not necessarily evidence that the individual hired will do well.

In fact, many people are hired who don't really fit their jobs. They have no special talent for the work, or they have the wrong temperament, or they lack interest. Some quit or are fired. Many stay on and "make the best of a bad situation." When this happens, everyone loses. They are unhappy, and the employer has a worker who is not fully productive.

How Good Is the Fit?

From one perspective, every step in the self-analysis process outlined in this chapter is directed toward preparing you for a successful employment interview. You want to show a prospective employer that you have carefully thought through what you have to offer, and how *your* skills fit *that* job. Employers see few people who are this thoroughly prepared. You want to be sure you are one of those few.

From another perspective, this process is designed to protect you. Good jobs are harder to get these days, and mistakes take longer to correct. If, as a result of this preparatory work, you obtain a job which interests you, and which is well matched to your talents, training and personality, then the likelihood you will do well is greatly increased. The potential payoff in income and personal satisfaction will more than justify the time invested. After all, it takes six to eight weeks for the average person to find a job. Managerial positions typically require four to six months. Even the shorter of these two periods is more than enough time to work through these exercises.

Skills, Marketable and Otherwise

A natural first question for anyone looking for work is, "What are your skills?" Employers, after all, hire people to *do* something. What is really being asked is, "What are you able to do?"

One common reaction to this question, particularly from women who have not worked for pay recently, or from those seeking a first job, is: "But I don't *have* any skills!" This is never true, but it suggests the need for at least some discussion of what is meant by a "skill."

When we talk about skills we refer primarily to the natural aptitudes or talents with which each of us is born. Learning and experience build on these natural gifts, and lead to real productivity. The difference is one of degree. Even a born swimmer has to practice regularly to win an Olympic medal. If you're not made to swim, however, all the practice in the world won't get you to the Olympics.

At first glance, it might seem that most adults should be well aware of their skills and talents. Our experience is the opposite. We are too close to ourselves to really appreciate many of our gifts. As the saying goes, "I don't know who discovered water, but it probably wasn't a fish." Precisely because some things come easily to us, we tend to discount them. We forget that the critical point is not how easy they are for us, but how much more difficult they are for others.

This chapter will, therefore, provide a framework for a careful review of what you do best. Your first goal is to become more fully conscious of your own strengths. Equally important, you want to increase your ability to describe these talents to others.

Build on Strengths

The reason a job exists is that an employer has something that needs to be done. There is a result that has to be produced. There is a problem that needs to be solved. To find the right job, you need to be clear about the kinds of results you are best at producing, and the problems you can most skillfully solve. Finding the right job involves matching an employer's needs with your ability to meet those needs.

It Can Hurt to Be Well Schooled

Unfortunately, the more time you've spent in schools, the more difficult this process may be. Schools *are* concerned with skills and aptitudes, but only with some of them. Many of the abilities critical to success in adult life (being able to negotiate well, a knack for sizing up other people, being able to think on your feet) are neither taught nor measured in schools. This gives students the implicit message that such skills are not important.

They are not only important, but essential in many jobs. When considering the challenges presented by the many occupations in our society, and where you would fit best, it is essential to think about the full range of adult capabilities, and not just the narrow set of competencies addressed by academic institutions.

Schools give another false message when they require students to excel in every academic subject to be considered truly successful. To make the Dean's List, or the Honor Roll, a student must read well, write well, be good at mathematics, science, languages, history and social studies, not to mention physical education and music.

The Well-Rounded Need Not Apply

It is important to note that this demand for universal talent is in striking contrast to what most jobs require. Employees must ordinarily have a much more limited set of gifts. You don't really care whether your mechanic can sing, or your barber can solve an equation, or your accountant appreciates history. All these things are fine, but what is important is how well they perform a more limited (specialized, if you will) range of tasks.

Jobs, unlike schools, do not demand that an individual be "well-rounded," attractive though that may be as a human ideal. Success in occupational choice lies in identifying as clearly as possible those few things which come easily to you, those specific tasks which you do quite well and enjoy doing well. You want to find a job which demands precisely those talents.

Norah Lofts, an English novelist, says of herself: "...in so many areas I am inept; I can't drive a car, read a railway timetable, tell a share from a stock, mend a fuse, or work out a date. I am 'innumerate,' just as some people are illiterate..." She is, however, the author of more than two dozen successful novels. It is doubtful whether she (or her banker) cares much about her lack of mechanical and mathematical ability. She is happy and successful doing what comes easily to her. There are plenty of people whom she can hire to take care of those tasks which she cannot do well herself.

Peter Drucker, one of the country's finest management consultants, argues that the search for only "well-rounded" employees is a formula for mediocrity. Strong personalities often have striking weaknesses, too. Effective executives do not ask, "What can a person do?" Instead, they ask, "What can this person do uncommonly well?" The whole value of being part of an organization rather than working alone is that you can use your greatest strengths most effectively, while others in the organization take care of the tasks for which you have no talent.

The Key to the Future Lies behind Us

Your talents do not exist somewhere in the abstract. Your natural gifts have been used and developed as you've lived your life to this point. You can most easily review them by looking carefully at your past experiences. A methodical consideration of what you have done successfully, and especially of those times you have thoroughly enjoyed something you did well, soon begins to show a pattern. The same skills and motivations come up again and again.

In reviewing your experience, look for the times when you produced specific *results*. Don't start with the abstract, but with the concrete. For any number of reasons you may now believe you are a leader, or good with money, or creative, or whatever. Yet an honest review of the times when you've been most productive may show that what you really have is the ability to contribute effectively to a group rather than lead it, a good sense of people rather than of finance, the ability to follow up meticulously rather than be creative and so on. *Much* self-delusion enters into self-descriptions. The best way to avoid self-delusion is to begin with concrete accomplishments, and patiently analyze them. Accurate self-knowledge will come, though it will come slowly, and you will need help from others.

Why Not Just Take Some Tests?

Given the importance of clearly and correctly identifying your skills, it is natural to ask if there are any tests which would do this for you. There are, but they have several limitations. Aptitude tests traditionally given in schools are almost entirely limited to school-oriented skills. Personality and interest tests can help measure other dimensions of your personality, but they too cover only some job-related personal characteristics.

Many of the factors which are crucial to success in various occupations are not easily measured. The capacity to deal well with a wide variety of people; a good feel for the balance between independence and supervision needed by children and adolescents; the ability to handle detailed follow-up; a feel for how machines operate and why they malfunction; a talent for negotiating successfully with people of diverse viewpoints and interests; an intuitive sense of how to resolve interpersonal conflicts; the ability to make shrewd judgments about people's motivations; an entrepreneurial urge to find unmet needs and fill them: these traits, each essential in some employment settings, are hard to capture in aptitude and personality tests.

The Self-Directed Search, an instrument developed by John Holland, is widely used in career counseling. So is the Strong-Campbell Interest Inventory. Some people find these instruments helpful. Others don't. It's not that they are badly designed. It's just that the human personality is too complex for adequate categorization by multiple-choice instruments. These inventories are more likely to be helpful when interpreted by a skilled counselor. However, even then they supplement rather than replace a review of your past successes.

If you want to take these or similar instruments, check with the counseling office at a nearby community college or other academic institution. Or, if you are interested in taking a more extensive battery of tests, write the Johnson O'Connor Research Foundation. Their materials include audio-visually based measurements and work samples which cover a wide range of aptitudes. For the address of the Johnson O'Connor Research Foundation, see the notes for this chapter.

Now to the List

In a few pages, forms will be provided for you to write down some of your past accomplishments. You can choose anything: work done in school, in an extracurricular activity, something done on the job, or at home, or in the armed forces, or in a volunteer organization, or whatever.

The accomplishments you list need not seem like major events to anyone else. What is important is that they are things you enjoyed doing, did well and felt good about. Examples might be successful competition in a spelling bee, designing a workbench for your garage, increasing corporate sales 20% through a new marketing program, selling more Girl Scout cookies than anyone in the troop, writing a thoughtful letter to the editor, reorganizing your division for more productivity, doing the art work for a local store or always being the one to whom people want to talk when they're upset and need a friend.

Think of each accomplishment as a story. You were the chief actor. You did something that had an observable result. Explain what you did, and the outcome, in simple language. Pretend you are talking to a foreigner who isn't totally familiar with American cul-

ture, and who won't understand unless you spell things out in detail.

Note that the emphasis is on what you did, not on what others did. Winning an award comes as a result of someone else's decision. The important thing is not that decision, but what you did which led to the award-winning performance. A competition in which you won no award, but where you did well and enjoyed the effort, would be equally useful for analysis.

If you have trouble making your list, try organizing it by time periods. List one thing you did well and enjoyed in the last three months, then something from the three months before that, and so on. As you get farther back in time, try to list at least one accomplishment per year.

Be sure the accomplishment is specific. Don't try to list something so global it's impossible to analyze in detail (for example, "raised two children," or "worked my way through school"). Instead, list specific accomplishments that were part of that global activity (such as "organized a successful girl scout troop for my eight year old daughter," or "scheduled my time carefully enough to work 20 hours a week during the first semester of my freshman year and still have time for homework").

Try to list at least 20 or 25 accomplishments. Describe them in enough detail so that what you did is clear. Then take them one at a time and ask yourself: "What in this activity did I most enjoy? What happened as a result of my actions? What does this say about my strongest gifts?" To bring out the answers to these questions, try to summarize each accomplishment in one sentence. Look at the verb in that sentence. What does it say about the intensity and nature of your action? The sentence should make the result of your action clear, as well as the benefits which came from those results.

The important thing, after you have analyzed several accomplishments, is to look for patterns. Is the same aptitude (for example, handling figures easily, or the ability to write clearly, or being able to sell others on your ideas) coming up again and again? Don't focus too long on any one accomplishment. What is important is finding what is common to your past successes. The abilities you used time after time in the past will also be central to your doing well in the future.

Some Examples

To provide some concrete illustrations before you start, here are three accomplishments and some skills they show.

Accomplishment

When I was a sophomore in high school, I noticed that the older students were using slide rules. I asked about them, and found out that using one saved time doing multiplication and division. (This was years ago, before the introduction of hand-held calculators.) I got a slide rule, and then found a book in the library that described how to use it. Following the directions in the book one step at a time, I figured out how it worked. Then I began doing my math and science homework with it. This saved a lot of time. I asked my teachers if I could use the slide rule during exams and they said all right. This gave me more time to concentrate on the problems themselves, since I could now do the arithmetic quickly. I offered to show a friend of mine how to use the slide rule, but to my surprise he was not interested. He said that when it was necessary, the teachers would show everyone how to use it.

Aptitudes or Skills Used

- *Ability to do library research.*
- *Good reading skills: able to read something and understand it; able to follow written directions.*
- *Good feel for numbers; natural aptitude for mathematics.*
- *Able to explain things to others (although in this case the offer to teach was refused).*
- *Able to take ideas and put them to new and practical uses.*

Accomplishment

I was in the sixth grade and we had to do several creative compositions. The teacher was demanding and gave praise only sparingly. He never gave perfect marks, he said, because perfection in creative writing was virtually impossible. Two of my compositions, however, won perfect marks. I remember what it felt like to write those stories: how careful I was about the words, and how, when they were done after an hour or two of intense concentration, I knew they were good. What the teacher thought of them really did not mean much to me. Those essays set an inner standard which I use constantly. If I get that certain feeling when I've finished a piece of work, I know it is good. My only disappointment in myself is that I

did not follow his advice and use my writing ability more consistently and creatively.

Aptitudes or Skills Used

- *Ability to write well, even under some pressure.*
- *Being emotionally involved in writing, leading to careful, thoughtful work.*
- *Good judgment about how well written work has been done.*
- *An ability to do written work carefully and to check it meticulously.*

Accomplishment

The most challenging and enjoyable job I have had was when I was the general manager for a small welding supply company. The owner hired me to run the company while he started another, totally unrelated business. My first task was to set up a new manufacturing facility. This required the establishment of manufacturing, quality control, safety and production-flow procedures. To do this, I first established my priorities in light of the company's goals. I established a step by step procedure that was safe and could be performed by anyone with minimal training. During the development phase, I had to handle multiple tasks and anticipate problems that could occur later, during the manufacturing phase. I had to write up procedures and instruct new employees on these procedures. I had to handle any problems as they occurred, until the new process was running smoothly.

Aptitudes or Skills Used

- *Can independently take on and keep track of a complex, many-dimensioned managerial task.*
- *Able to visualize an entire project and then work step by step toward the desired goal.*
- *Strong logical reasoning abilities.*
- *Able to foresee problems and take action to prevent them.*
- *Use writing skills to give clear directions.*
- *Teaching skills used to instruct new employees in necessary procedures.*
- *Direct others comfortably.*
- *Use problem-solving skills when difficulties occur.*
- *Deal with both plans and people in a coordinated, goal-directed way.*

Accomplishments Analysis Form

Accomplishment: My Actions, and Their Results   The Skills Used

_____

_____

_____

_____

_____

_____

_____

_____

_____

_____

_____

_____

_____

_____

_____

_____

_____

_____

_____

_____

_____

_____
_____
_____
_____
_____
_____
_____
_____
_____
_____
_____
_____
_____
_____
_____
_____
_____
_____
_____
_____
_____
_____
_____
_____
_____

_____

_____

_____

_____

_____

_____

_____

_____

_____

_____

_____

_____

_____

_____

_____

_____

_____

_____

_____

_____

_____

_____

_____

_____

_____

_____

_____

_____

_____

_____

_____

_____

_____

_____

_____

_____

_____

_____

_____

_____

_____

_____

_____

_____

_____

_____

_____

_____

_____

_____

_____

_____

_____

_____

_____

_____

_____

_____

_____

_____

_____

_____

Now, having seen some examples, it's time for you to begin listing *your* accomplishments. When you are finished, analyze each, looking for skills which played a major role in your past successes.

Don't Go It Alone

Because of the imperfect nature of self-knowledge, the process of skill identification needs to be carried on with the involvement of friends and relatives whose judgment you trust. They will often see your strengths and weaknesses more clearly than you do. They therefore function as a reality check. They can review your self-descriptions and help you answer questions such as: "Is this really me? Am I kidding myself? Have I left out something important? Am I exaggerating? Am I selling myself short?" Finding someone who knows you well and will take the time to review your self-analysis is an essential step in this process. A friend, spouse, parent, brother or sister, or past or present employer can provide a helpful outside perspective.

Another good thing to do is to ask three or four people who know you well to write a letter stating your greatest talents as they see them. It's useful to choose people who have known you in a variety of contexts (work, home, hobbies, social activities and so on). Let these letters guide you as you begin to inventory your accomplishments.

Getting a Group Involved

Another helpful way to involve friends in the skill analysis process is to use an exercise called "trioing." Get together with two other people who would also like to clarify their skills. Take one of your accomplishments. Relate in detail what you did and what happened as a result. List the skills you see yourself using. Then let the other two tell you the additional talents *they* believe were also involved. If you agree, add their analysis to your own.

Now let the next person have a turn at describing one of his or her accomplishments, and the skills used, followed by your comments and those of the third group member. Finally, the last of the group gets his or her turn.

As you do this for several accomplishments each, you should find that (1) your descriptions of what you did are becoming more explicit, (2) you are getting better at naming the skills you and the others used, (3) despite this, the group members are regularly able to point out abilities you didn't notice, and (4) the same talents keep coming up in many of your accomplishments.

Skills Are What You Can DO

Included for your use is a list of 244 verbs that describe functional or transferable skills. (These skills are transferable because they can be used in, or are transferable to, many different jobs or situations.)

You can use this list in several ways. As you look through the verbs, one of them may remind you of some past activity that you can add to your accomplishment list. Or, when analyzing what you have done, these verbs may help you to describe your behavior more accurately.

Finding Yourself on the Skills Grid

Another helpful tool when doing skill identification is the skills grid. The one at the end of this chapter is from Richard Bolles' *Quick Job Hunting Map*. Using this grid will help you to identify talents used in your accomplishments that you might otherwise miss. In addition, the list is a great vocabulary builder. The more you use it, the more fluent you will become at describing your skills accurately.

Now Pull Yourself Together

The final thing you need to do, once you have finished the various exercises described in this chapter, is to write several paragraphs which sum up what you learned. Remember, you are not, at this point, describing a job. You are describing yourself.

Discuss what you've done best when dealing with people. Do you want to help them? In what way? To lead them? In what context?

Look at the way you handle data and ideas. Are you good with numbers? With abstract concepts? With statistical data? Do you communicate your ideas most easily in written or spoken form?

Review your abilities with physical objects. Do you have a knack for running and repairing machines? For handling small items like electronic parts? For art?

As always, concentrate on those things that come easily to you and that you most enjoy. Then, when you've finished this first self-description, show it to at least two or three family members or good friends. Ask them if they think you have exaggerated, or have not said enough, or have left out anything important. Discuss it with them.

Your Functional/Transferable Skills In 244 Verbs

achieved	designed	headed	monitored	reasoned	summarized
acted	detected	helped	motivated	received	supervised
adapted	determined	hypothesized	moved	recommended	supplied
addressed	developed	identified	navigated	reconciled	surveyed
administered	devised	illustrated	negotiated	recorded	symbolized
advised	diagnosed	imagined	observed	recruited	synergized
analyzed	directed	implemented	obtained	reduced	synthesized
anticipated	discovered	improved	offered	referred	systematized
arbitrated	dispensed	improvised	operated	rehabilitated	talked
arranged	displayed	increased	ordered	related	taught
ascertained	disproved	influenced	organized	remembered	team-built
assembled	dissected	informed	oversaw	rendered	tended
assessed	distributed	initiated	painted	repaired	tested
attained	diverted	innovated	perceived	reported	told
audited	dramatized	inspected	performed	represented	took
budgeted	drew	inspired	persuaded	researched	took instructions
built	drove	installed	photographed	resolved	trained
calculated	edited	instituted	piloted	responded	transcribed
charted	eliminated	instructed	planned	responsible for	translated
checked	empathized	interpreted	played	restored	traveled
classified	enforced	interviewed	politicked	retrieved	treated
coached	established	invented	predicted	reviewed	trouble-shot
collected	estimated	inventoried	prepared	risked	tutored
communicated	evaluated	investigated	prescribed	sang	typed
compiled	examined	judged	presented	scheduled	umpired
completed	expanded	kept	printed	selected	understood
composed	experimented	lead	problem-solved	sensed	understudied
computed	explained	learned	processed	separated	undertook
conducted	extracted	lectured	produced	served	unified
conserved	filed	lifted	programmed	set	united
consolidated	financed	listened	projected	set-up	upgraded
constructed	fixed	logged	promoted	sewed	used
consulted	followed	made	proof-read	shaped	utilized
controlled	formulated	maintained	protected	shared	verbalized
coordinated	founded	managed	provided	showed	washed
copied	gathered	manipulated	publicized	sketched	weighed
counseled	gave	mediated	purchased	sold	worked
created	generated	memorized	questioned	solved	wrote
decided	got	mentored	raised	sorted	wrought
defined	guided	met	read	spoke	
delivered	handled	modeled	realized	studied	

By doing this you're not only subjecting your self-description to an important reality test. You're also becoming accustomed to talking about yourself in skills language. By beginning with those you know well, you will gradually become more comfortable using this approach. There is no better preparation for having similar discussions during employment interviews.

Knowing the Language

The importance of knowing how to discuss your skills with others comes through clearly in the experience of a woman who had worked for several years as a social worker. She wanted to move to the private sector and had obtained several interviews. None of these interviews had yet led to a job offer.

After completing the skill identification process, she arranged to talk to several people who could give her more information about occupations that attracted her (a process we will discuss in detail in Section III). She was particularly interested in learning more about public relations work. She was only seeking information about the requirements for a position, and not applying for an opening. Nonetheless, several employers began seriously discussing job possibilities.

When asked what made the difference, she answered that it was the change in her language. Before this, she had described herself by giving her degrees and past job titles: "I have a B.A. in history and an M.S.W. in social work. I've been a social worker for the Welfare Department, and also for Child Welfare." No one was interested in offering her a position in the private sector based on this information.

Now she explained her interest in learning more about public relations by saying, "I'm good at public speaking and I really enjoy it. I write well, and I have a facility for staying calm even when dealing with angry people."

She had switched her self-description from degrees and job titles to skills and personality characteristics. Her self-description related her past success to future potential doing public relations work. As a result, those to whom she was speaking began to see her as someone who might be good at the tasks such work requires.

An employer, after all, hires you to *do* something. When you are talking about your skills, you are talking about what you have done well before, and want to do well again. Employers will ask you, during a job interview, to "Tell me about yourself" (or "What are you best at?" or "What are you interested in?"). In this discus-

sion, you should be able to name several of your strongest skills without hesitation, giving one or two concrete examples of their use. Once you get into the job search process, this alone can mean the difference between an interview which leads to a job offer and one which does not.

The Case Studies

To give you some concrete examples of what can be gained from the exercises in this section, each chapter contains summaries done by people who have gone through them. These summaries, which we have labeled case studies, illustrate what you need to look for as you review your past experience.

Each of these case studies records forward movement in the process of self-understanding. If you read them carefully, you will also see occasional unanswered questions, apparent contradictions or conclusions which do not seem totally justified by the evidence. This is not surprising. Self-understanding is a slow process. These papers were written by real people as they worked through one stage of the challenging but rewarding task of self-analysis.

The skills you have, and the results you can produce using those skills, need to be summed up at this point. Later, as you work through the next two chapters, you will put your skills in the context of your personality traits and interests, and take a closer look at how they blend together. You can then summarize what you have learned about yourself in a paper similar to the case studies.

CASE STUDIES

Case Study 4-1

As you read this study, look for the way the author describes her skills. Is each rooted in something she actually accomplished? Does she focus on what she does uncommonly well? Her natural empathy for people and their problems combines with an interest in mental health to draw her toward psychology. At the same time, she has a combination of talents that would make a good manager. How do you react to her plans to aim first at being a therapist, with the later goal of managing a mental health facility? As she gathers more information on what these two jobs really involve, do you think her goals might change? Finally, look at how her talents, personality and interests blend together. Do they fit well? Are they moving her in more or less the same direction, or are there conflicts?

Reviewing the Options

Throughout the process of evaluating past jobs, projects and experiences, I have been surprised to find that I have used skills and talents that were never identified as such. The defining of my own aptitudes has been an enlightening experience. Now that I am aware of what they are, I can draw on them more purposefully and with much more confidence.

After considerable self-assessment, I have concluded that my strongest natural talent is my ability to identify with and understand other people's situations. This has emotional meaning for me because I have a natural inclination to want to help people improve the things that bother or hinder them. This can range from helping someone carry out a particular task to working through some personal problem. I would like to use this talent in a way that brings monetary reward, but the emotional payoff for me is seeing someone (or something) function more effectively.

Many of my personality traits reveal a tendency toward involvement with other people, usually in a helping capacity. While I like my personal space and time alone, I am aware that most of the things I do take on their fullest meaning in a person-to-person context.

One of my strongest personality traits is my ability to be empathic with other people's feelings. I am frequently sought out by friends to provide a listening ear or to discuss a problem. I think this is because I don't tell them what to do, take sides or talk to others about their issues. Basically, I listen and discuss options with them. I enjoy interacting with people in this way. I value their trust in me and like inspiring and motivating them.

Being approached for solace or help makes me feel important. I also like the actual process of helping another person to become more self-sufficient. It is a kind of brainstorming, sometimes on a very professional level. If I didn't have a good deal of personal contact in my work, I would become bored and unstimulated.

Another strong personality trait is my willingness to take on a challenge. I am able to accept responsibility for something meaningful and to persevere even when things are difficult

and confusing. I have done this in job-related areas by organizing new positions where there were no job prototypes and no precedents to follow. The challenge was in the organization of details. When I was in real estate, I was successful in selling homes to "difficult" clients who had frustrated and depleted the energies of numerous other agents. While I did view these clients as challenging, I liked working with them and getting to know them. I think this factor was critical in overcoming their resistance.

One other trait is my persistence. When I become interested and involved in a task or project, I feel a certain dedication to it. I frequently initiate things. When I do, I am very goal-oriented. Once I visualize some end-result, I am not easily discouraged. I tend to view setbacks as temporary lulls, and not as ultimate frustrations or failures. I've solved many a problem by using this trait. For example, sometimes real estate clients rejected property after property. I simply could not find anything that suited them. I handled this situation by reevaluating everything I knew about them and asking for more information, trying to find the critical element(s) that I was overlooking. Once I discovered what was missing, I was generally able to find the right home for them.

My own self-assessment, along with the comments solicited from long-standing acquaintances, reveals that one of my primary skills is an ability to organize. In the past, I have been attracted to new positions in which I not only worked out the initial job description, but organized procedures and systems to make the process itself as effective as possible. I am able to bring a definite structure and working order to a scattered assortment of data and material. In real estate, I was constantly organizing and correlating information from mortgage and title companies, buyers, sellers and other agents to bring about a successful closing. As I look back on these job responsibilities, it seems that the magic, for me, was in being able to make a situation or process "work." The organizing itself wasn't all that interesting. Setting my sights on the end result was the thing that motivated me.

My communication skills have been well-tested in these and other positions. My job at the executive headquarters of a large food chain involved questioning and interviewing division managers and other personnel in order to gather information for weekly in-house reports. Since I was not in a position to make suggestions based on the findings in my reports (though there were several I wanted to make) I was sometimes rather frustrated. My job was to compile and organize facts, not to comment on them. In keeping with my position, I responded to others with tact and objectivity and, in general, was diplomatic. Again, when I worked as a medical secretary, I dealt effectively with people who were upset and anxious and, in this way, was able to gain cooperation and promote a harmonious atmosphere in the office.

Another facet of this job entailed explaining the requirements of various insurance carriers to patients so that they could better understand their benefits and limitations. In high school, I used my communication skills to interview people at school and in the community, and to write articles about them in the school newspaper. I was responsible for asking questions in a way that would elicit the information I needed. I liked talking to people about themselves, and they seemed to enjoy it as much as I did.

My position at corporate headquarters also required management and supervisory skills. After the job was established I was given a secretary. I was able to oversee and coordinate her work so that our objectives were met in a systematic and harmonious way. Some years before, I managed a Campfire Girls group, and this required negotiating with the young members and deciding on goals. I was involved in planning and overseeing various group projects as well as working with the girls on a one-to-one basis. I have never before defined these organizing, supervising or managing abilities as actual skills. It is good to know that my skills go beyond the strictly social. I like communicating by inspiring and enabling, but I also like the idea of organizing and managing.

My problem-solving ability has developed through years of managing a family, and through personal trials of one kind or another. There was a period of time in my husband's career when our family made long-distance moves every few years. I single-handedly worked out problems with movers and schedules, and resolved the various dilemmas connected with relocation.

I have also learned to enjoy figuring things out on my own and searching out the resources to do so when necessary. For example, for most of my life I have been a very poor mathematician. I barely passed math in high school. When I was in undergraduate school a few years ago I spent an entire summer teaching myself basic math and college algebra. When I took the required course in the fall, I wanted to maintain a high average. When I could not work out a problem on my own, I found someone who would explain it to me. This was basically a self-educating process in which I "problem-solved" on two levels. The benefits were well worth the effort, although I much prefer to problem-solve with other people.

I've spent many hours on the Hotline with rape survivors, helping them to work out various issues related to their assaults. My work in the family therapy practicum has a similar theme. As the therapist, I help clients solve their problems through their own self-directed actions.

In reevaluating my accomplishments, I find that I have good skills in persuading others to move in a definite direction or to entertain a different point of view. In my real estate days, I helped clients to make decisions by evaluating with them the pros and cons of various properties. In this way, I was able to move them toward a course of action. Also, I am becoming more aware of my persuasive ability through my work with clients in therapy. Since changes are variously motivated and occur slowly, it is often difficult to recognize such movement as partially resulting from my (therapeutic) challenge and persuasion.

My primary interests are in the areas of mental health and physical fitness, and I see the two as very complementary. Professionally, I have chosen to pursue the field of psychotherapy, but I do not necessarily view physical fitness as secondary in importance to mental health. I am convinced that both are necessary to be well-functioning. After taking some required physical education courses as an undergraduate, I set up and carried out my own exercise program. In a very short time I noticed some important changes in myself, such as a greatly reduced level of anxiety and tension, more mental alertness, and an increased sense of overall well-being. As a result of my own experience, I often encourage clients *to take up some form of exercise.*

My interest in psychology has been evident for many years. When I was younger, I was attracted to any magazine or newspaper article on the subject, and I bought many "pop" psychology books. My recent efforts have been along more academic lines, and these have stimulated my interest even more. My fascination with human behavior is ongoing, and it seems to be a constant thread in much that I do.

I have other interests that I pursue in my spare time. I am interested in the Scriptures and other religious writings for their own value, and because I believe that these teachings make a significant impact on the belief patterns and behaviors of individuals. I have a strong interest in interior design, though I pursue it only marginally at the present time. Primarily, I am interested in color and symmetry and their use to create an environment with a positive effect on one's state of mind.

In summary, it seems that most of my interests are, in some sense, people-oriented. I am not particularly surprised at this discovery. The highest score on my Strong-Campbell Interest Inventory was in the social area.

My ideal job would allow me to work closely with different kinds of people. I would have plenty of opportunity to use my communication and problem-solving skills. I would meet people from all walks of life who have lots of problem situations to be worked out. I am good at reviewing options, and that would be a critical part of my ideal position. I would want to work on my own initiative for the most part, and would be required to organize many aspects of the job myself. I would be involved in activities such as workshops and seminars outside my office, for these would bring the additional challenges of creating, developing and organizing something.

At some point, I want to use my supervisory and organizational skills by managing a whole facility. My salary would be important, but not nearly as important as being recognized for my professional ability in relating to others, and in persuading people to make positive changes in their lives. My office would be comfortable and attractive, with tasteful furnishings and appointments. My hours could be fairly steady, although I want some flexibility in my schedule so that I

can opt for some exercise and relaxation. Most of all, I want to enjoy this job and have fun doing it.

Case Study 4-2

This paper describes a combination of skills which would be a good match to a variety of sales positions. The author's organizing and marketing abilities developed early in her life. Are her personality characteristics consistent with work in sales? How about her interests? Notice her healthy attitude toward the interest inventories she has taken. She relates the results from these instruments to her past accomplishments, and uses them to confirm and clarify what experience has taught her.

At the end of the paper she has an ideal job description. Read it carefully. Does it really spell out what she would be doing in her ideal job? We may have here an example of someone who has, on one level, recognized her sales talent. Because this work comes naturally to her, however, she still may not fully realize the value or strength of her abilities in this area. She seems to take it for granted, without explicitly spelling out how it will be used.

Coaching and Selling

One of the most frequent comments I hear about myself is how much potential I have. Various professors and professionals have told my family and friends that I will be a great success no matter what field I choose to pursue. At first, I am ecstatic from all the praise and from being held in such high esteem by those "who know these things." Then reality sets in.

There is no ready-made master plan for my life. I now recognize that work and life satisfaction depend on the extent to which I find adequate outlets for my skills, personality and interests.

I prefer situations where feedback is prompt, precise and unmistakable. I need to know how well I am doing. Sales is a profession that generally provides such immediate feedback. I am sure this is one reason I chose to remain in the business for six years.

In high school, I was involved in athletics. I especially enjoyed track, where I could immediately gauge how well I was doing and how much I had improved. Although I enjoyed the affiliation aspect of being on the team, I general-

ly felt secure enough in my own abilities to achieve as an individual regardless of how well the team was performing.

For me, growth is most likely when there is a great deal of freedom to experiment, to set my own pace and to select the specific jobs that I will work on. When I was a high school senior, my track team was forced by budget cuts to finance, on our own, a trip to the Junior Olympics in South Dakota. I developed a plan to make the general public aware of our achievements, and to solicit funds in order to finance our trip.

First, I worked through the appropriate channels to get the go-ahead to pursue the fund raising. Next, I implemented an effective, if amateurish, marketing strategy. Finally, I organized the track team and many other volunteers to canvas local neighborhoods door-to-door to ask the public for financial support.

The final outcome was much greater than anyone had anticipated. We raised enough money to pay for our five-day trip. In addition, we were able to purchase much-needed uniforms for the entire girl's high school track team. I relished the freedom to express initiative and ingenuity, to experiment, and to handle in my own way many of the problems that arose. Looking back, I think it was the control of my own work, rather than the tangible outcome of my effort, that was the ultimate motivator.

When I analyzed this accomplishment using the Quick Job Hunting Map, I was able to identify several of my strongest skill areas. I can creatively organize and plan, influence and persuade, communicate, advertise and motivate others. Both the Strong-Campbell Interest Inventory and the Self-Directed Search further indicated that I am an enterprising person. I scored extremely high in this area, and I believe this is a realistic assessment.

When I think of my interests, the phrase that first comes to mind is the "pursuit of happiness." An interest is an activity in which a person willingly takes part without ulterior motives. My interests make me smile, laugh and just feel good about doing them.

When analyzing my skills, I looked at two accomplishments that focused on fitness. That was not unintentional. When I began to identify my accomplishments, many of them related to the health and fitness field. A few years ago I volunteered to help coach a girls' high school track team. Professionally, I was not involved in the fitness arena. I thought it was just an "interest" and not a potential career.

I became very involved and committed to helping the girls achieve their goals. Today, I have warm memories of the special months in which I worked with that team. In addition, I now recognize that I made the transition from competing to helping others compete. Although I participate in many local fun runs and various athletic events, I believe my real interest lies in helping others achieve an increased level of fitness.

The aspect of my personality of which I am most aware is that I am very outgoing. I enjoy meeting people, and they are attracted to me. I contribute freely to conversations in either large or small groups. I am willing to share my experiences and am interested in hearing about the feelings and interests of others. I am an accepting person. I have a strong sense of self-respect, communicate that to others, and show respect for them as well. I possess a high level of energy and find it exciting to try new activities and develop new ideas.

My personality assessment was further helped by comments from friends and family. The letters that they wrote pointed out things to me that I never noticed, or perhaps failed to value in myself.

A review of my personality traits is helpful in identifying environments in which I would be most comfortable working. I am outgoing, persistent, acquisitive and self-confident. I need to work in an environment that accepts the independent side of my personality. As a student, the university setting is perfect for me. I can work independently. I have no difficulty with self-motivation. The enterprising and social side of my personality can flourish in this setting. My job in a university administrative office also fits my personality. Because I am a student, they respect my need for a flexible schedule and encourage me to work independently.

My ideal job will have a number of characteristics. I want to work in a smoke-free environment that stresses good health via fitness and proper nutrition. I would feel best in a small-to-medium-sized firm where I know the top management, but can work without a great deal of supervision. I prefer a flexible schedule. I'm willing to work evenings and some weekends. A good income is important to me; however, money is not a primary motivator. I would like a base salary, plus the option of commissions as well. I want to work for a firm that supports creative thinking and encourages brainstorming. Also, the company should support continuing education.

Life is change. I look forward to working in an environment that encourages this. My goal is to help people live healthier and longer lives.

Case Study 4-3

What is striking about this paper is how it, like the life of its author, is dominated by an unusually strong pattern of interests and values. The author is obviously a very talented person. Reading this paper, do you have a clear sense of his accomplishments? Of how well he has done at his various personal and professional activities? Can you identify his strongest natural talent? Are the outcomes of his activities clear? Look also at his new-found interest in counseling. What is the source of this interest? What evidence is presented that he has a natural talent for this activity? At the end of the paper there is a mention of workaholic tendencies. If you were advising the author, what would you suggest he do to enjoy his work more?

Sharing and Teaching

"And gladly would he lerne, and gladly teche"

— The Figure in the Tapestry of My Life

The various self-assessment activities in which I have engaged over the last several weeks have revealed little that is really new to me. I have, however, been struck by the clarity with which several recurring patterns have emerged in my life. The major themes which make up the dominant pattern of my life comprise a continuing emphasis on education, including both learning and teaching; a love of travel and of being outdoors in attractive natural surroundings; a virtual compulsion to help others in various ways; and a strong reformist tendency.

My primary skills are cognitive and communicative. I have had a strong intellectual orientation since childhood. One of my primary school teachers sent me to the library to avoid my insistence on answering every question she asked the class. I have read widely — if somewhat in-discriminately — throughout my life and have acquired a very considerable reservoir of eclectic knowledge, which I like to bring to bear on a situation at hand. I have a passion for ideas, both in the abstract and as ways of relating and organizing specific information I come across. My mind has a strongly analytical bent, to a degree that sometimes disturbs others who do not share the intensity of my passion to understand the meaning of things. It is not surprising, then, that I have spent most of my life around schools, to the extent of earning a doctorate in one field, participating in two postdoctoral NEH-sponsored summer seminars and recently beginning study toward another degree.

Acquiring knowledge is not enough for me. Since adolescence, I have sought to use my ability to articulate ideas and information. I want to share what I know or believe with others. While in high school, I spent a summer as a counselor at a camp for crippled children, helping handi-capped youngsters discover how much more they could do with their bodies than they had ever thought possible. Most of the time, however, I have helped others learn to develop their in-tellectual and spiritual rather than their physical capacities. I spent another summer on the edge of an Indian reservation in New Mexico teaching Bible school to Indian and Hispanic children. My honeymoon was spent teaching Bible school to minority children in East Los Angeles and then in Compton, California (next to Watts) the year before the riots.

Since I left graduate school twenty years ago, I have been teaching college English. I am extremely skilled at making ideas clear, vivid and alive for students. I help them discover and understand patterns of meaning in literature and in their own lives. I try to be a model for them of homo sapiens, man seeking to know, man thinking. Life is seldom more intense or satisfying for me than when I am sharing with others the process of discovering meaning, order and value.

Even though I write well and enjoy periods of intense, secluded study, I am not really a pure scholar, for I would not wish to spend all my time studying and writing. Rather, I think of myself as a scholarly teacher, with a great desire and ability to help others discover what their minds are capable of.

46

Whenever possible, I have combined my learning and teaching activities with travel. New places and new peoples fascinate me. My family moved several times during my early childhood, and I have moved around at intervals ever since. I spent a couple of summers away from home as an adolescent, went to graduate school in California, took my first teaching job in Alabama, and later another in Liberia, West Africa. Since returning, I have spent summers studying in Los Angeles and Philadelphia, with one fifteen-month unofficial sabbatical in West Germany. I prefer roving vacations, during which I often drive several thousand miles, preferably in the western mountain states.

Those roving vacations serve another persistent need. Although I have always (with the exception of my two years in Africa) lived in cities, as a child I was at times lucky enough to live near open fields and woods and small hills. I loved roaming them, either alone or with friends. I was a Boy Scout and then an Explorer, primarily for the pleasure of outdoor camping, and my wife and I found camping vacations both affordable and enjoyable. I take photographs, mostly when on vacations, and my hundreds of slides are largely of scenery rather than people. Even between vacations I have a strong need to get out of town periodically and into the countryside.

My interest in teaching ties into another, more comprehensive theme in my life. My father was a very moral man with a lot of inhibitions. He expressed his moral sense by helping others unobtrusively. I recall especially that for years he took care of an old woman whom he found in a filthy hovel near our church. He cleaned her, fed her, got her medical attention and helped her use some money she had to make herself more comfortable. I have modeled myself on that aspect of him by developing a virtual compulsion for helping needy people, especially if they belong to a group which is ignored or rejected by most folks.

I volunteered to work in hospital emergency rooms on weekend nights. While in college I tutored children in a public housing project. I pick up hitchhikers. One year I gave my fellowship money to a fellow graduate student with two young children because my new bride was supporting me (and because I was vexed that my fellowship had been reduced). I helped a poor

woman buy food for her family while I was teaching in Alabama.

To my wife's considerable distress, over the years I have loaned students and friends hundreds of dollars, most of which has never been repaid. And I long ago made a deliberate commitment to offer my teaching skills to people in whom most other teachers showed little interest. Almost all my professional teaching has been in Black schools in this country and in Africa.

Recently I have become interested in another way of helping others, as I learned what it could do for me. My interest in psychology has been a long one, but — except for one short episode fifteen years ago — that interest remained academic. During divorce proceedings about two years ago, however, my wife and I began (too late) marriage counseling. She soon dropped out, but I continued, delighted to have someone to whom I could pour out my miseries. Those counseling sessions contributed to an increasing sense of liberation, enhanced self-esteem and emotional growth. I began participating in a peer counseling program, which I still continue. In that program, I learned to counsel as well as to be counseled, and I loved it. I also did well at it and gradually have decided that I want to become a trained professional counselor. It is for that reason that I am returning to school.

One more theme in my life's pattern is a persistent desire to improve things. I can seldom leave well enough alone. I can always find something unsatisfactory, and envision something better. Tinkering with my cars to improve them has been a sort of hobby with me. But I also tinker with thermostats in the building where I teach and even at professional conferences when the temperature is too warm or too cold. Through membership in faculty organizations and by publishing newsletters I have been trying to improve my university, and public higher education in the state generally, for fifteen years.

In the '60s and early '70s, I participated in civil rights and anti-war demonstrations. A reformist streak runs deep in me. I still want to make life better for everyone around me, especially for those who are not in a good position to help themselves. I am, however, trying to outgrow my messianism and my tendency to sacrifice my own needs and desires in order to serve others. I am learning that it is really all right to enjoy myself, and to see to it that my own needs are met.

At the moment I do not intend to quit university teaching to undertake full-time counseling. I still love teaching English and want to continue doing it for the foreseeable future. On the other hand, I would not mind a change of working conditions or a considerable increase in income or a lot fewer papers to grade. What I envision for the future is a situation in which I can both teach and counsel (and, of course, continue to learn in both capacities). I do not have to teach English or necessarily even teach in a university classroom. Perhaps workshops or public lectures would satisfy that craving to lead a group by enlightening it. Yet I do not desire to work in isolation. I like to be around educated, sophisticated colleagues who also love to learn and teach and help others.

I would like to have students more eager to learn and better prepared than most of those I now deal with. Now, however, I am increasingly interested in promoting emotional as well as intellectual growth and health, in others as well as in myself. That means counseling. I am seeking a state license because I want to be able to practice on my own, as well as in concert with other professionals. I do not want to be a mere assistant.

I have intermittent, fleeting visions of working in a spacious, light, airy office instead of my current cramped, windowless cubbyhole, though that point is not necessarily critical. I would also like to live in a geographic area within easy reach of beautiful, rugged mountain terrain. Mountains near a beautiful (rocky) seacoast might be a special treat. I want to make enough money to allow plenty of travel, including intercontinental travel. It would be fine if such travel were part of my job, as long as the pace was not too hectic.

That sounds like a very busy life, especially if teaching and counseling involved two different jobs instead of one. Yet I would like to live at a somewhat more leisurely pace. I think I have been a workaholic long enough, though I can hardly imagine not working at all.

The work situation I have just described would afford me a great deal of satisfaction, combining all my major skills with the opportunity to help others in ways I consider important. Moreover, a combination of teaching and counseling would encourage me to continue my own personal growth, intellectual and emotional. And I might find myself being paid rather well for playing, since both teaching and counseling are a kind of playing for me.

The Quick Job-Hunting Map
Functional/Transferable Skills Inventory

The "Quick Job-Hunting Map" is one of the many creative tools developed by Richard N. Bolles for use by job-seekers and career changers. His permission to use the Skills Inventory here is much appreciated.

Instructions for filling out the skills inventory:

Take seven sheets of paper and describe your seven most satisfying accomplishments or achievements. Or, if the word "accomplishment" or "achievement" makes you uncomfortable, then, as an alternative, just describe seven jobs you have had, paid or unpaid, one on each sheet. Give each a brief title. Or, if you haven't had seven jobs yet, or you hated them, try instead to describe seven ROLES you have had in your life. Go back over each sheet of paper and be sure that you have enough detail, so that you can see what it is you really did. How much detail? See the samples below. Then turn the page and write your seven titles at the top of the Skills Inventory and proceed.

<table>
<tr><td align="center">**Sample**
(This won't do):</td><td align="center">**Sample**
(This will do):</td></tr>
<tr><td>*"The Halloween Experience. I won a prize on Halloween for dressing up as a horse."*</td><td>*"My Halloween Experience — When I was seven years old, I decided I wanted to go out on Halloween dressed as a horse. I talked a friend of mine into being the back end of the horse. But, at the last moment, he backed out, and I was faced with the prospect of not being able to go out on Halloween. At this point, I decided to figure out some way of getting dressed up as the whole horse, myself. I took a fruit basket and tied string to both sides of the rim so that I could tie the basket around my rear end. This filled me out enough so that the costume fit me, by myself. Then I fixed some strong thread to the tail so I could make it wag by moving my hands. When Halloween came, I not only went out and had a ball, but I won first prize as well."*</td></tr>
</table>

Your Functional/Transferable Skills Inventory

Webster's dictionary says: "**function**: *one of a group of related actions contributing to a larger action.*"
And, "**transferable**: *usable in any occupational field.*"
You are now about to take each experience of your own (your accomplishment/job/role), by title,
and do an Inventory of it.

DIRECTIONS. This Skills Inventory is essentially a Coloring Book.
● Let's try it out with the sample we just saw on the previous page. We write the title in at the top: "The Halloween Experience". Then we start down the grid.

● The first "paragraph" or "box" of skill words has: "Designing_____ ; Molding _____ ; Shaping_____ ;" etc. So we ask ourselves, did we—in doing the Halloween Experience—use ANY or ALL of those skills? The answer is: "Yes". So, we do two things:
(a) We *color in* the square (sort-of) next to that paragraph, to indicate "this experience used one or more of these skills in this paragraph": AND THEN
(b) We *underline*, within the paragraph, the skill(s) used. In the case of the Halloween Experience, it was "designing"—so, we underline it. (That is, you will underline. We have put it in italics here, for our sample, so as not to confuse you when you come to your own underlining.)

● Then we go on to the next "paragraph", which begins with "Preparing_____ ; Clearing_____ ;" etc. We ask ourselves, did we use ANY or ALL of these skills in doing the Halloween Experience? The answer is "No" so we leave it blank and go on to the next. The answer there is "No" also.

● We go on to the paragraph which begins with "Handling/fingering/ feeling _____ ;" etc. We ask ourselves the same question again, and here the answer is "Yes". So, (a) We *color in* the square, and
(b) We *underline*, within the paragraph, the skills used in the Halloween Experience. Several here appear relevant: "Handling, Manual dexterity, and Manipulating". We underline, therefore, these words (we have italicized them, again, so as not to confuse you). And so on to the end of page 79.

SKILL PARAGRAPHS	SAMPLE The Halloween Experience	1	2	3	4	5	6	7	Additional thoughts that occur to me about other times when I used these skills
●A¹ **MACHINE OR MANUAL SKILLS** I CAN DO BECAUSE I DID DO:									
*Designing*___ ; Molding ___ ; Shaping; Developing___ ; Composing ___ (e.g. type)	▓								
Preparing___ ; Clearing___ ; Building___ ; Constructing___ ; Assembling___ ; Setting Up___ ; Installing___ ; Installation of___ ; Laying___									
Lifting/Pushing/Pulling/Balancing___ ; Carrying___ ; Unloading/ Moving/Shipping ___ ; Delivering___ ; Collecting___									
Handling/fingering/feeling___ ; Keen sense of touch; Keen sensations; Finger dexterity (as in typing, etc.); *Manual*/hand *dexterity*; Handling___ ; *Manipulating* ___ ; Weaving/Knitting; Handicrafting/ craft skills; Making models	▓								
Precision-working; Punching___ ; Drilling___ ; Tweezer dexterity; Showing dexterity or speed									
Washing; Cooking/culinary skills									
Feeding ___ ; Tending ___									
Controlling/Operating ___ ; Blasting___ ; Grinding___ ; Forging___ ; Cutting___ ; Filling___ ; Applying___ ; Pressing___ ; Binding___ ; Projecting___									

MACHINE OR MANUAL SKILLS *continued*

	Sample	1	2	3	4	5	6	7	Additional experiences
Operating tools; operating machinery (e.g. radios); operating vehicles/equipment; Driving ___ ; Switching ___									
Fitting ___ ; Adjusting ___ ; Tuning ___ ; Maintaining ___ ; Fixing/Repairing ___ ; Masters machinery against its will; Trouble-shooting___									
Producing___									
Other skills which you think belong in this family but are not listed above:									

AND I USED THE ABOVE SKILLS WITH:

Tools (specify kinds):									
Work aids (what kinds?):									
Trees/stones/metals / other:									
Machines/equipment/vehicles:									
Processed materials (kinds?):									
Products being made (kinds?):									
Other:									

A² ATHLETIC/OUTDOOR/TRAVELING SKILLS I CAN DO, BECAUSE I HAVE PROVEN:

	Sample	1	2	3	4	5	6	7	Additional experiences
Motor/Physical coordination & agility; *Eye-Hand-Foot coordination*; Walking/Climbing/Running									
Skilled at general sports: Skilled in small competitive games; Skilled at___(a particular game)									
Swimming: Skiing/Recreation; Playing. Hiking/Backpacking/Camping/Mountaineering; Outdoor survival skills; Creating, planning, organizing outdoor activities; Traveling									
Drawing samples from the earth; Keen oceanic interests; Navigating									
Horticultural skills; Cultivating growing things; Skilled at planting/nurturing plants; Landscaping and groundskeeping									
Farming; Ranching; Working with animals									
Other skills which you think belong in this family but are not listed above:									

B¹ DETAIL/FOLLOW-THROUGH SKILLS I CAN DO, BECAUSE I DID DO:

	Sample	1	2	3	4	5	6	7	Additional experiences
Following-through; Executing _____ ; Ability to follow detailed instructions; *Expert at getting things done*; Implementing decisions; Enforcing regulations; Rendering support services; Applying what others have developed; Directing production of___ (kind of thing)									
Precise attainment of set limits, tolerances or standards; Brings projects in on time, and within budget; Skilled at making arrangements for events, processes; Responsible; Delivering on promises, on time									
Expediting ___; Dispatching ___; Consistently tackles tasks ahead of time; Adept at finding ways to speed up a job; Able to handle a great variety of tasks and responsibilities simultaneously and efficiently; *Able to work well under stress, and still improvise*; Good at responding to emergencies									
Resource expert; Resource broker; Making and using contacts effectively; Good at getting materials; Collecting things; Purchasing___; Compiling___									
Approving___; Validation of information; Keeping confidences or confidential information									

continued next page

Skill	Sample	1	2	3	4	5	6	7	Additional experiences
A detail man or woman; Keen and accurate memory for detail; Showing careful attention to, and keeping track of, details; Focusing on minutiae; High tolerance of repetition and/or monotony; Retentive memory for rules and procedures (e.g. protocol); *Persevering*____									
Checking____									
Explicit, ordered, systematic manipulation of data; Good at the processing of information; Collates data accurately, comparing with previous data; Tabulation of data; Keeping records (time, etc.); Recording____(kinds of data)									
Facilitating/Simplifying other people's finding things; Orderly organizing of data or records									
Organizing written and numerical data according to a prescribed plan; Classification skills; Classifying materials expertly; Filing; Filing materials; Retrieving data									
Clerical ability; Typing; Operating business machines and data processing machines to attain organizational and economic goals; Copying; Reproducing materials									
Other skills which you think belong in this family, but are not listed above:									

•B² NUMERICAL/FINANCIAL/ACCOUNTING/ FINANCIAL (MONEY) MANAGEMENT SKILLS I CAN DO, BECAUSE I DID DO:

Skill	Sample	1	2	3	4	5	6	7	Additional experiences
Numerical ability; Expert at learning and remembering numbers; number memory; Remembering statistics accurately, for a long time									
Counting; Taking inventory; Calculating; Computing; Arithmetic skills; High accuracy in computing/counting; Rapid manipulation of numbers; Rapid computations performed in head or on paper									
Managing money; Financial planning and management; Keeping financial records; Accountability									
Appraising____; Economic research and analysis; Doing cost analysis; Effective Cost Analyses, Estimates, Projections, and Comparisons; Financial/Fiscal Analysis and Planning/Programming									
Developing a budget; Budget Planning, Preparation, Justification, Administration, Analysis and Review									
Extremely economical; Skilled at Allocating Scarce Financial Resources									
Preparing financial reports; Bookkeeping; Doing accounting; Fiscal Cost Audits, Controls, and Reductions									
Using numbers as a reasoning tool; Very sophisticated mathematical abilities; Effective at solving statistical problems									
Other skills which you think belong in this family, but are not listed above:									

•C¹ INFLUENCING/PERSUADING SKILLS I CAN, BECAUSE I DID:

Skill	Sample	1	2	3	4	5	6	7	Additional experiences
Develop rapport/trust; Inspiring trust in the minds and hearts of others; Encouraging people									
Helping people identify their own intelligent self-interest									
Persuading____; Expert in reasoning persuasively/developing a thought; Debating, Influencing the attitudes or ideas of others									
Recruiting talent or leadership; Attracts skilled, competent creative people; *Enlisting*; Motivating others; Mobilizing____; Stimulating people to effective action *continued next page*									

52

INFLUENCING / PERSUADING SKILLS *continued*

	Sample	1	2	3	4	5	6	7	Additional experiences
Promoting____ ; (Face to face) Selling of tangibles/intangibles; Selling ideas or products without tearing down competing ideas or products; Selling an idea, program or course of action to decision-makers; Developing targets/building markets for ideas or products; Fund-raising/money-raising									
Getting diverse groups to work together; Wins friends easily from among diverse or even opposing groups or factions; Adept at conflict management									
Arbitrating / mediating between contending parties or groups; Negotiating to come jointly to decisions; Bargaining; Crisis intervention; reconciling____									
Renegotiating____ ; Obtaining agreement on policies, after the fact									
Charting mergers; Manipulating____ to achieve____; Arranging financing									
Other skills which you think belong in this family, but are not listed above:									
AND I USED THE ABOVE SKILLS WITH:									
Opinions									
Attitudes									
Judgments, Decisions									
Products									
Money									
Other:									

C² PERFORMING SKILLS
I CAN DO, BECAUSE I DID DO:

	Sample	1	2	3	4	5	6	7	Additional experiences
Getting up before a group; Very responsive to audiences' moods or ideas; Diverting; Contributes to others' pleasure consciously; Performing									
*Demonstrating*____ (products, etc.); *Modeling*____ ; Artistic (visual) presentations	▓								
Showmanship; *A strong theatrical sense*; Poise in public appearances	▓								
Addressing large or small groups; (Exceptional) speaking ability / articulateness; Public address/public speaking/oral presentations; Lecturing; Stimulating people/stimulating enthusiasm; Poetry reading									
Playing music; Making musical presentations; Singing; Dancing									
Making people laugh; Understands the value of the ridiculous in illuminating reality									
Acting; Making radio and TV presentations/films									
Public sports									
Conducting and directing public affairs and ceremonies; Conducting musical groups									
Other skills which you think belong in this family, but are not listed above:									

C³ LEADERSHIP SKILLS
I CAN DO, BECAUSE I DID DO:

	Sample	1	2	3	4	5	6	7	Additional experiences
Initiating____ ; Able to move into totally new situations on one's own; Able to take the initiative or first move in developing relationships; Skilled at striking up conversations with strangers									

Skill	Sample	1	2	3	4	5	6	7	Additional experiences
Driving initiative; Continually searches for more responsibility; Persevering in acquiring things (like_____)									
Excellent at organizing one's time; *Unusual ability to work self-directedly, without supervision*; (Very) self-directed at work									
Unwillingness to automatically accept the status quo; Keen perceptions of things as they could be, rather than passively accepting them as they are; Promoting and bringing about major changes, as change agent; Planning for / and effecting / initiating change; *Sees and seizes opportunities*									
Sees a problem and acts immediately to solve it; Deals well with the unexpected or critical; Very decisive in emergencies; Adept at confronting others with touchy or difficult personal matters									
Showing courage; No fear of taking manageable risks; Able to make hard decisions; Adept at policy making; Able to terminate projects / people / processes when necessary									
Leading others; guiding____ ; Inspiring, motivating and leading organized groups; Impresses others with enthusiasm and charisma; Repeatedly elected to senior posts; Skilled at chairing meetings									
Deft in directing creative talent; Skilled leadership in perceptive human relations techniques									
Other skills which you think belong in this family but are not listed above:									

•C⁴ DEVELOPING / PLANNING / ORGANIZING / EXECUTING / SUPERVISING / MANAGEMENT SKILLS
I CAN DO, BECAUSE I DID DO:

Skill	Sample	1	2	3	4	5	6	7	Additional experiences
Planning____ ; Planning and development____ ; Planning on basis of lessons from past experience; A systematic approach to goal-setting									
Prioritizing tasks: Establishing effective priorities among competing requirements; Setting criteria or standards; Policy-making; Policy formulation or interpretation									
Designing projects; Program development / Programming; Skilled at planning and carrying out well-run meetings, seminars or workshops									
Organizing____ ; Organizational development; Organizational analysis, planning and building; adept at organizing, bringing order out of chaos with masses of (physical) things									
Organizing others, bringing people together in cooperative efforts; Selecting resources; Hiring; *Able to call in other experts / helpers as needed*; Team-building; Recognizing and utilizing the skills of others; Contracting / Delegating____									
Scheduling____ ; Assigning____ ; Setting up and maintaining on-time work-schedules; Coordinating operations / details; Arranging / Installing____									
Directing others; Making decisions about others; Supervising others in their work; Supervising and administering____									
Managing / Being responsible for others' output; Management____ ; Humanly-oriented technical management; Real property, plant and facility, management; R & D Program and Project Management; Controlling____									
Producing____ ; Achieving____ ; Attaining____									
Maintaining____ ; Trouble-shooting____ ; Recommending____									
Reviewing____ ; Makes good use of feedback; Evaluating____ ; Recognizes intergroup communication gaps; Judging people's effectiveness									
Other skills which you think belong in this family but are not listed above:									

continued next page

DEVELOPING / PLANNING / ORGANIZING / SUPERVISING *cont.*

AND I USED THOSE SKILLS WITH:	Sample								
Individuals	▨								
Personnel									
Groups									
Organizations									
Management systems									
Office procedures									
Meetings									
Projects / Programs									
Educational events									
Other:									

•D¹ LANGUAGE / READING / WRITING / SPEAKING / COMMUNICATIONS SKILLS
I CAN DO, BECAUSE I DID DO:

	Sample	1	2	3	4	5	6	7	Additional experiences
Reading; Love of reading voraciously or rapidly; Love of printed things; Relentlessly curious									
Comparing____ ; Proofreading ____ ; Editing effectively____ ; Publishing imaginatively____									
Composing____ (kinds of words)									
Communicating effectively; Expresses self very well; Communicates with clarity; Making a point and cogently expressing a position; Thinking quickly on one's feet; Talking / Speaking; Encouraging communication									
Defining____ ; Explaining concepts; Interpreting____ ; Ability to explain difficult or complex concepts, ideas and problems									
Translating____ ; Verbal / linguistic skills in foreign languages; Linguistics; Teaching of languages; Adept at translating jargon into relevant and meaningful terms, to diverse audiences or readers									
Summarizing____ ; Reporting accurately; Very explicit and concise writing; Keeping superior minutes of meetings									
Outstanding writing skills; Ability to vividly describe people or scenes so that others can visualize; Writes with humor, fun and flair (related to *Diverting*, below); Employs humor in describing experiences, to give people courage to embrace them									
Uncommonly warm letter composition; Flair for writing reports; Skilled speech-writing									
Promotional writing; Highly successful proposal writing for funding purposes; Imaginative advertising and publicity programs									
Other skills which you think belong in this family but are not listed above:									

AND I USED THE ABOVE SKILLS WITH:

Ideas									
Feelings									
Facts									
Articles									
Reports / Newsletters									
Brochures / catalogs / journals									
Books									
Other:									

•D² INSTRUCTING / INTERPRETING / GUIDING / EDUCATIONAL SKILLS
I CAN, BECAUSE I HAVE:

Skill	Sample	1	2	3	4	5	6	7	Additional experiences
Proven myself to be very knowledgeable; Having a commitment to learning as a life-long process									
Briefing____ ; Informing____ ; Enlightening ____ ; Explaining ____ ; Instructing ____ ; Teaching____ ; In-Service training ____									
(Unusually) skillful teaching; Fosters a stimulating learning environment; Creating an atmosphere of acceptance; Patient teaching; Adept at inventing illustrations for principles or ideas; Down to earth; Adept at using visual communications (charts, slides, chalkboards, etc.); Instills love of the subject; Conveys tremendous enthusiasm									
Coaching about____ (finances, etc.); Advising/aiding people in making decisions; Giving advice about____; Giving insight concerning____									
Encouraging____; (cf. Influencing/Persuading Family of Skills, above)									
Adept at two-way dialogue; Communicates effectively; Ability to hear and answer questions perceptively; Acceptance of differing opinions; (Keen) ability to help others express their views; Consulting									
Enabling/Facilitating personal growth and development; Helping people make their own discoveries in knowledge; Helping people to develop their own ideas or insights; Clarifying goals and values of others; Counseling; Putting things in perspective; Brings out creativity in others; Shows others how to take advantage of a resource									
Group-facilitating; Discussion group leadership; Group dynamics; Behavioral modification									
Empowering____; Training and Development____; Training someone in something; Designing educational events; Organization and administration of inhouse training programs									
Other skills which you think belong in this family but are not listed above:									
AND I USED THE ABOVE SKILLS WITH:									
Information									
Ideas / Generalizations									
Values / standards									
Goals / decisions									
Other									

•D³ SERVING / HELPING / HUMAN RELATIONS SKILLS
I CAN, BECAUSE I DID:

Skill	Sample	1	2	3	4	5	6	7	Additional experiences
Relates well in dealing with the public / public relations									
Servicing____ ; Customer relations and services; Attending____ ; Adjusting____ (e.g. bills); Referring (people)____									
Rendering services to____ ; Being of service; Helping and serving____									
Sensitivity to others; Interested in/manifesting keen ability to relate to people; Intense curiosity about other people—who they are, what they do; Remembers people and their preferences; Adept at treating people fairly; Listening intently and accurately; A good trained effective listener; Good at listening and conveying awareness; Consistently communicates warmth to people; Conveying understanding, patience and fairness; Readily establishes warm, mutual rapport with____; Able to develop warmth over the telephone									

continued next page

56

SERVING / HELPING / HUMAN RELATIONS SKILLS *continued*

Skill	Sample	1	2	3	4	5	6	7	Additional experiences
Interpersonal competencies; (Unusual) perception in human relations; Expertise in interpersonal contact; Keen ability to put self in someone else's shoes; Empathy: instinctively understanding how someone else feels; Understanding; Tact, Diplomacy and Discretion; Effective in dealing with many different kinds of people / Talks easily with all kinds of people									
Caring for / Nursing children or the handicapped; Watching over___; Love of children; Guiding___									
Administering a household; Hostessing; Shaping and influencing the atmosphere of a particular place; Providing comfortable, natural and pleasant surroundings; Warmly sensitive and responsive to people's feelings and needs in social or other situations; Anticipating people's needs									
Works well on a teamwork basis; Has fun while working, and makes it fun for others; Collaborates with colleagues skillfully; Treats others as equals, without regard to education, authority, or position; Refuses to put people into slots or categories; Ability to relate to people with different value systems; Motivates fellow workers; Expresses appreciation faithfully; Ready willingness to share credit with others									
Takes human failings/limitations into account; Able to ignore undesirable qualities in others; Deals patiently and sympathetically with difficult people; Handles super-difficult people in situations, without stress; Handles prima donnas tactfully and effectively; Works well in a hostile environment	▓								
Nursing___; Skillful therapeutic abilities; Curing___; Gifted at helping people with their personal problems; Raises people's self-esteem; (Thorough) understanding of human motivations; Understands family relationships and problems; Aware of people's need for supportive community; Adept at aiding people with their total life adjustment / Mentoring									
Unusual ability to represent others; Expert in liaison roles; Ombudsmanship									
Other skills which you think belong in this family but are not listed above:									

AND I USED THE ABOVE SKILLS WITH:

	Sample	1	2	3	4	5	6	7	Additional experiences
Children									
The young									
Adolescents									
Adults or *Peers*	▓								
The aging									
All age groups									
Other:									

•E¹ INTUITIONAL AND INNOVATING SKILLS I CAN DO, BECAUSE I DID DO:

Skill	Sample	1	2	3	4	5	6	7	Additional experiences
Imagining___; Highly imaginative; *Possessed of great imagination and the courage to use it*	▓								
Ideaphoria / Continually conceiving, developing and generating ideas; Conceptual ability of the highest order; Being an idea man or woman; Inventing; *Inventive; Ability to improvise on the spur of the moment*	▓								
Innovating; Having many innovative and creative ideas; Creative, perceptive effective innovator; *Willing to experiment with new approaches*; Experimental with ideas, procedures, and programs; Strongly committed to experimental approaches; Demonstrating continual originality; Love of exercising the mind-muscle	▓								

I CAN, BECAUSE I DID:	Sample	1	2	3	4	5	6	7	Additional experiences
Synthesizing perceptions, etc.; Seeing relationships between apparently unrelated factors; Integrating diverse elements into a clear coherent whole; Effective dissolution of barriers between ideas or fields; Ability to relate abstract ideas; Balancing factors / Judging / Showing good judgment									
Deriving things from others' ideas; Improving___ ; Updating___; *Adapting* ___ ; Reflection upon___ ; Sees the theoretical base in a practical situation; Significant theoretical modeling; *Model developing*; Developing___ ; Formulating___ ; Developing innovative program ideas	▓								
Generating ideas with commercial possibilities; Able to see the commercial possibilities of abstract ideas or concepts; Applying___ ; Applying theory; Applied research; Creating products; Entrepreneurial									
Form perception; Perception of patterns and structures; *Visualizing shapes*; Graphing and reading graphs; Visualizing in the third-dimension; Able to read blueprints	▓								
Spatial memory; Memory for design; Able to notice quickly (and/or remember later) most of the contents of a room; Remembering___ ; Memory for faces									
Showing foresight; Recognizing obsolescence before compelling data is yet at hand; Instinctively gathering resources even before the need for them becomes clear; Forecasting									
Perceiving intuitively; Color-discrimination (of a very high order)									
Other skills which you think belong in this family but are not listed above:									

•E² ARTISTIC SKILLS

I CAN, BECAUSE I DID:	Sample	1	2	3	4	5	6	7	Additional experiences
Shows strong sensitivity to, and need for, beauty in the environment; Adept at coloring things; instinctively excellent taste									
Expressive; Exceptionally good at facial expressions used to express or convey thoughts, without (or, in addition to) words; Ability to use the body to express feelings eloquently; Uses voice tone and rhythm as unusually effective tool of communication; Skilled in telephone-voice; Can accurately reproduce sounds (e.g. foreign languages spoken without accent); Mastery of all forms of communication									
Good sense of humor / *playfulness*	▓								
Creative imagining / Creating original___ ; Operates well in a free, unstructured, unsupervised environment; Bringing new life to traditional (art) forms; Translating___ ; Restoring___	▓								
Aware of the value of symbolism, and deft in its use; Skilled at symbol formation (words, pictures, and concepts); Visualizing concepts; Creating poetry, or poetic images; Designing and/or using audio-visual aids; Photographing									
Visual and spatial designing; Artistic talent (drawing, etc.); Illustrating; Mapping; Drafting / Mechanical drawing	▓								
Fashioning / Shaping things; *Making*___ ; Designing in wood or other media; Redesigning structures; Styling___ ; Decorating___									
Writing; Playwriting; Assisting in / directing the planning, organizing and staging of theatrical productions									
Musical knowledge and taste; Tonal memory; Uncommon sense of rhythm, Exceedingly accurate melody recognition; Composing									

continued next page

58

ARTISTIC SKILLS *continued*

Other skills which you think belong in this family, but are not listed above:

AND I USED THE ABOVE SKILLS WITH:

	Sample	1	2	3	4	5	6	7	Additional experiences
Colors									
Spaces									
Shapes, faces	▨								
Handicrafts									
Arts, drawing, paints									
Fashion, jewelry, clothing, furs, furniture									
Music									
Other:									

•F¹ OBSERVATIONAL / LEARNING SKILLS
I CAN DO, BECAUSE I DID DO:

	Sample	1	2	3	4	5	6	7	Additional experiences
Observing____ ; (Highly) observant of people / data / things; (Keen) awareness of surroundings									
Reading____ ; (e.g., dials); Adept at scanning radar or other sophisticated observational systems; Estimating____ (e.g., speed)									
Listening skillfully; Hearing accurately; Keen sense of smell; (Tremendously) sensitive sense of tasting									
Perceptive: Perceiving____ ; Detecting____ ; Discovering____ ; A person of perpetual curiosity / discovery, delighting in new knowledge; Continually seeking to expose oneself to new experiences; Highly committed to continual personal growth and learning; Learns from the example of others; Learns quickly									
Alert in observing human behavior; Studying other people's behavior perceptively; Perceptive in identifying and assessing the potential of others; Recognizes and appreciates the skills of others									
Appraising____ ; Assessing____ ; Screening applicants; Realistically assessing people's needs; Accurately assessing public moods; *Quickly sizes up situations* and instinctively understands political realities	▨								
Exceptional intelligence, tempered by common sense									
Other skills which you think belong in this family, but are not listed above:									

AND I USED THE ABOVE SKILLS WITH:

	Sample	1	2	3	4	5	6	7	Additional experiences
Data (what kinds?)									
People (any special kinds?)									
Ideas	▨								
Behavior									
Procedures									
Operations									
Phenomena									
Instruments									
Other:									

F² RESEARCH / INVESTIGATING / ANALYZING / SYSTEMATIZING / EVALUATING SKILLS I CAN, BECAUSE I DID:

	Sample	1	2	3	4	5	6	7	Additional experiences
Anticipates problems before they become problems; Recognizing need for more information before a decision can be made intelligently; Skilled at clarifying problems or situations									
Inspecting____ ; Examining____ ; Surveying organizational needs; Researching exhaustively; Collecting information / Information gathering; Academic research and writing									

Surveying___ ; Interviewing___ ; Adept at gathering information from people by talking to them; Researching resources, ways and means; Researching personally, through investigation and interviewing; Inquiring									
Analyzing___ ; Dissecting___; *Breaking down principles into parts*; Adept at atomizing / breaking down into parts; Analyzing community needs, values, and resources; Analyzes communication situations; Analyzing manpower requirements; Analyzing performance specifications									
Diagnosing___ ; Organizing / Classifying___ ; Identifies elements, relationships, structures, and organizing principles of organizations to be analyzed; Isolating elements; *Able to separate 'wheat from chaff'*; Reviewing large amounts of material, and extracting essence; Perceiving and Defining Cause & Effect relationships; Ability to trace problems, ideas, etc. to their source									
Grouping___ ; Perceiving common denominators; Systematizing / Organizing material / information in a systematic way									
*Testing*___(e.g. an idea, or hypothesis)									
Determining / Figuring out___ ; Solving___; Problem-solving; Trouble-shooting									
Reviewing / Evaluating___ ; Screening___ (e.g., fund proposals); Critiquing___ ; Evaluating by measurable or subjective criteria; Accurately evaluating___ (e.g., programs administered by others; experiments; loan applications; papers; quizzes; work; records; staff; program bids; evidence; options; qualifications; etc.)									
Decision-making skills; Re-evaluating									
Other skills which you think belong in this family, but are not listed above:									
AND I USED THE ABOVE SKILLS WITH:									
People (what kinds?)									
Data (what kinds?)									
Things (what kinds?)									
Ideas (theoretical, abstract, symbolic, systematic?)									
Articles, artifacts, or processes									
Matter (inert or moving) or Energy									
Phenomena (physical, biological, scientific, mathematical, or cultural?)									
Other:									

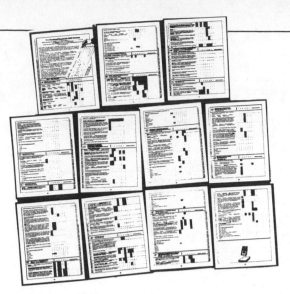

When you've finished this whole Inventory, for all seven of your accomplishments/achievements/jobs/roles or whatever, you want to look for PATTERNS and PRIORITIES.

    a) For Patterns, because it isn't a matter of whether you used a skill once only, but rather whether you used it repeatedly, or not. "Once" proves nothing; "repeatedly" is very convincing.

    b) For Priorities, because the job you eventually choose may not be able to use all of your skills. You need to know *what you are willing to trade off, and what you are not.* This requires you to know what your priorities are: i.e., which skills, or family of skills, are most important to you.

PHOTO-COPY, DOUBLE-COLOR, PRIORITIZE

We therefore suggest you tear out the preceding pages of the Skills Inventory, *arrange to photo-copy the opposite side of each page*, and then spread them all out on a table or on the floor.

Now you have a complete "aerial view" of all the skills you have. At this point, we suggest you use a second color (like red) and go back over all the "squares" you colored in. Ask yourself, do I enjoy this skill/these skills still today? If the answer is "Yes", DOUBLE-COLOR that particular square. And DOUBLE-UNDERLINE, in red, the particular skills you ENJOY, in each corresponding Skill Paragraph.

When you are all done, look at the total "aerial view" of your skills, to see which family of skills has the most DOUBLE-COLOR (say, red); put it up at the top of the table or floor lay-out. Which family of skills has the next most DOUBLE-COLOR? Put it next. Thus, you will quickly see which skills are most important to you.

Five. Personality and Priorities

The first requirement for success in a job is that you be able to do what the job requires. There is more to being in the right job than having the skills to do it, however. A position which matches your personality is equally important, especially over time. It is not unusual for someone to be unhappy with a job despite being successful at it. Getting caught in such a situation is doubly painful, since other people can't understand why you want to quit when you're doing so well.

Suppose you're shy, and yet take a position in which you must constantly meet new people. You will often feel uncomfortable, even if you can handle the work with ease. Similarly, if you don't work well under pressure, you won't make a good air traffic controller, even if you have all the physical and mental abilities needed to do the job. On the other hand, if you are an independent, self-directed person, you should find being a college professor a good fit.

What is at issue is not the goodness or badness of the job itself. The same position which will raise one person's blood pressure, thereby increasing the probability of heart disease, will lower that of another. An individual who is warm and accepting may make an excellent scout leader but an uncomfortable Marine drill instructor. A worrier can expect real problems as a stock market advisor, whatever degrees in finance he or she may have earned. Someone who bores easily will be driven mad by a repetitive job, even if the job is not difficult and pays well.

Although personality traits are difficult to define precisely, what we are talking about is the way you typically feel about other people; how you react emotionally when angry or threatened; how you handle risk, danger, uncertainty and pressure; and how you feel about yourself. Some people are cool, some are explosive; some are introverts, others extroverts; some worry a great deal, others very little. The critical issue is how your personality fits the demands of a given job.

As a practical matter, skills and personality traits often blend in ways that make them difficult to separate. Being a good negotiator, for example, is as much a matter of personality as it is of having specific negotiating skills. You may therefore have some problems separating your skills from your personality traits. This is a common experience, and no cause for concern. Do the best you can, keeping in mind that skills refer to what you can *do*, and do easily and well. Personality traits, on the other hand, involve your emotional needs. These needs determine how you *feel* about what you're doing, and about the context in which you're doing it.

Some Examples

To provide some concrete illustrations before you start, let's take the same three accomplishments used as examples in the last chapter. There we looked at what these accomplishments showed about the person's abilities. This time through, let's look instead at what they say about the individual's personality and emotional needs.

Accomplishment

When I was a sophomore in high school, I noticed that the older students were using slide rules. I asked about them, and found out that using one saved time doing multiplication and division. (This was years ago, before the introduction of hand-held calculators.) I got a slide rule, and then found a book in the library that described how to use it. Following the directions in the book one step at a time, I figured out how it worked. Then I began doing my math and science homework with it. This saved a lot of time. I asked my teachers if I could use the slide rule during exams and they said all right. This gave me more time to concentrate on the problems themselves, since I could now do the arithmetic quickly. I offered to show a friend of mine how to use the slide rule, but to my surprise he was not interested. He said that when it was necessary, the teachers would show everyone how to use it.

Personality Traits Shown

- *Curious about how things work*
- *Seek the excitement of learning new and better ways to do things*
- *Enjoy sharing what has been learned*
- *A self-directed learner; enjoy figuring out things on my own*
- *Like to make decisions independently*

- *Willing to ask those in authority to do things differently*
- *Persistent*
- *Become frustrated when others don't share my willingness to do things differently.*

Accomplishment

I was in the sixth grade and we had to do several creative compositions. The teacher was demanding and gave praise only sparingly. He never gave perfect marks, he said, because perfection in creative writing was virtually impossible. Two of my compositions, however, won perfect marks. I remember what it felt like to write those stories: how careful I was about the words, and how, when they were done after an hour or two of intense concentration, I knew they were good. What he thought of them really did not mean much to me. Those essays set an inner standard which I use constantly. If I get that certain feeling when I've finished a piece of work, I know it is good. My only disappointment in myself is that I did not follow his advice and use my writing ability more consistently and creatively.

Personality Traits Shown

- *Willing to rise to a challenge without feeling threatened or discouraged by it*
- *Proud of my good work*
- *Need for intense concentration*
- *High inner standards of accomplishment*
- *Willing to trust my instincts*
- *Enjoy producing excellent results*

Accomplishment

The most challenging and enjoyable job I have had was when I was the general manager for a small welding supply company. The owner hired me to run the company while he started another, totally unrelated business. My first task was to set up a new manufacturing facility. This required the establishment of manufacturing, quality control, safety and production-flow procedures. To do this, I first established my priorities in light of the company's goals. I established a step by step procedure that was safe and could be performed by anyone with minimal training. During the development phase, I had to handle multiple tasks and anticipate problems that could occur later,

during the manufacturing phase. I had to write up procedures and instruct new employees on these procedures. I had to handle any problems as they occurred, until the new process was running smoothly.

Personality Traits Shown

- *Enjoy complex and challenging managerial work*
- *Lead others (the owner, in this case) to trust and have confidence in me*
- *Able to direct others; not shy about being in charge; in fact, enjoy being in charge*
- *Prefer non-routine, novel work rather than routine, repetitive work*
- *Need to bring order from complexity*
- *Enjoy problem-solving as a personal accomplishment, and as a means to managerial control*

Now You Do It

Your next step is to jot down a short summary of each of the accomplishments you listed in Chapter Four. Then, on the Personality Analysis Form (Exercise 5-1), write out the personality traits you observe in each accomplishment. Ask yourself, as you review your past successes, what emotional needs were met by what you did. Do not dwell too long on any one incident. What is important is to find the personality characteristics that come up again and again. As Richard Bolles puts it, "Your deepest purpose is to identify the core of your life, the constant thread, the constancy in you that persists through all the changing world around you." If you find this pattern, or even make progress toward clarifying it, you will have a much clearer idea of who you are and what you are made to do.

Personality and Skills Together

The interaction of personality characteristics and natural talents plays an important role in determining job satisfaction. An outgoing person with mathematical talent will not want the same job as a shy person with mathematical talent.

How do you move from skills and personality characteristics to specific occupations? One useful exercise involves filling in a grid. In Exercise 5-2 list five of your strongest skills down the left side of the grid, and five major personality characteristics across the top.

Exercise 5-1

Personality Analysis Form

Accomplishment
(Summarized from last chapter)

Personality Traits Shown
(Emotional Needs Met)

_____

_____

_____

_____

_____

_____

_____

_____

_____

_____

_____

_____

_____

_____

_____

_____

_____

_____

_____

_____

_____

_____

_____

_____

Accomplishment
(Summarized from last chapter)

Personality Traits Shown
(Emotional Needs Met)

_____

_____

_____

_____

_____

_____

_____

_____

_____

_____

_____

_____

_____

_____

_____

_____

_____

_____

_____

_____

_____

_____

Accomplishment
(Summarized from last chapter)

Personality Traits Shown
(Emotional Needs Met)

_____

_____

_____

_____

_____

_____

_____

_____

_____

_____

_____

_____

_____

_____

_____

_____

_____

_____

_____

_____

_____

_____

_____

Such a 5 × 5 grid produces 25 possible combinations. Look at each of these combinations, and try to name or invent a job for as many as you can.

To illustrate how this grid works, let's see how two opposite personality needs combine with several skills to produce a variety of job possibilities.

Skills	Personality Traits	
	1. Need for individual accomplishment	2. Team player
1. Good writer	Reporter, with own byline	Congressional staff member
2. Top athlete	Golf, runner, tennis	Baseball, hockey
3. Sales ability	Manufacturer's rep, on commission	Salaried sales coordinator
4. Scientific talent	Research scientist at independent lab	Government scientist
5. Mathematician	Professor	Member of corporate research team

After doing Exercise 5-2, look over all the possibilities you have generated. If any of these jobs are positions you would be seriously interested in investigating, make a note of them. Chapters Seven and Eight will discuss how to research them to see whether they are worth pursuing.

The Intuitive Too

The whole approach we have taken up to this point has been highly analytical. Useful though this analysis is, there is also a place for the intuitive and creative in setting employment goals which we explore in Exercise 5-3.

One way to tap into your inner sense of a fitting life is by visualizing yourself doing what you would really find satisfying. Sit back, relax, turn on some inspiring music and picture yourself going to work several years from now. Assume that everything has worked out well. You have a job, and a life, which is a fine match to your skills and personality.

Don't try to plan out what you will imagine. Simply begin your day and let yourself picture what feels right. Just see what happens.

Be sure to include the weekend in your imagining. A job is part of an entire lifestyle. Anything you really enjoy doing that's not part of your job can become a

leisure activity. Accountants also paint, and cab drivers are weekend referees. Barbara Sher quotes a Mexican saying: *La vida es corta, pero ancha* — Life is short, but it is wide.

Getting Things in Order

The last chapter stressed the importance of reviewing your past accomplishments so that you become more aware of your skills. You have now taken a look at these same accomplishments to see what they show about the needs of your personality. The next step is to get your findings into priority order.

It is one thing to generate long lists of skills or personality traits. Realistically, however, you also need to see clearly which skills you most enjoy using, and which personality traits are dominant.

One handy mechanism for ranking a list is the "decision tree." It is a procedure that allows you to break a list of many items into a series of choices between two options. You then sum the net effect of these choices, and thereby find those items on the list that are really most important to you.

Putting in Priority Order

Look at the form in Exercise 5-4. List, under "Jobs," eight jobs you *have* had. If you have not had eight, first list the jobs you have had and then finish with some you think you might like. List only the job titles.

For each job title, in the space labeled "Attractive Features," put down those things you liked about the job. For positions you have not actually had, list the things you think you would like.

If Bob Wegmann were making out this list, for example, he would begin with his present position, professor. Then he would put down the things he likes about this job: flexible hours, independence, respected status, time to do research and write, opportunity to work with adults who are making critical personal decisions, job security and a beautiful working environment.

Do the same for your jobs. List as many features as you can for each of the eight jobs. Sometimes you will be listing characteristics such as pay or the type of workplace. At other times you will be listing things you like to do. You may want to draw on the list of 244 verbs in Chapter Four to remind yourself which skills each job requires.

Now review the attractive features you listed for all eight jobs. Do some come up more than once? Do any come up over and over?

Personality Traits and Skills

On top of this grid, list five of your dominant personality traits. Then, on the left side of the grid, list five of your strongest skills. Now try to jot down a job title in which the skill would be used, and the personality need met, for as many of the 25 combinations as you can.

Jobs Combining Personality Traits and Skills

Skills	Personality Traits				
	1._____	2._____	3._____	4._____	5._____
1._____	_____	_____	_____	_____	_____
2._____	_____	_____	_____	_____	_____
3._____	_____	_____	_____	_____	_____
4._____	_____	_____	_____	_____	_____
5._____	_____	_____	_____	_____	_____

Dreaming

Assume it is five years in the future, and your hopes and dreams have come to fruition. Close your eyes, and picture yourself waking up in the morning. Look around and see where you find yourself. Are you single or married? To whom? Go through the morning routine. What is your house like? How is it furnished? What is the neighborhood like? Go to work. How do you get there? Where do you go? What do you do? Who are you working with? What is the workplace like? How are people dressed? Go through the day, the evening that follows, and then the weekend.

Don't try to plan out what you will see. Just let yourself dream. Then write out below what your life was like.

_____

_____

_____

_____

_____

_____

_____

_____

_____

_____

_____

_____

_____

_____

_____

_____

_____

_____

What Attracts You in a Job?

Jobs   Attractive Features

1. _____   _____
                              _____
                              _____
2. _____   _____
                              _____
                              _____
3. _____   _____
                              _____
                              _____
4. _____   _____
                              _____
                              _____
5. _____   _____
                              _____
                              _____
6. _____   _____
                              _____
                              _____
7. _____   _____
                              _____
                              _____
8. _____   _____
                              _____
                              _____

Most Attractive Features

1. _____   6. _____
2. _____   7. _____
3. _____   8. _____
4. _____   9. _____
5. _____   10. _____

From all the features you listed, choose the ten which are most important to you. Write these at the bottom of the page under "Most Attractive Features." You don't have to put them in any particular order. The only requirements are (1) that each should be distinct from the others, and (2) that each is something that would make a job attractive to you. Don't leave out anything important, even if, for some reason, it's not among the characteristics of your past jobs.

You now have a list of ten features, numbered one through ten. Each is different from the others, and each (to you, at least) is an attractive characteristic.

Review the list. Be sure you have been specific enough to be clear. "Good working conditions," for example, covers too much, and is too vague. Be more explicit. "A quiet, uncrowded work area" or "easy access to co-workers" might be what you really mean. Or you might have in mind "a new, attractively furnished office," or "many other single workers of both sexes." Be as specific and descriptive as possible.

The next step is to use the decision tree, Exercise 5-5, a structure for putting these ten attractive features in priority order. The decision tree focuses your attention on every possible pairing of the ten factors, one pair at a time. In each case, you must choose which of the two is more important to you.

Suppose the first five items on your list of ten are as follows:

1. Involves working with children
2. Flexible hours
3. Regular raises for both inflation and experience
4. Allows me to use my artistic ability
5. Entails responsibility for managing a budget

The first pairing on the decision tree has you choosing between items 1 and 2. If you could have only "working with children" or "flexible hours," but not both, which would you choose? If you had to choose between two attractive jobs, with all other things equal, would you prefer a position that lets you work with children but has fixed hours, or one which has flexible hours but no contact with children? If working with children is more important to you, circle the 1. If flexible hours are more important, circle the 2.

The next pairing involves 1 and 3. Now you must choose between working with children and having regular raises for both inflation and experience. If everything else about the jobs were acceptable, circle the choice you would make, either 1 or 3.

The decision tree similarly pairs factors 1 and 4, 1 and 5 and so on up to 1 and 10. It then, in the second row, pairs factors 2 and 3 (note that 2 and 1 are omitted because they have already been compared in the first row), 2 and 4, 2 and 5 and so on to 2 and 10. The third row does the same with factor 3. Altogether there are 45 pairs.

It sometimes helps to work down the left edge of the decision tree (choosing between 1 and 2, 2 and 3, 3 and 4 and so on). This way you are not considering the same feature in decision after decision, as you are if you work straight across each row.

When you have finished making all 45 decisions, choosing which factor in each pairing you prefer, you need to add up the number of times you have circled a 1, then how often you circled a 2 and so on. Enter these totals in the column headed "How Often Chosen?" As a check, add them up. The total should be 45.

Now look over the list and see which of the ten factors you chose most often. This is your top priority in a job, something which is more important to you than anything else. The factor you have chosen second most often is your second priority, and so on. (If two factors tie, go back to the pair where you chose between those two. See which one you circled. List that one as the higher ranking of the two.)

One objective in your job search will be to find a job which involves at least your top two or three priorities.

Other Uses

This same "decision tree" method of analysis works where more than one person is involved. You and your spouse, for example, can make separate lists of every city in which you've lived or would like to live, and what you found attractive about each. Using separate decision trees, each of you can put the attractive features of these cities in priority order. After you review your own priorities and those of your spouse, your goal will be to locate a city which has the top two or three priorities from both lists. This would be a place you would both really enjoy.

If you want to get a clearer idea of what attracts you to people, list your friends, past and present, and then spell out what you like about each. After selecting ten particularly attractive personal characteristics, use the decision tree to rank them.

The value of this process is that it gets you away from merely dealing with labels (the name of the person or city or job or whatever). It leads you instead to a detailed consideration of the specific features which are really important to you. It then has you rank them.

The Decision Tree

Features					Priorities					How Often Chosen?	Rank
1	1 2	1 3	1 4	1 5	1 6	1 7	1 8	1 9	1 10	_____	_____
2		2 3	2 4	2 5	2 6	2 7	2 8	2 9	2 10	_____	_____
3			3 4	3 5	3 6	3 7	3 8	3 9	3 10	_____	_____
4				4 5	4 6	4 7	4 8	4 9	4 10	_____	_____
5					5 6	5 7	5 8	5 9	5 10	_____	_____
6						6 7	6 8	6 9	6 10	_____	_____
7							7 8	7 9	7 10	_____	_____
8								8 9	8 10	_____	_____
9									9 10	_____	_____
10										_____	_____

Total   45

Doing this with a computer, by the way, is both faster and more fun. There is information on a helpful (and free) computer program which will do this for you in the notes at the end of this book.

Specifying factors and putting them in priority order are essential steps in choosing and finding employment. Someone who says, "I want to be a doctor," has only one vocational possibility. The person who says, "I want to help others, preferably in a medical setting, in a respected and responsible role which provides a steady and secure income," has a much greater range of options to consider.

In an ideal world, we could get all we wanted. In this far from ideal world we often cannot. But most of us have at least a reasonable chance to obtain our top priorities, either immediately or after taking some intermediate steps. This will not happen, however, unless those priorities have been clearly identified.

This means you need to use the decision tree (which works with a list of any length; there's nothing magic about ten factors) over and over again in the job choice process. Of my personality needs, which are the most important? Of the things I do best, which do I most enjoy doing? Of the working environments that attract me, which would be the most satisfying? Of the areas where I have experience, which are those I have most totally mastered? Working out these priorities can be tedious at times, but the payoff is a clear sense of what you really want.

People sometimes take jobs thinking their personalities will change to fit the position. Other assume they can change the way the job is done to suit their personalities. Both of these approaches are formulas for trouble. Far better to find a position where your skills and personality work together to help you do what the employer needs done.

As you read the case studies, ask yourself which jobs would be a good fit, and which would not. Try to see as clearly as you can what it is about both the person and the position that would lead to either a good fit or a mismatch.

CASE STUDIES

Case Study 5-1

In this chapter we shifted our focus from skills to personality traits. One of the important ways that personalities differ is the degree to which people prefer to act alone, as one partner in a pair or as a member of a larger team. Where do you think the author of this paper falls? Given her compassionate nature, it is understandable that she is attracted to the helping professions. These professions, however, cover a wide range of possibilities. Would her skills and personality fit the demands faced by a therapist in private practice? A nurse? A nursing home administrator? A psychology professor? Is there any additional information you would need to judge the appropriateness of the person/position match for these jobs? Given her interest in both understanding and helping, how do you think she can find a position which would allow her to do both?

Empathy, Courage and Caring

Human behavior, and the feelings and needs behind people's actions and interactions, have long intrigued me. At the heart of this interest is a need and desire to understand myself and the influences that have contributed to my own personality. Because of these interests, I have pursued a degree in the behavioral sciences with a concentration in psychology. This course work, additional reading, private introspection and job experience have all increased my fascination with the way people behave. My desire now is to increase my knowledge by working in some type of social service setting while continuing my formal education.

For as long as I can remember, I have had a deep concern for people who are disadvantaged in some way. In high school I served as a hospital volunteer. Later, after marriage, I worked as a missionary in some of the poor areas of Rio de Janeiro in an attempt to bring both physical and spiritual relief to the underprivileged people there. A number of years ago I earned an Associate Degree in the field of nursing. I have worked since that time in the area of pediatrics, with both physically ill and mentally retarded children. Three years as a staff nurse on the pediatric unit of a hospital for the indigent increased my awareness of the innumerable physical and emotional deficits that exist for multitudes of children and their families.

Working as a member of an interdisciplinary team for the treatment of the mentally retarded further acquainted me with the needs of the handicapped. I encountered whole families who were in deep despair over the illness or retardation of their loved ones. Often these families had weak or no support systems to sustain them, and had become maladaptive in their own lives. When counseling them I was often instrumental in helping them find relief by encouraging verbalization of their concerns, and by putting them in touch with other sources of help.

More recently I have developed a heightened concern for the plight of the elderly in our society. I have participated in community and church projects for senior citizens and presently serve as a volunteer for the Hospice organization (a group of people united for the purpose of providing physical, emotional and spiritual support for the dying and their significant others).

Being aware of my own need for supportive community makes the knowledge that I am part of a respected team important to me. Support from other team members is reassuring, and association with them gives me an opportunity to learn new ideas and skills. With each new experience I am made more aware of the concept that "the more I know, the more I know I don't know."

Many of my personality traits further exhibit my interest in the problems of others. I am intensely compassionate with either animals or people who are hurting in some way. As a child growing up on a farm, I frequently attempted to nurse an injured bird or sick, stray cat or dog. When a new child entered school I often appointed myself as a committee of one to make her or him feel accepted.

Today I am repelled by cruelty to animals, and have a keen sense of wanting to protect and help abused children, neglected or lonely elderly people, and individuals who are discriminated against in some way. I frequently participate in projects designed to increase public awareness of child abuse and am currently planning to help in a community effort to teach parenting skills to parents.

My sensitivity to the feelings of those around me is evidenced by the intuitive and insightful assessments I am often able to make. Creative problem identification and problem-solving skills further enhance my ability to perceive distress in another person and to guide her or him in the direction of finding a solution.

Recently I sensed that one of my co-workers was deeply distressed. Upon expressing my concern, I discovered that many facets of her life were in turmoil. Together we examined options that could lead to a resolution of some of her problems. Within a short time she was able, with continuing support, to make a number of important decisions that will affect her life for many years.

Quite often family members and friends seek me out to ask for an answer to a personal problem. On numerous occasions I have acted as "confidant and counselor" to my teenage children and their friends, as well as to co-workers. On these occasions I am usually able to offer encouragement, or to influence their ideas and attitudes in a manner which contributes to a resolution of their problems.

The ability to communicate seems to be a natural talent for me. This skill has improved with time and training. In addition to actively listening, I am also good at sharing my ideas, both verbally and in writing. It has been my habit for many years to write short notes to my children, other family members and friends. I place them in shirt pockets, lunch pails, mirrors, desk tops, steering wheels or school books. These communiques have expressed encouragement, sympathy, empathy, apology or just reminders of love and concern, and have often initiated dialogue when feelings had put a damper on constructive communication.

My ideal job would place me in a team environment, working with other competent and professionally trained people who share my concern for those in our society who are disadvantaged in some way. My ability to be sensitive to the needs and feelings of those who are physically, emotionally or socially handicapped would be of value. I am particularly concerned about the very young and the elderly. My tendency to be compassionate, and my need to be nurturing, suggest employment in one of the helping professions. This job should provide me with an opportunity to use my communication and problem solving skills, and allow me to improve these skills and learn from those around me.

I can work well under stress, responding calmly to unexpected or crisis situations. I am *able to prioritize needs in an emergency situation, after quickly grasping and assessing the circumstances. Almost daily, the Intensive Care Nursery where I now work presents such situations, sometimes of a life threatening nature. Responding to the needs of each emergency has required me to "think on my feet."*

While able to work independently, I appreciate being able to ask for help or advice from co-workers. A job requiring me to do a variety of tasks simultaneously would be a welcome challenge, particularly if proficiency in decision making is involved.

Case Study 5-2

The author of this paper is old enough to be able to look back and reflect on what has changed in his life, and what has remained constant. Interests and values clearly change. Do skills and personality evolve as dramatically? Notice the important contribution other people made to the process of clarifying his strengths. Note also how his priorities have sharpened and simplified over the years. How important is his evolution from an emphasis on technical ability to people skills and managerial expertise? How do you think he will use his willingness to take risks in his new career directions? Look closely at his discussion of an ideal job. How closely has he integrated his new self-knowledge? How clear are his goals? The author of this paper is a thoughtful and intelligent person. The process of matching self and a work role, however, is a complex one. In a later chapter we will see how additional information about the labor market leads this person toward some interesting and desirable options.

Mid-Course Correction

"Who am I?" is an extremely complex and difficult question. As a result of exploring myself and my history, however, I have been able to identify the basic motivational patterns which are the constant threads in my life that have persisted even as I have grown and changed. I have been able to identify the combination of interests, skills and personality traits that are uniquely mine. While searching for my identity and examining my past life are not new experiences, I have for the first time paused long enough to carefully listen to and accept what others have said about me.

I took the Strong-Campbell Interest Inventory, but found that the questions did not seem to fit this phase of my life. The results were very general, and in many cases in opposition to the other information and data that I collected. I am aware that my life is in a major transition, however. Many things I have tolerated in the past are no longer acceptable. The Strong-Campbell did make me think about my interests, and in that respect it was useful.

The most helpful exercise or aid that I used was one that I accidentally discovered myself. After reading the letters from friends and classmates, I remembered that I had copies of "Military Performance Reports" for the past 20 years. These reports, written annually, even though often inflated, provide a vivid picture of how I have been described by superiors, peers and subordinates. For the first time I examined them collectively, looking for trends and patterns in my successes and accomplishments as seen by others.

The reports define and spell out the core of my life, the forces that have motivated me, and the tasks that I do well. I admit that I am amazed that a writer in Heidelberg, Germany, when I was 23, saw the same things in me that another writer did in Dover, Delaware, when I was 43. How seemingly easy it has been for others to identify character traits, skills and motivating forces that I have been unaware of or unwilling to admit.

During this life/work planning search I have become acutely aware of the degree of change and growth I have experienced, although my basic motivations have changed little. I seem to have three primary motivating forces in my life: family, interactions with the people around me and risk-taking. These seem to be the essence of my personality, extending back to my first success at age 11 when I mowed lawns, to age 14 when I worked at an amusement park, to age 26 as an air traffic controller in Vietnam, and now at age 46 as a mid-life student.

Like many men in the United States, there was a time when I put career and earning a living ahead of the emotional needs of my family. I felt that I was meeting my family's major needs by being a good provider. I thought little of my values until they were put to the test. At age 26, when I went to Vietnam, I saw my priorities in life as career, duty to country, family and then my own personal needs. When faced with death, dying and unbelievable personal stress, I found that career and duty to country were, for me, superficial. I began a long journey toward understanding that I was significant, important to myself and to others, and that my first priority was to care for myself. Then I would be able to care for my family. Today self and family have merged and become one, making it difficult to see where one starts and the other ends. Career and patriotism are still important, but well down the list of what is most important in my life. Family and self are my primary values.

Interaction with the people around me is my second most important motivator. As a young adult I focused on improving my technical skills. I saw that as the route to success. Later in life, I discovered that technical expertise must be combined with managerial skill if I expected to advance. I also found that once I became an expert in my field, the job itself was no longer a challenge. My real growth on the job did not come from increased technical skill or my ability to organize, but rather from my people skills, my ability to interact with others and my relationships. Job satisfaction started with task accomplishment, but ultimately meant little unless accompanied by a sense of fulfillment rooted in my relationships with those with whom I worked and interacted. Who I am is reinforced by the people around me; they constantly assure me that I am okay.

I am a skillful, patient, down-to-earth teacher and leader. I enable, motivate and empower personal growth and development in others. People who have known me state that I demonstrate extreme protectiveness and loyalty to others who, in turn, give me the same. I enjoy being needed and respected. It is also significant that I like people who are most like myself. The people whom I enjoy the most are those with whom I share a common core of experience, and those with whom I share a common bond of interests, goals, hopes and dreams. Even though I enjoy working independently, it is quite clear that I am very much a social animal.

The third major motivator in my life is risk taking, and this is the motivator that I knew the least about before beginning this exercise in self-

discovery. I have found that my fears and feelings about myself have often stimulated me to take risks that extended my abilities well beyond what I considered my limits. I have always enjoyed new people and new places and have functioned exceedingly well in new situations. I am a dreamer of sorts, with a keen perception of things as they could be. In each new environment and situation, I start out by questioning the system, weighing the risks and eventually resisting the established boundaries by formulating and implementing change.

When I am sure of my cause, I become totally involved and determined to see the task accomplished. The limit I most challenge is my own fear. I have long been aware that as an air traffic controller my greatest attribute has been my ability to remain calm in extremely complex, dangerous, high density traffic situations. What I have not been aware of was that all my successes and accomplishments have been a direct result of my facing and attempting to overcome my own fears. One example occurred when I volunteered to work at the busiest airport in the world. I did not have the education or experience for the job and I was very afraid that I would not be "able or capable," but I was compelled to take the risk. The victory over my own fears and perceived limitations was that much sweeter and satisfying. This pattern of risk taking and using my secret fears has generated personal growth.

I chose my first career, and it was extremely satisfying, meeting my emotional needs as I matured and changed over the years. But like all jobs it had its disadvantages. Now I am looking for a more ideal job. It will have to meet my needs, especially in the three areas I have recently identified as my primary motivators. While these motivators are simply a way to explain how I view the world, they have not changed over time and seemingly will remain important well into my old age. At this moment in time I am motivated and stimulated by family, personal relationships and by risking myself in both relationships and task accomplishment.

For me the perfect job would be a balance of work and leisure that assures maximum contact with my family. This connectedness with my family may include working together in joint enterprises or simply time spent together. In this *perfect job I see myself as a member of an egalitarian group or network where I lead by example, and where each member is responsible for his/her own efforts. I want to be able to promote growth in others in a climate that makes it possible for me to grow and develop. One of my goals is to empower people with a better sense of self, and awareness of their own personhood and unlimited potential. I need people around me and I need to be needed.*

I also need to be financially successful. Money equals power, and I see them both as absolutely necessary. While personally satisfying, my first career made very little money. For the next 20 years I must make enough to carry me and my wife through old age, and that's a big order.

The ideal job will also have to be global in scale, because new places, people and situations are very important to me. I feel much more comfortable living and working in different countries rather than just visiting them.

The ideal job must offer me the challenge of being on the cutting edge of human development, testing boundaries and ideas. This job will require me to risk myself. I must also retain the flexibility necessary to adjust my work, hours and energy output, leaving the uninteresting and mundane tasks to others.

At first glance all these requirements for my ideal job seem overwhelming, but on closer inspection I see that combining them into one career or position may not be as difficult now that the job description has been spelled out.

"Who am I?" is still a difficult question, but now that I have stopped long enough to listen to others and explore some continuing skills and basic motivations, I am closer to an answer. I am at a point in my life where looking back is important, and these self-exploration exercises have indeed been beneficial for that task. Now I must apply this information while developing my life course for the future.

Case Study 5-3

The organizing and administrative skills of this author at first suggest that he would do well as a corporate executive. Before ordering a gray flannel suit, however, he (and we) must obviously take into consideration his

personality and values. They, clearly, do not suggest the executive suite. This paper is, therefore, a nice illustration of the inadequacy of focusing only on a person's skills, without also looking at personality and values. As you review the author's wide-ranging interests, do you have a clear sense of which are the most important to him? Similarly, which needs of his personality are most dominant? Do you think he has a good sense of how his skills, interests and personality needs blend together? Are you clear on what he would be doing in his ideal job?

Organizer/Mystic/Life of the Party

It was initially very hard for me to sum up, in a few neat and logical pages, what I learned about myself. I reviewed all of my lists, exercises and surveys to discern my basic motivational pattern. I was at first unable to pin down one, two or three major variables in either skills, interests or personality traits. It appears that I have been constantly seeking new experiences, new challenges and new ideas. As a result, I continually acquired new skills, new interests and new personality traits along the way.

In reviewing the major phases of my life I can see, from an overall perspective, how my interests changed, my skills developed and my personality traits began to broaden and refine. I would be selling myself short, or doing myself an injustice, if I were only to include in this paper four or five little stories about myself and say that this is "me."

But I must say that writing this paper has accomplished its purpose. Now I can readily recall a great many stories which I will be able to relate quickly and simply to others in future job interviews as examples of my marketable skills.

These days my primary area of interest (besides academics and survival in general) is in intercultural affairs, with emphasis on the different religious belief systems inherent in different cultures. This interest has led me to a concern with spirituality in general, and Sufism in particular.

My explorations into the Christi Order of Sufism as manifested today in the West have produced a marked change in my basic motivational pattern over the last seven years. I left a highly promising career as an officer in the United States Army Air Defense Artillery to devote my energies toward helping accomplish what an Indian Sufi mystic (and greatly honored singer and musician) came to the West to do in 1910. After becoming terrifically inspired by this fellow's writings, I decided to assist him in his work in whatever way seemed helpful, with the overall purpose of spreading the message of Sufism in the West.

At one time I considered my organizational skills to be my greatest asset. Since that time I have been able to work at different tasks which have developed my intuitive faculties. I have functioned comfortably and effectively in leadership and staff roles for a multitude of projects. These have included supporting Alpine summer camps involving 500 to 600 people each year, singing and dancing in an eight-month-long theatrical production, assisting in the restoration of an ancient building complex, living in two different Sufi communities for five years, editing an English charity's quarterly magazine for 18 months and being the camp director of my order's USA Leader's Retreat in New Mexico's wilderness in 1982.

I really enjoy working around "Sufi" people. They are generally hard to typecast outwardly. They seem to possess a fairly tolerant attitude toward others. They also usually possess a better than average internal, intuitive sense of what direction to take in their lives.

I have experience working with many different types of people here and abroad. I have found that I get the most satisfaction working with ambitious, creative high achievers who are oriented positively toward their lives and work, and also possess idealistic tendencies toward perfection (politically, spiritually, etc.). I feel comfortable acting in the role of "being the boss." I feel uncomfortable acting under superiors who are tyrannical, insecure, intolerant and inconsiderate.

In order to discuss what I have rediscovered about my personality traits, it will be helpful to mention first the results of the Self-Directed Search and two different Strong- Campbell Interest Inventories. Both of these exercises placed me in the Enterprising-Social-Artistic areas.

Since early childhood I have always received straight A's in art. It was recognized often and publicly in my schools that I and another student (a girl) were the best artists. I thrived on that recognition and became more creative. I even received a first place award in the prestigious annual Boston Globe Art Competition.

I am also very social, gregarious and humorous. I am proud of the number and quality of friendships that I have been able to make and maintain through the years. Friendship is very important to me. I used to be considered the "life of the party" among my adolescent peer group. I was always doing things to make people laugh. My mother says she first noticed this trait in me as a very young child when I put on puppet shows for my neighborhood friends.

Much later, as a captain in an advanced military six-month course, I was made the social chairman for my section of 40 officers. In other words, I was the fellow who organized the parties for my group and coordinated with the social chairmen of the two other groups. I have done some absolutely outrageous things at parties, almost always spontaneously, just to make people laugh and become more at ease and comfortable. I also relish the attention this brings me.

This ability to make people laugh has served me extremely well throughout my life. It has proven very valuable in many quite dramatic, dangerous or difficult life adventure situations where I was able to diffuse personal tensions before they passed into a critical and destructive phase. I feel good about my abilities as a peacemaker and mediator. I have often found myself in these roles in group situations throughout my life.

I have also noticed how enterprising I have been on many occasions, often to a fault. I always seem to be aware of my ability to inspire others to agree with my point of view, often through a creative use of language and rational thought. This is in some ways manipulative but probably very good if one wants to be in sales. I have never been interested in selling things I did not believe in, but I have done quite well at fayres and festivals in England selling-bartering-trading all sorts of odd things like food, books, jewelry and so forth.

I once made $1200 in a four-day weekend, working with a lady partner at a festival. I enjoyed the fast pace and social interface with the passing public: telling spontaneous jokes, feeding the stomachs, hearts and minds of many, many people and juggling all sorts of other things at the same time. We would then throw everything in the back of a van and drive off to another festival site after a couple of days of baking and cooking up more goodies. I appreciate being my own boss, working outside and working with my lady-love every day. I don't know if there are many corporations which would allow me to do this.

I would have to say that I am definitely an organizer. From earliest childhood I can remember organizing interesting games for my playmates and making sure that they were modified as necessary to keep things fair for participants of all ages. This fairness thing in me persisted up through high school, where I can remember receiving compliments from other student court judges about how remarkably fair I was.

Getting the Student Court established in my school was one of the least publicized but most rewarding accomplishments of my senior year. I was able to persuade my friend, the student president, to persuade the principal to approve the establishment of a never before done Student Court. Two of my other great interests are law and politics.

Another personality trait that is a little difficult to talk about from my present, more humble point of view, is leadership. Looking back over my life I would have to say that I operated in leadership roles throughout Cadet Corps life at Texas A&M University, my follow-up mini-career in the army and on into Sufi life.

I can't say that I'm a natural born leader. I wasn't the captain of the baseball/basketball/track & field teams in junior and senior high schools. But I did participate in those sports, learning how to become a good team member.

After this experience, and the marvelous socialization process of thriving through what many others considered to be an amazingly difficult "fish" year at A&M, I began to be noticed by others as a leader. Many more times than I would care to remember I have been given awards, recognition and responsibilities for projects, programs and personnel requiring multiple leadership skills.

In the army I was given command of a tactical missile air defense battery. I had less than three years active service at that time. All of a sudden I was responsible for many millions of dollars worth of equipment and, more important, responsible for the lives of more than 200 United States and Korean support personnel. During my tenure I had to supervise a complete change in our primary weapon system and integrate a new package of improved equipment and personnel.

The old-timers and new-bees inevitably developed a significant and serious "us versus them" mentality, which threatened the overall morale of the unit and, by association, our combat readiness. I found myself in just the right place at the right time to use my harmonization skills of fairness and good judgment to diffuse a potential crisis.

Later, during a USO show, I had to use my showmanship and humorist skills to MC the opening and closing of the show. This required grace and humor in front of a very large audience of troops, a general and other officers and local Korean dignitaries. I really had to think on my feet when, in the middle of that show, one of the showgirls (who must have been told who the battery commander was) came off stage and dragged me up there to dance with her, which I did very well, to the roaring amusement of my troops and significant others.

My "ideal job" would have to include some of the personal penchants I have already mentioned. Some form of weekly travel would be nice. A total change of scenery every so often would be necessary. There is not much money in Sufism, which must come first in my life's priorities. A creative opportunity, in service to others, where I can more or less "be my own boss," is important. I seem to enjoy some productive routine, balanced by a little outdoor physical work. I want to experience a challenge now and then to keep me on my toes. The ability to make a total break with the past now and then, and with my work, would also be refreshing. Sufis occasionally enjoy going on spiritual retreats in order to refresh and rejuvenate their personal perspectives.

Given my slightly extroverted, active and industrious nature, it may also be good for my ideal job to be one of great activity among people and with things. I have found great satisfaction in creating order out of chaos — and vice versa when appropriate. I seem to be able to do well at work which is action oriented, real life, high pressure and requires spontaneous, spur-of-the-moment thinking.

It would be nice if this job required adventurous sojourns in exotic and beautiful foreign lands. Some form of independent consulting or marketing/sales work might be worth investigating. It would also be good if my accomplishments were recognized by others.

I would enjoy working on a daily basis with my female partner. Perhaps some form of homespun occupation might suit my needs and also satisfy my intense desire to be my own boss and manage my own time.

Six. Interests:
Meaning and Magic at Work

For reasons which are not entirely clear, some people feel a strong attraction to a particular environment, or a specific kind of work. There is something about these places or activities that has a certain magic for them. They may be excited by the process of government, or deeply attracted to religious ceremonies. They may deeply value children and how they react and think. They may have dreamed since childhood of being a teacher, star athlete, medical doctor or pilot.

In this chapter, we use the word "interest" to refer to the attractions, ideals, values and dreams that can, for some individuals, give special meaning to certain occupations and work environments.

Probing your interests is a challenging task. For one thing, everyone has skills, and everyone has personality characteristics. Not everyone has strong interests, however. Still, when interests *are* strong, work which connects with them is important to your happiness and well-being.

Making this connection can be difficult. It is not unusual to be attracted to a job without having the skills or personality necessary for success. Bob Chapman has always felt deeply about music, and would love to be a musician. Unfortunately, he cannot carry a tune. Bob Wegmann dreamed as a child of being a United States senator. He knew more about the members and their political positions than most adults. Having worked in the senate, however, he now knows he could not possibly tolerate such a pressured existence, with almost no time alone to read, reflect, or think things through.

When our dreams are inconsistent with our talents or personality, we need to transform them. This can mean writing political commentary instead of running for office, or being an airport administrator instead of flying. For Bob Chapman, it means listening to music rather than playing it. For Bob Wegmann, it has meant being elected to a Board of Education, and a Faculty Senate.

Many people ignore their dreams, thinking them impractical. They take whatever job is available and provides them with a good living. At first this may seem to work out. To ignore one's dreams, however, is to ignore a deep source of motivation. If some area of life is emotionally significant for you, then some part of your happiness will lie in working (or using your leisure time) in that area.

What You Will Be when You Grow Up Is Not the Question

The process of finding an occupation which pays enough and is a good match to our talents, personality and interests is, for most people, slow and difficult. False starts and wrong turns are common.

One of the recurring horrors of childhood is dealing with that old standby, "What do you want to be when you grow up?" Children who decline to answer are wiser than they know. Two extremely misleading assumptions lurk behind this apparently simple question. The first is that there is some magic age when we are "grown up." The second is that, as an adult, there is one occupation which will determine what we will "be" throughout all of our adult years.

With the exception of a small part of the upper middle class, most people are employed at several occupations during their working lifetimes. Such occupational switches can be healthy. It is unreasonable to expect someone in his or her early twenties to make a firm occupational choice. At this age we know far too little about either the world or ourselves.

We have, for example, often seen students abandon career goals and change college majors once they interviewed several people who worked at the occupation for which they were preparing. When they found out what they would really be doing all day, they realized this was not what they wanted.

The problem goes beyond avoiding obviously bad occupational choices. Many people are deeply attracted to more than one occupation. It can take years for them to find a way to express their multiple interests in some combination of work and leisure activities. There are also individuals who find they are very successful at occupations which they do not enjoy. They must then come to terms with the conflicts this causes.

Furthermore, the "magic" that you find in a job may disappear over time. People burn out. For years, someone loves teaching. Then, one day, it is all over. It's just a job, and a boring one at that. When this happens, the wisest course is to leave and go on to something else.

Changed beliefs can also eliminate much of the satisfaction found in a job. Many managers and professionals see particular positions as stepping stones to higher responsibility. They believe getting to the top will eventually bring them real satisfaction. It may be years before they get close enough to their goals to realize that happiness is different from success. Shocked to see that some highly placed people are bitterly unhappy, they then have to reconsider their objectives, and the meaning of their work.

It is thus perfectly normal for the process of shaking off youthful illusions to continue into the thirties and forties. As a result, our first occupational choices are likely to be abandoned or significantly modified as the years go by. It appears that the Pennsylvania Dutch are right: "Ve get too soon old, und too late schmart."

We Mislead the Young

It is a great shame that the young are not more aware of these facts. One poll in Minnesota had 1100 high school students discuss jobs and careers. These young people consistently thought of a career decision as a life-long commitment to one occupation. They also believed that a person's interests should point to only one "correct" occupational choice, rather than to a set of possibilities. These widely held student views are frighteningly inaccurate.

As a consequence, young people often look on career decisions as terrifying, believing that an error could permanently ruin their lives. The choice of an occupation, seen as an event instead of a process, becomes something to be put off for as long as possible. Not a single student suggested that it is common for adults to change occupations, or even total career direction.

Let's Work on It

The main purpose of this chapter is to provide a series of exercises to help you think through your values and interests. These exercises approach your dreams and concerns in a variety of ways. They are intended to help you clarify this part of your life.

As you do this work, you should find your goals, values and interests becoming more explicit. We do want to stress, though, that not every exercise works for each person who uses it. One person may find a particular exercise of special value, while another will not. If you do the whole group, however, you should find several that draw out your interests and values in a helpful way.

Try to avoid the mistake of reading each exercise, thinking of a few answers mentally, and then moving on. There is a value in putting your thoughts down on paper. The process of writing things out helps make explicit what would otherwise remain fuzzy. Experiences, objectified in writing, change. Writing creates understanding.

Career Anchors

One instrument that can help you begin comes from research done by Edgar Schein, working with graduates of the Sloan School of Management at Massachusetts Institute of Technology. Professor Schein found that, after some years of work experience, a pattern of self-perceived talents, motives and values begins to guide a person's career. Whatever else might change, this "career anchor" or basic orientation toward work is what an individual wants to hold onto. We have taken this concept, modified it somewhat, and produced a list of "Key Job Characteristics" in Exercise 6-1.

Review these features of various occupations to see which most appeal to you. This should begin to clarify some of the values and job characteristics that are of particular importance to you.

Other Views

One way to see your life as a whole is to write your obituary (Exercise 6-2). Although this may seem strange (or even a little frightening), it can be an effective way to put things in perspective. Seeing your life in its entirety helps you to highlight the concerns you want your life to express. The key question then becomes: if this is what I want my life to be at the end, what do I need to do today?

Another useful activity is to look back over the past year, listing those events in Exercise 6-3 which gave you the most satisfaction, and also those which generated the most anger. Although the second list may seem negative, it is an equally valid way of getting in touch with what is important to you. Looking at what makes you angry can help to identify areas of emotional involvement. All jobs require you to solve problems. If you are emotionally involved with the problems you are solving, your work is likely to mean more to you.

Suppose you were put in charge of a charitable foundation, and given the opportunity to dispense a sizable sum of money. To what persons, institutions or

Key Job Characteristics

1. In this job you will be responsible for a technically demanding task. The attractive feature of this position is the feeling of being competent. With each additional project, your skill and experience at this kind of work will grow.

2. In this position you will be dealing with a wide variety of challenges, people and places. This is a job for a very flexible person. There is no set routine; each day will be different.

3. This job allows you to use your talents and gifts to be of service to those most in need of your help. Your work will be appreciated because of the important assistance you give.

4. What is attractive about this job is that it is predictable, secure and relatively free from stress. It is good work with good people, and allows you to enjoy a settled life as a respected member of your community. There may not be a lot of variety, but there aren't a lot of nasty surprises either.

5. This is a demanding management position which requires constant problem solving and good interpersonal skills. Decisions regularly have to be made with only incomplete information. You will take some heat in this job. Crises arise, and you must handle them without becoming paralyzed or feeling guilty when difficult choices must be made.

6. In this line of work you will operate independently. You can set your own agenda and your own pace. Your life is not determined by someone else's decisions.

7. This position has real power. Someone has to make the critical decisions, and you will be the one who makes them. Hence the position has a good deal of clout, and so will you when you fill it.

8. In this position you will know that what you produce comes from your own efforts. You can enjoy the challenge of what you do, knowing that the results you see are clearly linked to your own creative work.

9. The great thing about this job is that you can identify with it. The uniform lets people know that you are part of an important organization. It's not so much the particular job you do that's important. Rather, it's being part of a group recognized and respected by everyone.

10. This position requires you to be constantly learning. You will regularly need to seek out new information, master new subjects, and then put this knowledge to work.

Decision Matrix

To help you remember them, each of the ten key job characteristics is summed up in one or two words:

1. Technical Competence
2. Variety
3. Service to Others
4. Security

5. Top Management
6. Independence
7. Power
8. Creativity

9. Organizational Identification
10. Constant Learning

Each of the job characteristics above is numbered. Below are 45 pairs of numbers (every possible combination of two numbers between 1 and 10). For each pair, assume that you have been offered two attractive jobs. In each case, you are choosing between two of the job descriptions you have just read. If you had to choose, which of the two would you prefer? Circle that number and then go on to the next pair of numbers, again making a choice. Continue until you have made all 45 choices.

1	2	3	4	5	6	7	8	9	1	2	3	4	5	6
2	3	4	5	6	7	8	9	10	3	4	5	6	7	8
7	8	1	2	3	4	5	6	7	1	2	3	4	5	6
9	10	4	5	6	7	8	9	10	5	6	7	8	9	10
1	2	3	4	5	1	2	3	4	1	2	3	1	2	1
6	7	8	9	10	7	8	9	10	8	9	10	9	10	10

Now count how many times you chose each of these ten jobs, and then rank your choices. (Give rank 1 to the job chosen most often, 2 to that chosen second most often, and so on.)

Job	How Often Chosen?	Rank	Job	How Often Chosen?	Rank
1	_____	_____	6	_____	_____
2	_____	_____	7	_____	_____
3	_____	_____	8	_____	_____
4	_____	_____	9	_____	_____
5	_____	_____	10	_____	_____

Total   45

Looking Backwards

It is the year 2030. You are suffering from a disease which, unfortunately, is terminal. The doctors give you about a week to live.

Naturally, you are looking back on your life. Begin somewhere in the mid-1980s and write what happened to you from then to the present (2030). Describe what you did. What do you feel best about in your life? What will people be saying about you at your funeral?

It is important, in writing this autobiography/obituary, that you not plan ahead what you want to say. Rather, begin by describing the recent past (the mid-80s) and then write whatever comes to you. Just let the ideas develop as you write.

What Most Affects You Emotionally?

On the left side of this page, list some occasions and experiences which you have thoroughly enjoyed. Then, on the right side, list any events which have angered or upset you. Look over both lists. Is there a pattern? Do your reactions and concerns suggest an occupational area which would have special emotional meaning for you?

This Made Me Really Happy: This Made Me Really Angry:

_____   _____

_____   _____

_____   _____

_____   _____

_____   _____

_____   _____

_____   _____

_____   _____

_____   _____

_____   _____

_____   _____

_____   _____

_____   _____

_____   _____

_____   _____

_____   _____

_____   _____

You're One with a Million

You have just been named trustee of a charitable foundation set up by a wealthy relative of whom you were previously unaware. You suddenly find yourself in charge of $100 million.

The terms of the bequest are that you must spend $1 million on yourself, and give the remaining $99 million to others. You can give your family part of your million, but the $99 million must go to persons, organizations or charities outside your family.

List what you would do with your money, and how you would allocate the $99 million that would go to others.

With my million dollars, I would:

_____

_____

_____

_____

_____

_____

I would allocate the $99 million as follows:

_____

_____

_____

_____

_____

_____

What does this list say about your interests, values and needs?

_____

_____

_____

_____

_____

A Style Identification Exercise

Walk through your home or apartment as if you had never seen it before. Pretend you are an anthropologist from another country. Look carefully at how things are decorated, what clothes are in the closet, what books and magazines are around, what records or tapes are on the shelf, the kind of food in the refrigerator, and so on.

If you had no idea of who lived here, what would you guess about the occupant? What pattern of interests would you see? What personality and lifestyle would you assume?

What does all of this say about you and the kind of person you are? What job would fit someone like you? In what environment will you do your best work?

_____

_____

_____

_____

_____

_____

_____

_____

_____

_____

_____

_____

_____

_____

_____

_____

_____

_____

groups would you make the bequests? Reviewing the choices you made in Exercise 6-5 can give you some indication of the concerns and values which are particularly important to you.

Another way to take a fresh look at yourself involves reviewing your house or apartment for clues to your personal characteristics. How do you choose to dress? How do you decorate your living space? What colors and foods and music and books do you most like? What kind of people do you invite into your home? Based on the answers to these and similar questions, what work environment would fit you best?

What Jobs Are Emerging?

When you have finished these exercises, review them. Take a close look at the employment implications of your major interests and values. Try matching these interests with some of your strongest skills, and see what kinds of jobs would fit both. A grid for this, much like the skills/personality grid in the last chapter, is provided in Exercise 6-6.

As you did then, try to generate job titles for as many of the combinations as you can. Writing ability and an interest in government would suggest a speech writer for an elected official, for example. Mathematical skill and an interest in the needs of children could fit being a middle school math teacher, or a statistician for a child psychology research team. A desire to help the poor, combined with carpentry skills, might suggest a job rehabilitating old buildings in an urban homesteading program.

When you have finished producing as many combinations as you can, compare the results with the job titles generated by the grid in Chapter Five. If you're really up for a challenge, try doing a three-dimensional grid. Look for occupations that combine your strongest skills, dominant personality traits and major interests and values.

The Merging of Personality, Interests, and Talents

An essential part of the meaning of work is the context in which we experience it. There is an old story about a man walking along a road. He notices a group of workers chipping away at some large pieces of rock, and asks them what they are doing. One replies, "I'm cutting rock." Another, "I'm earning a living for my family." The third, "I'm building a cathedral."

We don't all need or want to build cathedrals. In the long run, though, we do need to find significance in our work beyond the weekly or monthly paycheck.

Roger Gould, a psychiatrist with a particular interest in adult development, argues that finding personal meaning in work is particularly important in midlife. When we are young we work to feel bigger and more adult, because we have to for survival, and because we identify with the organization which employs us. These motivations, however, will not carry us through our entire lives. As we grow older, we come to realize that we must work at what we do best because it is inherently enjoyable to use our greatest strengths. Similarly, we must find work which has emotional meaning for us.

The Blend

The chapters in this section have provided a framework for you to consider your skills, personality needs and interests. What is really important is how these aspects of your humanity blend together to determine what you do best, enjoy most, and really care about. Two career counselors, Arthur Miller and Ralph Mattson, report working over the years with more than 3000 people. In each person they found a pattern of "motivated abilities" — the talents that the individual most wanted to use.

Our own experience is consistent with theirs. People have patterns of behavior which they typically exhibit whenever they are free to act as they choose. This pattern of motivated abilities comes from each individual's blend of interests, talents and personality traits.

What is fascinating is how people follow this pattern in almost any situation, whether appropriate or not. A person who is motivated to teach others will do so whether or not any teaching is needed. The individualist, promoted to a managerial position, will find some way of performing as an individual, despite his or her official duties as "team leader." The team worker, given a solo assignment, will find someone with whom to work. The person who is motivated to work on problems will look for some to solve. The individual who is turned on by stress and competition will gravitate to "wherever the action is."

If the demands of a job contradict a person's motivational pattern, the result will be irritation, frustration, anxiety and depression. A person motivated to create or innovate will break new ground where this is unnecessary, or make moderate improvements at unreasonable cost. The individualist, made part of a team, will ignore the need for teamwork. He or she will seek out some task which can be performed alone, where individual results will stand out.

Interests and Skills Grid

On top of this grid, list your five strongest interests. Then, on the left side, list the five skills you most enjoy using. Now try to jot down a job title for as many of the 25 combinations as you can.

Jobs Combining Interests and Skills

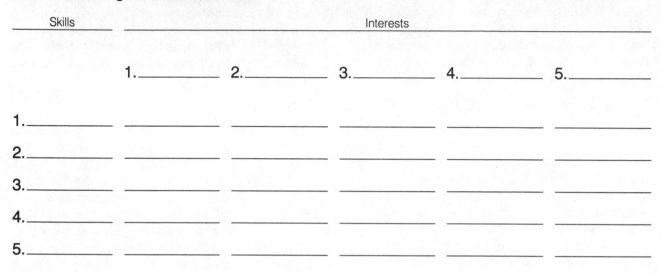

Skills	Interests				
	1._____	2._____	3._____	4._____	5._____
1._____	_____	_____	_____	_____	_____
2._____	_____	_____	_____	_____	_____
3._____	_____	_____	_____	_____	_____
4._____	_____	_____	_____	_____	_____
5._____	_____	_____	_____	_____	_____

Misplacement therefore becomes counterproductive for both the individual and the organization. An essential task for an effective manager is to get the right people into the right assignments. As Peter Drucker once put it, being responsible for a person who's in the wrong job is like cleaning up after an elephant.

Many managers are insensitive to the importance of this person/position match. You cannot depend on others to be sure you are hired for, or are assigned, a position that fits you. Your goal must be to discover for yourself what work is most congruent with your motivational pattern, and to find a position where you can do that work.

Now What?

Before proceeding further, you should stop and sum up what you have learned. Put in writing a summary of your interests, skills and personality traits. Show this to several people who know you well, and ask for their comments.

The Ideal Job Advertisement

To help express what you are seeking, in Exercise 6-7 try writing an advertisement for a job you would love to have. The advertisement should be one which, if you actually saw it in a newspaper, would immediately excite you. You would be perfect for such a job.

The ad need not have any traditional job title heading it (teacher, salesperson, police officer, executive or whatever). Instead, just describe what has to be *done* in the job, under what conditions, and by what type of person.

This advertisement can be an excellent starting point for a conversation when you begin interviewing people to get the labor market information you need, as you will be doing shortly. You may find to your surprise that your ideal job really exists, and has a title.

Summing Up Section II

If you are going to be successful at a job, you want one which draws on your strongest skills, training and experience. To be comfortable at a job, you are looking for something which is consistent with your personality. And to be really satisfied with a job, you want work which taps emotionally significant areas of interest.

The ideal is to find a position which does all three of these, or at least comes as close as possible. One set of jobs is realistic given your skills. Another set would fit your personality. A third would be consistent with your interests and values. You want to generate a list of possible occupations which are part of all three sets. You can then research these occupations in more depth, to see which are realistic for you, given today's labor market conditions.

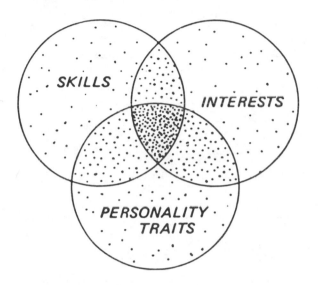

The search for the right job is a search for the best match. The work done so far has been oriented only toward the first element of that match: yourself. Now a similar effort must be put into researching the second element: available jobs. You have a clearer idea of what *you* want. You must now move to checking out what *employers* want. Where are your interests, talents, experience and personality most in demand?

If people exhibit extraordinary variety, the labor market offers equally varied opportunities. How do you find what you want? There are two key tools: library research and interviewing. Used together, they will help you search effectively for the best possible person/position match.

Before beginning Section III, however, it is worthwhile to review three final cases. Reading these papers can help give you a practical, "hands-on" feel for the impact of interests on career decisions. Each paper was written by someone whose concerns and values play an important part in his or her life. The importance of these interests grows as the years go by. Constructing a life which expresses them is a significant goal of life/work planning.

The Ad I Want to Answer

Review what you've learned about your skills, interests and personality traits. Then write a help wanted ad that describes what would be, for you, an ideal job.

_____

_____

_____

_____

_____

_____

_____

_____

_____

_____

_____

_____

_____

_____

_____

_____

_____

_____

_____

_____

CASE STUDIES

Case Study 6-1

For most of us, any first job is exciting. Initially, our focus is not primarily on obtaining the maximum satisfaction from work. At this stage, we are more concerned with survival, with not failing, and with breaking into the adult world. The author of this paper has now passed through that stage. Having been successful in a number of positions, she wants to find something which suits her better than the work she has done so far. She has clear values (though not all of them need to be expressed in her work). What are her strongest interests? Her skills seem to cluster around two areas: organizing and supervising, and promoting. Which is her stronger suit? Will any of her personality characteristics eliminate some jobs which she would otherwise consider, or suggest a particularly good match? Is her ideal job description focused enough to allow you to name one or several occupations which would likely fit her requirements?

Service and Structure

I have been fighting a secret battle all of my adult life, trying to appear perfectly suited to virtually every job I ever stumbled on. Some jobs fit better than others. I remember my stint as an army laundry clerk in Germany. My job was to compare the number of bedsheets recorded with the number received. I stood with a clipboard eight hours a day, watching GI's troop in with enormous bundles of laundry — like olive-drab ants carting broken pieces of bread.

The factory itself was a steamy, sprawling maze of activity. Bundling, washing, pressing and hanging were conducted under a steady roar of machinery and the swelling babble of a dozen different languages. Spaniards, Greeks, Germans, Italians and that peculiar brand of American, the stoned GI, joined in the common task of keeping the army well-dressed. If Kanter, in her book Life in Organizations, *was correct in assuming that one's importance in the organization decreases as the noise level increases, then I was truly at the bottom of the corporate ladder.*

I was satisfied for awhile, since certain needs were being met. On the Strong-Campbell Interest Inventory, I learned that military activities and adventure fell among my top nine interests. The

laundry certainly had that. It even had a high sociability quotient (S-theme). Of all general occupational categories reviewed, I most enjoy those that are people-oriented. This is probably the strongest and most consistent characteristic of my personality.

Perhaps Holland's definition of the "social" personality best explains my major incompatibility with the laundry factory. I simply have "an aversion to explicit, ordered, systematic activities involving materials, tools or machines." On the Strong-Campbell inventory, "accountant" was the lowest item on my basic interest scale. The Self-Directed Search suggested foreign language instructor, foreign service officer and language interpreter as feasible career paths.

The lure of new experiences and the challenge of establishing common bonds without the benefit of a common language or culture kept me counting sheets far longer than expected. As a single parent in Europe, I was able to utilize my abilities as a creative and resourceful problem-solver. My excellent communication and social skills enabled me to maximize benefits in the most ingenious ways. A quick review of my twenty accomplishments revealed an emerging personality pattern. I am an enthusiastic participant in those activities to which I have become committed. My optimism and flexibility enable me to adapt to change with ease. Perseverance is a significant component in the pursuit of my identified goals. It is because of the depth of my commitments that it is so important for me to define my values, goals and aspirations clearly.

Job satisfaction can be maximized by pursuing a vocation that has meaning, that carries emotional weight. I've been happiest working for the welfare of my family, as well as for the local and international community. Travel and continuing education have been recurrent pleasures in the course of my life. I now realize that I experienced my greatest difficulties when facing direct confrontation, social injustice, betrayal of loyalty and financial insufficiency. Among my key values are: 1) improved relationships between people, 2) better cultural and artistic opportunities and 3) improved health and environmental conditions.

Upon reflection, I have derived most satisfaction from paramilitary employment such as with the fire department or the county probation department. I find it an odd attraction, considering my deep need for personal freedom in directing my own activities.

There is a certain sturdiness and clarity in the structure of these organizations. However, they still allow for autonomy and flexibility in exercising authority, and they have a need for acceptance by people as a whole. In many ways, I'm motivated toward service. I have a natural interest in developing opportunities to help others.

My major accomplishments occurred when I was able to develop and implement an independent course of activity utilizing direct action and authority. Group projects stimulate me and encourage me to act on broad objectives. For example, as a recruiter for the fire department, I interacted with many colleges in the setting up of recruitment booths, lecturing, speaking with career placement officials and instituting direct out-reach programs to recruit young people into the department. I expanded these duties to local high schools and civic groups, addressing classes and promoting interest at "career days," scouting groups and technical/vocational workshops.

I utilized extensive promotional skills in this position, and was primarily responsible for instituting a new advertising package for the fire department. I appeared on virtually every area radio program, and several television stations, and was chosen to be the recruitment spokesperson on two television commercials. I organized and disseminated public service announcements on a regular basis to all local media outlets.

The decision tree helped me to focus on vocational features that I find most attractive. "Flexibility," again, was prominent. I'm happiest when my day-to-day activities and relationships offer novelty and change. "Good pay" was a close second, but only as an external factor. It is relatively easy for me to take charge and direct activities, so "assuming supervisory responsibility" was number three in the hierarchy. "Socialization" and "travel" were equally important in establishing my ideal work environment. Other factors such as "creativity, opportunities for learning, attractive surroundings" and just "being busy" rounded out my major criteria.

My employment, thus far, has not been well related to my needs. Art, children, nutrition, criminal justice and traveling are among my most compelling interests. As far back as I can remember, I've derived great pleasure from art. When I was a teenager, I would save my allowance for a weekly train ride to the Chicago Museum of Fine Arts. For hours I would wander in that great kaleidoscope of colors and forms — bathed in the golden glow of Rembrandt and the neon of Edward Hopper. My father, firmly rooted in Mexican tradition, was suspicious of my "real" reason for these weekly junkets, but that reason really was love of art. Even now, I find myself constantly organizing my environment to include an eclectic array of pleasing sounds, colors and shapes.

A local juvenile detention facility has a poster that reads "Need: something you must have in order to be healthy, happy and secure." Of course we all strive for the universal goals of love, respect and independence. But it is the concept of individuation that ultimately defines "the core of your life."

I have discovered that my basic friendliness and social traits enable me to grasp the overall thoughts of groups and interpret them in practical and reasonable terms. Because I'm sensitive to social needs, people tend to relax in their dealings with me. This is an ideal trait in my potentially explosive employment as a probation officer for adult felons.

Most organizational projects would benefit from my greater than average ability to bring order out of chaos and to adapt to changing conditions. I function best in situations where I have direction, but not restrictive supervision. I think in practical and competitive terms; however, I avoid direct confrontation. I have a sense of adventure and enjoy new and exciting experiences.

My ideal job would be in government service at the state or federal level, with an office location in Austin, Texas or Washington, D.C. I would prefer a position that offers the opportunity to travel, particularly in Spanish-speaking countries. The key requirements would be excellent communication skills, confidence and a sense of adventure, as well as the ability to manipulate limited resources in a creative manner. Flexible hours and responsibility for a wide range of projects are important. I thoroughly enjoy working with the community and would be most effective in a position where I could facilitate meaningful change.

Case Study 6-2

The author of this paper has recently left a job which he found totally uninteresting. Is it clear why the job had no interest for him? Is sales work (for which he has obvious talent) without attraction, or was it the product, or the customers and territory? In his ideal job description, can you tell the kinds of problems he would like to solve? The kind of service he would like to offer? At the end of his paper he mentions real estate and finance. Can you suggest any other fields which might fit his blend of skills, interests and personality characteristics?

Cash and Competition

To be properly prepared for a successful job search, I have learned that one of the most important steps is clarifying my interests, skills and personality traits. I have found that I must satisfy myself in these three areas in order to enjoy any job.

I found this out the hard way. I recently left a job for which I had the right skills and personality traits, and at which I was very successful. My interest level was so low, however, that I chose to resign. I did this not just to maintain my sanity and to complete my M.B.A., but also to give myself time to step back and take a good look at my interests, skills and personality traits. I want my next job choice to be more rewarding.

The exercises showed that I have many interests. These interests are best grouped into three main divisions: competing, traveling and learning.

I love to compete in almost any way possible, learn everything I can and travel anywhere. This was made very clear to me on a recent Club Med vacation I took with my wife in Ixtapa, Mexico. During this vacation, part of each day was spent meeting people from all over the world, competing in a number of different sports and learning about the local villages. Many of my friends felt that this sounded more like work than a vacation. However, for me it was the most exciting and rewarding vacation I've taken. I realize now that the reason I enjoyed it so much was because it included all of the activities that interest me the most. I should also mention that I realized that I will have to make quite a bit of money in order to accomplish doing many of the things which interest me. Thus, making money has be-

come a much stronger desire in my life.

To identify my skills, I found the exercise which was the most helpful to me was the Quick Job Hunting Map. In doing this exercise, I found the skills that I am strongest in are: athletics, leadership, observation, learning, follow through, working under pressure, influencing, persuading and gaining people's trust.

A perfect example of how I have used these skills took place in my last job, where I was a commodity chemical sales representative. A good prospect, whom I had developed from a "cold call," ran into a problem. He needed a large amount of a certain chemical very quickly, and he needed to meet a very tight specification.

At the time, my manager was out of town. So, using my leadership abilities, I immediately organized a group of people to finalize delivery dates and shipping arrangements, while I got agreement on the pricing. This required me to persuade a supplier to give our company a below market price, enabling me to get this order. I had also found that this chemical would require special handling, so I learned the procedure and made the necessary arrangements. My actions under pressure were successful and this "prospect" became a good customer of ours.

In working through the exercises, one personality trait came through loud and clear. I found that I can't stand to lose or fail. This is especially true when seeking to accomplish goals that are very important to me. Other personality traits that I possess are perseverance, inquisitiveness and an "outgoing" personality. I also found that I very much enjoy the recognition that goes along with the accomplishment of goals and objectives. My intense interest in competing is a strong factor in the molding of my personality. I have found that to win or to accomplish my goals, I must feel I have an edge; and I believe my personality gives me that edge.

An example of how I use these traits took place when I was a senior in high school. I had been told that I had the ability to play college level competitive golf, so I decided to seek and obtain a scholarship from a top college in the area. I used my outgoing personality to become acquainted with as many of the college and university coaches as possible over a six-month period. While doing this, I gained the knowledge I would need to accomplish my goal. After many acquainted with as many of the college and university coaches as possible over a six-month period. While doing this, I gained the knowledge I would need to accomplish my goal. After many rejections, my persistence and ability to persuade finally paid off, and I received a four-year scholarship to a local university.

The exercises which I have done to find my true interests, skills and personal traits have been very helpful to me in getting myself back on the right track after my previous job experience. The exercises gave me a clear idea of what is necessary if a job is to satisfy my personal needs. I now realize that these needs must be met in order for me to enjoy my work.

The perfect job for me will call on my inquisitive nature and outgoing personality. It will be a job in which I will constantly meet new people, and be required to learn all I can about both the clients and their difficulties. I will then be able to use my persuasion skills and persistence to convince them that what I can do for them will solve their problems. This job will take place in a highly competitive environment where the rewards for accomplishing goals involve both a great deal of money and considerable recognition. Thus, this job will satisfy my intense desire for competition, while also enabling me to earn the money needed to travel and enjoy the lifestyle I want.

In conclusion, I suspect the job that would fit this description is one in which I would be the owner of my own service organization. Therefore, I have begun to investigate the avenues which could lead to the accomplishment of my goals in real estate and finance.

Case Study 6-3

The young woman who wrote this paper identifies her family background as a very strong influence on her values and approach to employment. Do you agree? What influence does this have on her attitude toward the corporation for which she works? How does it affect her consideration of other career possibilities? Does it put any limits on how she expresses her sympathy for the underdog? Look closely at her strongest skills, both as she summarizes them and as they are expressed in her ideal want ad. Do they translate into a job title? Can you tell from the ad what she might actually be doing all day?

Working for the Underdog

As Barbara Sher points out in Wishcraft, *an important step in explaining anyone's personality is understanding the environment in which he or she developed. I am no exception.*

My early background was very unstable. My parents were divorced when I was ten. My mother became the sole support, both financially and emotionally, of myself and my two younger brothers.

In order to pay the bills for this family of four, my mother had to enter the job market at the age of 38. I watched her frustration and hopelessness as she, an uneducated, unskilled, insecure housewife, tried to obtain a decent paying position to provide for her family. I also saw her determination as she progressed from part-time typist into a successful, well paid executive secretary in a large corporation.

My mother was a wonderful role model when I was growing up. She is still an inspiration, exemplifying the virtues of determination and hard work. She was supportive and encouraging. I grew up believing I could be whatever I wanted to be. What my mother didn't tell me was how to be whatever I wanted to be.

Neither my mother, father nor grandparents had a college education. My paternal grandfather came to the United States from Eastern Europe. He didn't know how to read or write. He built a transportation company with no formal education. He died a multi-millionaire without ever knowing how to write a check or read a book.

My father followed in my grandfather's footsteps. Education was never a high priority in my family. They believed that hard work, foresight and common sense made a fortune, not a college degree.

While my mother encouraged and supported me, she herself didn't know how to go about obtaining the things, like education, that I needed to fulfill my goals. Having never experienced the benefits of an education, she wasn't equipped to guide me towards a particular field or major, nor even to instill in me the importance of a college education. When she entered the job market, she considered herself fortunate to have a skill — typing.

With her entry into the workforce, I was left

in charge of myself and my two brothers, and given a lot of responsibility. As an example, when the three of us would return home from school, it was my responsibility, being the oldest, to make certain homework was finished, household chores were completed and dinner started before anyone could go outside to play.

I remember one afternoon when my brother begged me to allow him to go out and play before he finished his household duties. I resisted. He told me he would take my turn at doing the dishes for two weeks if I "covered" for him and ran the sweeper so he could go outside. Knowing a good deal, I agreed.

There were many deals made to my advantage because I was in control and had the authority over my two younger brothers. To be a leader to my brothers required a lot of responsibility as well as the ability to be a negotiator. Many afternoons I broke up disagreements between the two of them so life could return to normal before my mother came home from work.

These experiences have contributed to my acceptance of responsibility, and the leadership and negotiating skills that I use successfully on my current job. As Employee Relations Representative for 200 hourly employees, negotiating and leadership are a necessity for survival. I am thankful for the amount of responsibility I had when I was younger.

There were other advantages in watching my mother worry about employment, and be rejected for positions. One of the major characteristics this experience instilled in me was a great sympathy for the underdog or underprivileged. It was through no fault of my mother that she had to struggle to maintain a house over our heads. My father was, and still is, a practicing alcoholic. Alcoholism was a battle my mother couldn't win, no matter how hard she tried.

As a result, today I feel great compassion for the underdog or the underprivileged. The situation my mother and my family faced, through no fault of our own, motivates me to help others who, through no fault of their own, find themselves in a trying time in their lives. To be able to help a person who is a victim of circumstance, and traumatized, fulfills me.

To help people in such a situation — rape victims, abused women and children, employees who are left without a job because of the corporate system — makes me feel happy. To me, these are worthwhile causes that make life worth living. By comparison, to see these same individuals taken advantage of makes me furious.

My husband tells me I am a "crusader" and always on a "soap box." He thinks — probably correctly — that I am out to change the world. One particular incident showed me how unique my motivation and feelings are. I'll illustrate in the following example how I was enlightened.

One night, I came home from work and told my husband about an employee who refused the special retirement package the company was offering him. The company was going to close the office he was located in. He was unaware of the company's strategy. I had done my best sales job on three separate occasions to convince the employee to take advantage of the "special" retirement package. Each time he refused, stating he wanted to continue to work. He didn't know he would soon have no position with the company.

I knew that, because of his refusing the special package that he was being offered, he would receive only a normal retirement allowance when the office closed. As a result, he would lose approximately $80,000 in incentive benefits.

When I told my husband how frustrated I felt in not being able to disclose this information and prevent him from making a mistake, my husband couldn't understand my frustration or concern. He told me to quit being a "bleeding heart"; if the man refused the deal it was his own fault when he ended up with less money.

At that point, I realized that not everyone feels the same compassion or motivation toward helping people who are victims of circumstances outside their control. My husband, who came from a stable, secure family, couldn't identify or understand my motivation.

It's this motivation that makes me feel unique, needed and successful. One of the most satisfying accomplishments of my life took place during a tragedy. The corporation I work for decided to close their Pittsburgh office. Roughly 250 employees were affected, through no fault of their own. Of the 250, about 175 were separated, through severance or retirement, because no positions were available for them. In many cases these were good, loyal, dedicated employees.

As the only Employee Relations Representative in Pittsburgh, I handled the counseling for these 175 people. I believe my sincere sensitivity and compassion for these individuals motivated me to go above and beyond the call of duty. I tried to help each person make the transition from being an employed individual to being unemployed without being devastated. I felt they were victims of circumstances and the corporate system. I enjoyed giving of myself, through my position, to help them.

Along these same lines, I believe I personally am one of my biggest accomplishments. Through no fault of my own, the advantages of a college education were never explained to me. After watching my mother struggle for job security, I returned to night school eight years ago with a high school education. Next summer I will receive my bachelor's degree in psychology.

The job I held for four of these eight years required 40% travel. I also got married, had a child, and relocated. Moving set me back 24 credit hours, since the new university had different requirements. I drive a long distance to take classes. Next semester I plan on leaving my little girl with my mother in Pittsburgh so I can work full time and carry 15 credits. Most of my family and friends don't understand my motivation. They tell me I have my corporation's motor oil in my veins.

My motivation is not external, it's internal. As I see it, I was a victim of circumstance, and never had the opportunity to make a decision about an education. I lived through the gloomy situation my mother was in when she had no degree or experience. I am realistic when I defend myself and state that by leaving my child for four months I am helping her in the long run.

To attend night school for the past eight years during the situations I previously mentioned — traveling, marriage, pregnancy, motherhood and a relocation — required a lot of organization, time management, determination and the ability to handle numerous unrelated tasks at the same time. It is these very characteristics, along with my motivation to help others, that constitute the "core of my life."

No matter what accomplishment I look at, these same characteristics were utilized. As a result, I was a success. The accomplishments can be totally different, such as going to night school or completing an assignment at work, but the skills and motivations that contributed to my achievements are the same.

The Strong-Campbell Interest Inventory, Holland's Self Directed Search and the Quick Job Hunting Map are all consistent with this pattern. They describe me as social, responsible, humanistic and concerned with the welfare of others. I am more interested in people than in analytical or mechanical tasks. Two of the positions which these instruments suggested were social worker and special education teacher. Both occupations involve helping people who are victimized. Both are positions that I believe I would find fulfilling, if the money and benefits were adequate.

In summary, my childhood has ingrained in me the importance of authority, money, security and education. Compassion and a motivation to help people who are victims of situations beyond their control are instilled in my mind and heart. The ability to handle many tasks simultaneously has been a challenging and fulfilling way of life for me. I've proven my determination, organization and time management skills in both my personal and professional life.

An ideal position which would utilize all the above skills, interests and personality characteristics and provide job features which would be especially attractive to me would be advertised as follows:

WANTED: A sincere, humanistic individual who is concerned with the welfare of people who are victims of circumstance. Must be able to handle many diverse tasks simultaneously in a fast paced, pressured environment. Must be willing to assume authority and remain calm in emotionally disturbing situations, and to advise clients on the most rational courses of action. Candidate must possess excellent self-starting ability, since little supervision is given; must be organized and manage time efficiently. Good communication skills are required. Candidate must possess a B.S. degree in psychology and a willingness to obtain a master's degree in a social science.

In return, we will provide an excellent salary and benefit package, 100% paid educational assistance, security and recognition for a job well done. We will create an environment that will provide the successful applicant the opportunity of experiencing fulfillment by making a positive impact on a needy individual's life.

SECTION III.

LABOR MARKET RESEARCH

Introduction to Section III

The two chapters in this section discuss how to find the labor market information necessary for informed career decisions. What you need ranges from statistical data to company gossip, so you will have to contact a variety of sources to get what you want.

It takes some effort to find this information, but the effort pays off. These are the steps that many people skip. That's what gets them in trouble. Anxious to get a new job, they immediately begin mailing out their resumes, answering ads and so on. This is an error we urge you to avoid. What we have seen, over and over again, is that desirable job offers are not received when the information-gathering stage is omitted. Instead, the whole job search process bogs down. To be blunt: you can do this work initially, or you can come back and do it after a futile attempt to get the position you want, but unless you are extraordinarily lucky you will have to do it sooner or later.

There are two ways to approach the information-gathering methods discussed in this section, depending on your situation. If you are deciding what occupation you want to pursue, and Section II generated a list of possibilities, you now need to narrow your list. Section III will show you how to do that. Case studies at the end of each chapter give concrete examples of how this selection process works.

If, on the other hand, you have already decided on an occupation, then you need to locate the best places to begin looking for employment. You may want to be an elementary school teacher. Before you apply for specific positions, you need to know as much as possible about the local public school districts, private and parochial schools, university lab schools and so on.

Or you may have a degree in accounting. Now you have to decide whether to use that degree in an accounting firm, as part of the accounting division of a major corporation, as the accountant for a medium sized business, or as a self-employed person running your own accounting practice. You need to know the tradeoffs involved in each of these possibilities, and which would best suit your personality and interests.

What Section III discusses, essentially, is the last set of activities before you actually begin seeking employment: gathering the labor market information you need for informed decisions about both your occupational goals and specific employment objectives.

Accurate, detailed information is the foundation for your job search activities, and research *is* necessary. When examined closely, many jobs turn out to be surprisingly different from our preconceptions. Even the same job title can have different meanings, depending on the setting. Secretaries in a university, a major insurance company, a local charitable foundation and a small real estate office lead very different worklives. They have different co-workers and customers to deal with, a variety of tasks peculiar to the setting and a range of pay and benefits. The same job title does not necessarily mean the same job.

So you need to get the lay of the land. The employment interview is *not* the place to do that. Instead, your goal is to learn as much as you can *before* the interview. During the interview you want to come across as informed and knowledgeable. You also want to concentrate on communicating who you are and what you have to offer the employer.

If you are surprised or discomfited by something you learn during the interview, it will show. Your negative reaction will raise questions in the interviewer's mind. Given several candidates for the job, it is quite possible that, as a result, the employer will offer the position to someone else. It's much better to get the information you need ahead of time.

There is an interesting little book by Max Gunther entitled *The Luck Factor*. For years, Gunther was curious about people who were described to him as being very "lucky": people who made the right decisions at the right time and as a result became wealthy. What Gunther wanted to know was this: what do lucky people do that other people don't do?

One of the consistent characteristics he noticed was a pattern of gregariousness. These individuals loved to talk to people, wherever they met them: on trains or planes, in chance meetings or at social gatherings. Often these chance meetings and conversations brought information which turned out to be valuable, provided a contact which led to hiring a key person or stimulated the beginning of some new and successful venture.

Finding this information can be the result of pure chance and natural friendliness, but it does not have to be. The library research/interviewing process described in this section allows you, in effect, to organize your luck. You can proceed, in a careful and methodical way, to gather the facts and opinions needed for an informed employment decision.

This Is Intelligence Work

This process can be more enjoyable if you make a game out of it. Assume you are a spy. Your mission, should you accept it, is to discover a position which meets your needs on as many levels as possible: interests, skills, social relationships, pay, potential for advancement, consistency with your personality and so on. To accomplish this you need to "penetrate" an attractive organization where such a position can be found or created.

This is a challenging game. Our complex economy provides thousands and thousands of job possibilities. There are many traps for the unwary. Jobs are not always what they seem. Employers promise promotions, but do not always follow through. What looks like a great opportunity can become a dead end.

To be successful, therefore, you need to know what you're getting into before you make a decision. An army that marches forward blindly may walk into an ambush. To avoid this, scouts and spies are sent ahead to check things out.

You are in the same position. Like all good intelligence agents, you will first check any maps, reference books or other written materials to see what you can discover about the employment territory ahead. You need to read all you can about the culture and language of the industry and the different approaches, situations and styles of individual companies. Then it will be time to go out and take a look for yourself.

How will you find this information? Most of what is in print can be found in a good library. Chapter Seven outlines what to look for, and how to find it. Then, when you have learned as much as you can from printed materials, you need to talk to knowledgeable people. Who should be seen, how you find them and some of what you need to ask are described in Chapter Eight.

Many people go into job interviews with little preparation. They "wing it." Occasionally they're lucky. Most of the time they aren't. As a result, the position is not offered to them. Better to do your homework first. The two chapters in this section will help you gather the background information you need, and do it as quickly and efficiently as possible.

Seven. A Librarian, You Say?

A job search is, to a surprising extent, an information search. Many employment possibilities are lost because people don't know an opportunity exists, or don't know how to get through to the person doing the hiring. So we need at this point to focus on the apparently simple question: if a job search is an information search, how do you get the employment-related information you need?

Some of this information is in libraries, and so the use of library resources is the primary focus of this chapter. Chapter Eight will discuss the next step: how to interview people to learn all the important things that are never put in print. These two steps are part of the same process. The library research lays the foundation for really effective personal interviews.

First, Find a Library

For most of your library work you will not have to check out books. Because of this, you shouldn't be hesitant about using a library whose borrowers are limited to a group to which you do not belong. No one minds if you use a college library even if you aren't a student. Similarly, you can use a public library in the closest large city even if you don't live within the city limits. Just do all your work there, so you don't need to check anything out.

Most of what you will be reading will be short articles or reference items. If you haven't been in a library for some years, don't worry. This isn't like writing a term paper. You'll only need to take a few notes on key pieces of information, or photocopy an occasional article or table of data. What counts is finding what you need to make informed career decisions.

Although libraries are great places once you're familiar with them, we know many readers will be resistant to doing library research. It has been our experience that using a library is a little like going to church. If you've been away for a long time, you may feel awkward about going back.

The best way to overcome this awkwardness is to attack it head on. Phone and make an appointment with the person who runs the business section of the closest large library. Explain that you need to gather information on occupations, industries and specific companies. Be candid: admit that you are unfamiliar with what the library has and how to use it.

When you arrive, allow the librarian to show you what is available and where it is located. Our experience is that librarians are eager to work with you, and will happily go out of their way to be of assistance. You will be shown books, reference works, newspaper files, journal collections, directories, technical reports, the annual reports of publicly traded corporations and so on. One value of reading this chapter is that it will give you an overview, so some of what you're shown will be familiar.

Some of the library's holdings will be in print, some on microfilm or microfiche; much will be easily available on open shelves, but some items will be kept in back rooms and storage areas. Anything not at a particular library will usually be available through interlibrary loan.

As you dig into the available information, you will learn from experience what meets your needs and what doesn't. The case studies at the ends of both chapters in this section illustrate what can be found and how it helps prepare you for interviews.

Some specialized libraries are privately owned by industries and businesses. They are typically found at corporate headquarters and research and development facilities. Their collections can be excellent sources of information on specialized topics, but they often require an appointment to use them. The *American Library Association Directory* lists these libraries, their holdings and regulations. If they can help you, don't be bashful about asking to use them.

Then You Need a New Friend: A Reference Librarian

Once you are familiar with the business section of the most convenient large library, make it a point to introduce yourself to the reference librarian. Reference librarians specialize in finding information. They are familiar with the major directories, government publications and other sources you will need. Their role in the library system is to help people find the facts they are looking for. All the books and journals in the world aren't much help unless you can find what you want, and helping people do that is the reference librarian's calling.

Be sure to get his or her name. Write it down. Explain the research you're doing. Mention what

103

you've already read and what you're looking for, and ask for suggestions. Let the reference librarian know you will be coming back periodically as your job search proceeds. Ask if he or she would mind your phoning occasionally if you need to check something quickly.

Most research librarians (like the rest of the human race) appreciate it when someone takes the trouble to learn their names, and shows some appreciation for their expertise. Finding information is their specialty, which they enjoy practicing. They will gladly help you find what you need if you take the trouble to explain what you're seeking and why. And if they know you'll be coming back, they'll keep an eye out for things that might interest you.

What will you be reading? That will vary depending on the size of town in which you're seeking employment, whether you've worked before in the industries that interest you, the occupation or occupations you are considering and so on. In the rest of this chapter we will outline some commonly used sources for business information. This is only a sampling; there are many more. We've tried to walk a middle road, listing a variety of resources without bogging down in too much detail.

Some of the references we discuss may not be relevant to your situation. We suggest you read this chapter selectively, skimming rapidly when appropriate. Other information will be just what you need, in which case you can start with the references listed, and then get help finding more.

Check Out the Occupation First

For any occupation you want to learn more about, begin with the Department of Labor's *Occupational Outlook Handbook*. In this standard reference you will find a short description of most common occupations. Information is given on the nature of the work, working conditions, typical places of employment, the training needed, the future employment outlook, typical earnings and one or two places to write for additional information.

The Department of Labor revises this handbook every other year. Some information may, therefore, be a bit out of date by the time you read it. Also, the statistics are averages for the entire country, and may not be accurate where you live. Wages and salaries, particularly, can vary widely from region to region. You need to verify whether the information given holds true for your area. The national figures, however, will give you a good benchmark to use for comparison.

Another government publication, *Occupational Projections and Training Data*, supplements the *Occupational Outlook Handbook*. It too comes out every other year, and provides additional information about most common occupations (the proportion of women and minorities with a given job title, for example).

The American Almanac of Jobs and Salaries, by John Wright (New York: Avon, 1984) is, in effect, a private sector version of the government publications just mentioned. It contains excellent discussions of what people do and earn in most common white collar and service sector occupations.

There are chapters on government jobs, positions in the world of entertainment and the news media, the five standard professions (accounting, architecture, dentistry, medicine and law), science and technology jobs and general white collar employment, including representative career possibilities in American business, unions and the health care industry. There is information on the most widely held jobs as well as discussions of relatively uncommon but important occupations such as the clergy, agents and brokers, writers and so on. There is a surprising amount of information about salaries in individual states, and even in specific cities.

This is definitely a book worth consulting before beginning your interviewing. The amount of information on any one job or set of jobs is not great, because so many occupations are covered in one volume. What is there, however, is quite helpful.

These volumes, and the journals read by those in the occupation you are researching, should give you the basic information you need. At a minimum, before you begin interviewing, be sure that you know:

1. The essential skills, training, education, licenses and other requirements of the occupation.
2. The industry or industries in which the occupation can be found.
3. Typical salaries and fringe benefits.
4. The opportunities for advancement (in some occupations it is common to be promoted rapidly, in others slowly, and in others hardly at all).
5. The supply/demand ratio in the labor market, so that you have an idea of how much competition there is for openings.
6. The time typically spent in this occupation (engineers, for example, frequently move on to positions in sales and management; it is more common for an M.D. to remain a physician until retirement).

7. Vulnerability to economic downturns (aerospace engineers, for example, will earn good pay when working but may lose their jobs if the economy turns down or a contract is lost).

Learning Where To Go

Your next stop should often be the *Encyclopedia of Business Information Sources* (Detroit, Michigan: Gale Research Company, 1983). This book, in effect, presents a series of mini-bibliographies on a wide variety of business topics. The information on periodicals and almanacs is especially helpful. The headings under which you can find the information you need range from Arsenic Industry and Atomic Power through Mental Health and Mortgage Bonds to Zinc Industry and Zoological Gardens.

A parallel reference work is *Where to Find Business Information* (New York: John Wiley, 1982). It is designed, says the preface, "to show precisely and quickly where current business information is located and how to get it." More than 5000 newsletters, trade periodicals, general business periodicals, computerized data bases, yearbooks, directories, government publications and other sources are indexed.

Another reference volume to use during your career research is the *Guide to American Directories* (Coral Gables, Florida: B. Klein Publications, Inc.). This is a "Directory of Directories." It indexes over 5000 of them, arranged by type of business or area of professional concern. Want to get a stockbroker's job overseas, for example? You can start with *The International Directory of Stock Exchanges* to get some names and addresses.

Part of the art of finding information is knowing who to phone. A knowledgeable person can tell you in a minute where to find something which could take you a day to find on your own. When you are wondering who to phone, try *The National Directory of Addresses and Phone Numbers*. This is, in effect, a national phone book. It provides the names, addresses and phone numbers of over 150,000 businesses and government offices. Somewhere, in one of those offices, is someone who can tell you what you want to know.

Take a Close Look at the Industry

Many occupations (sales, accounting, computer programming) are found in a wide variety of industries. Other, more specialized positions (wholesale clothes buyer, stock and bond analyst) are found in only one.

In either case, research on the industry or industries is important. Many persons, before accepting a job offer, will do some checking on the firm, but not bother to read anything about the entire industry. This is a major mistake. It is possible to locate a company you like and even a supervisor with whom you get along unusually well, and still have a bad experience because the entire industry is in trouble. You should not seek a job at Suburban Savings & Loan without some research on recent trends in the financial sector. Similarly, an apparently desirable position at Local Lighting and Power may look different to you once you've read about the pressures on the electric utility industry. It might look better, or it might look worse. In either case, you will have a better understanding of what you would be getting into.

You cannot, in other words, evaluate the long term attractiveness of working for a specific firm unless you know the economic context within which that firm operates. Such information is easy to find. One standard source is *U.S. Industrial Outlook* (Washington, DC: U.S. Government Printing Office). This annual Commerce Department publication provides a short but fact-filled article on each major U.S. industry. It will let you know whether a particular industry is growing, stable or declining, and it includes projections for the years ahead.

Standard and Poor's Industry Surveys (New York, NY: Standard and Poor's) represent a good private sector source for similar information. These volumes are issued four times a year, which means they are more up-to-date than most reference works. Here you will find an overview of each basic industry (aerospace, banking, chemicals, food processing, insurance, and so on), along with data on specific major corporations.

At a minimum, before you begin interviewing, be sure you know the following things about the industry in which your informant works:

1. The primary products (automobiles, petroleum, electricity or whatever). Are there any new products being produced by this industry? Are there limits on the natural resources needed to produce these products? Do they cause environmental or health problems?
2. The financial condition of the industry. How high are profits, and are they increasing or decreasing? How sharply does the industry react to economic downturns? How much is being invested in new buildings and equipment? Are there a few large

corporations, hundreds of firms or thousands of small enterprises?

3. How the product is marketed. Who decides to buy the product, and why? Is the decision to buy based largely on quality or price? Are products largely sold to the public, or to other industries? How dependent is this industry on the financial health of other industries?

4. The level of competition. Are there potential new competitors? Who has the major market share? Have some firms been having problems and going out of business?

5. The amount of research and development. How important is the development of new products? Where is this research done: by the firms themselves, in universities, research laboratories or where? Have there been any important breakthroughs lately?

Don't Fail to Check the Journals

Be sure to ask the reference librarian about any relevant trade journals the library receives regularly. The most recent issues of some of these, such as *Advertising Age, World Hospitals, Bankers Monthly, Computer Design* or *Industrial Marketing* should be on the shelves. Find out where the back issues are stored.

If the reference librarian is aware of the journals you need, he or she can let you know which other libraries in the area receive publications his or her library doesn't have. Most libraries today have computerized list of every journal received by every library in the state.

Another useful source of information now available in many libraries is the *Business Index*. Updated regularly, this index lists, by topic, every article which has appeared in recent issues of business magazines and journals. Ask the librarian about it.

Here's Where the Networks Gather

One thing you'll always want is detailed data on the professional associations in your fields of interest. Members of these associations, and particularly their officers, are prime sources of information about both firms and people. The reference room of the library will have several volumes with information on these groups.

National Trade and Professional Associations (Washington, DC: Columbia Books) is an annual

publication. It will give you the name and address, president's name, number of members, size of staff, budget, phone number and publications of 6000 business-related organizations, along with information on annual meetings. The groups covered range from A/C Pipe Producers Association to the Zirconium Association. There is a geographic index, a budget index and a subject index.

Now, by the way, is the right time to get into the habit (second nature to any good spy or investigative reporter) of always confirming facts with at least two sources. So, for another look at trade group listings, try the *Encyclopedia of Associations* (Detroit: Gale Research Company).

This work is published annually in five volumes, with information on over 18,000 active groups. Included are legal, governmental, scientific, educational, cultural, health, public affairs, religious, hobby, athletic, veterans and many other types of organizations. Listings include the address, phone number, executive secretary, date founded, membership size, divisions, publications (including newsletters), affiliations, annual conventions and other useful information. Chambers of commerce are among the groups listed. An alphabetical and key word index is included in Volume I.

Now that you have the organizations which serve people in industries and occupations that interest you, write a short note to each. Ask for membership information and a sample copy of their newsletter, journal or other similar publication. Pay particular attention to these publications. They are an important source of information on recent developments and potential job opportunities. Also, be sure to ask if there is a local chapter, or at least some active local members, and how you can get in touch with them.

Sometimes a chamber of commerce or other organization can provide a directory of local voluntary and professional organizations. Such groups are worth joining. They are the natural place to find lists of people active in the industry, salary surveys or other useful facts and figures, helpful talks at monthly meetings and an opportunity to meet people you want to know. These informal meetings are very useful chances to ask questions and meet those who are most active in the areas that interest you. They can also easily lead to later interviews at the other person's place of business.

In a large metropolitan area, there is a tendency for the central city chamber of commerce to be dominated by the city's major corporations. Suburban and outlying areas, however, often have their own chambers of commerce, and here you can expect to find a much stronger representation from small business. Depending on whom you are trying to meet, the central city chamber or the smaller chambers might be best.

How about Specific Firms?

Both to obtain information and to identify places where you might seek employment, you need a list of specific firms which hire for the jobs you are considering. Here we run into a problem. Today, many job opportunities are found in smaller businesses. Most of the printed information, however, is about large, publicly traded corporations.

When stock in a corporation is traded on one of the country's stock exchanges, the Securities and Exchange Commission requires the corporation to publish information about sales and profits, the salaries of top executives and so on. Much of this information can be useful to you in deciding whether this is a firm where your talents would be well used. Corporations that are privately held (that is, whose stock has not been sold to the public) have no legal obligation to make such information public, and usually don't. You will find some things in print about these firms, but nowhere near as much.

Finding printed information on small businesses can also be a challenge. There is usually at least one directory in any city which will give you some basic facts about every business in town. In some cities, the local newspaper can provide an index to business stories about all firms, no matter how small.

Inc. magazine publishes an annual report on the 500 fastest growing small companies in America. Here you can find information on what kinds of small firms seem to be doing best, and where they are located. Some universities are establishing small business or entrepreneurial programs within their business schools. The professors who teach in these programs often gather helpful data on small businesses in the area. Chambers of commerce and other business groups sometimes sponsor small business seminars or similar groups which can provide useful printed materials.

As all of the above indicates, there is more information available on smaller firms than there used to be, but it will require some digging on your part to find it.

The Big Ones

A good first source of facts on major corporations is Standard and Poor's *Register of Corporations, Directors and Executives* (New York, NY: Standard and Poor's). This standard reference is issued annually in three volumes. Volume I is an alphabetical listing of approximately 45,000 corporations with addresses, phone numbers, names of officers, directors and other principles; annual sales and number of employees; division names and functions; and subsidiary listings. Volume II lists over 70,000 directors and officers alphabetically, and gives residence addresses, year and place of birth and college attended. Volume III provides industry cross-indexing, geographical indexing, new additions and other information.

Another standard source of information on individual businesses is the set of reference works published by Moody's. These volumes cover the areas of: Banking and Finance, Industrial, International, OTC Industrial, Public Utilities and Transportation. Each provides detailed information on corporate history, offices, financial status, corporate officers, stocks and bonds outstanding, and so on.

Many American firms are owned by other corporations. If you want to see whether a particular business is so controlled, the standard reference is the *Directory of Corporate Affiliations* (Skokie, Illinois: National Register Publishing Company, 1985). Each parent corporation is listed alphabetically, with its subsidiaries, groups and divisions. A second section allows you to look up a subsidiary and identify the parent company. Addresses, phone numbers and the names of chief executives are given for both parent companies and subsidiaries.

This is important information. It can make a great deal of difference to you, when working at a local firm, whether decisions are made locally or must be referred to executives living elsewhere. This is particularly important when budget decisions and layoffs are being considered.

Be sure, as you look over these sources, to ask the reference librarian if you can see whatever is available about businesses in your area. Many chambers of commerce put out guides to local firms, or at least to the firms which have joined the chamber. Businesses which sell mailing lists have computerized records of every firm in town, and sometimes publish these lists. *Polk's City Directories* can be useful if you want to generate a list of businesses found within a certain area (within commuting distance, for example).

Many libraries have various publications issued by the corporations themselves. Although they tend to stress the positive and downplay any problems, they are still valuable sources. Annual reports and other publications contain a great deal of factual information, and the way this information is presented can often tell you much about the corporate culture, and how the people in the corporation see themselves.

For an outside view, it is helpful to supplement this information with research reports done by the major stock brokerage firms. Some reports of this type can be found in the library. Value Line, for example, publishes one-page discussions of most major corporations. Although these analyses are intended to help investors decide where to put their money, they are equally useful to you in deciding where to invest your time and energy.

Government Information

If you want to check on some of the employment possibilities in state and local government, ask if there is a state directory. Many states have them, and the reference librarian will be familiar with what is available. City and county officials can provide organization charts and other facts on local government units if the state does not publish this information.

For federal employment, begin with the *U.S. Government Manual* (Washington, DC: U.S. Government Printing Office). Updated annually, this volume describes the purposes and programs of each government agency. It lists the leadership of each department and agency by name; gives locations and addresses of regional offices; has their phone numbers; and provides a name index, a subject index and an agency index. It is an invaluable resource for anyone seeking a federal position, or using people who work there as sources of information.

There is a parallel book to use if you are dealing in any way with the Congress: the *Congressional Staff Directory* (Mt. Vernon, Virginia: Congressional Staff Directory). Updated annually, this source lists the staff members serving in the offices of individual members of Congress. It also has information on House and Senate committee and sub-committee staff. Biographical information is given for key staff personnel, as are phone numbers, room numbers and so on.

Congressional staffers, by the way, are often unusually well informed and can be excellent sources of information on a variety of topics.

People and Printed Information Make a Dynamite Combination

It is important, as you zero in on an industry and occupation, to obtain back issues of trade journals and spend a few hours reading them. Here you will find articles on both new developments and the major problems a field is facing. There will also be information on the people who are most active in the profession. Pay particular attention, of course, to anyone from your area. Make notes on their activities, and any information that would help you to find them.

You will need this information to help you decide whether this is the right time for you to enter this field. You will also want these facts as background so you can talk knowledgeably with the people whom you will be interviewing.

Finding Out about People

Just as it can be difficult to find much in print about small, local businesses, you will also usually find little in print about the people who own and manage these concerns. The same will be true of those in lower-level positions in major corporations. There is some information in print, however, and it is worth the effort to get what you can.

When you begin interviewing, you will find that university professors can sometimes be useful sources. They are often able to refer you to people in the business community whom they know because of a shared professional interest, and to brief you on what they're like.

Before going to see a professor, check a series of volumes published by R. R. Bowker and Company. *American Men and Women of Letters* and *American Men and Women of Science* provide biographical information on many professors (as well as on other scientists and professionals working in industry).

For the business community, you can try the various Who's Who publications put out by Marquis Who's Who. Contrary to popular impression, you do not have to be nationally famous to be included in these volumes. Thousands of people are included in the regional editions, and they aren't all company presidents or millionaires. These reference works give the name, position, parents, educational background, date and place of birth, marital status, career, civic activities, political affiliations, awards, religion, home and office address and other information on leading citizens who live in the area covered by the directory. In addition to the regional directories, there are other publications such as *Who's Who in America; Who's Who in American Politics; Who's Who in American College and University Administration;* and *Who's Who in Finance and Industry*.

Some daily papers are now routinely stored and indexed in computers. This makes it possible to pull out any stories which have appeared on a specific person.

Any information you can find on business people, using any of these methods, can help you in two ways. First, they suggest people whom you should go to see. Second, once you have an appointment to see someone, they can help you to learn as much as possible about that person before the interview.

This Is Just a Start

Of necessity, this chapter has primarily discussed the library references most commonly used in the job search process. There will undoubtedly be specialized journals and reference works of interest to you as you study a particular industry, occupation, firm or group of individuals.

When doing the interviewing discussed in the next chapter, one topic you should regularly raise with your informants is what journals are most worth reading, what recent books are good and with what reference works you should become familiar. This, along with a librarian's advice, will help you zero in on what is most appropriate for your specific interests.

CASE STUDIES

Case Study 7-1

This case study provides a good example of how to seek a job in a part of the country which is some distance from where you live. There are three things to note: (1) library research can provide helpful information even at a distance, (2) interviewing can also begin where you live, since basic occupational and industrial information can be obtained anywhere and (3) once the basics are out of the way, though, you do need to interview people on site. Notice, too, how this person kept at his search, despite initial discouragements, until he hit the magic combination: rapport with the individual who hires, and a good match to his skills and interests. As you read through this paper, you will see some employment possibilities which were *not* pursued. Are any of them attractive enough to be a good "Plan B"?

A Desert Search

To summarize what I have learned about myself: my basic motivational pattern is creative problem-solving. My ideal job would be as a consultant. However, two of my interests complicate this. First, I thrive on intense personal contact. Second, I have a burning desire to relocate to a low population area in the southwestern United States.

The community college, including continuing education, was a possibility that had already occurred to me. In addition, two new directions came to mind that seemed to offer possibilities. Community-based organizations seemed especially relevant. Government positions, such as county agricultural agent, merited looking into. All three directions offer a chance to work with adults in an information-sharing role, and each can be found in low population areas.

My next task was to gather information. I needed information not only to find the proper job match, but to fulfill my interest in a particular area of the country. The area of the country would have a big impact not only on available jobs, but also on my wife. Therefore, she and I spent time in the library going over all the geographical material we could find. We combined this information with our own experience, and used the decision tree. This resulted in a target area 100 miles either side of a line between Albuquerque, New Mexico, and Kingman, Arizona.

I could now focus on job information. Of the possible directions, I was leaning toward teaching. In Peterson's Annual Guide to Undergraduate Study, *I found a listing by state of all the schools offering two-year degrees. It contained information that allowed me to focus on eight schools within the target area. Next, I tackled the* Microfiche College Catalog Collection *and read the most recent catalog of each of these institutions. The search was narrowed to four that taught a substantial number of courses in the area of my major. Each employed faculty with the M.A. degree.*

Just knowing there were places in the real world that seemed to match my skills and desires gave me the confidence to start my interviews. The first was with a professor at a local community college. It provided a wealth of information. He had taught for twenty-two years, in several in-

109

stitutions. He told me what a typical day was like and how it varied from place to place.

The starting salary at this institution was extremely good; however, it was an exception. We talked at length. The only negative aspects were the policies and bureaucracy. These seemed no worse than the business world I had left. Then we discussed job opportunity. I had already discovered that the employment outlook was poor while reading the Occupational Outlook Handbook. I was informed that open positions in the behavioral sciences usually drew several hundred applicants. At this institution it had been nine years since the last person was hired in the department. The only encouragement he could offer was that demand varies from place to place, and some areas offer opportunities because of lower pay and remoteness. Though discouraged, I left realizing this was but the first of many steps.

My next interview, with a conservationist for the Agriculture Department, was more disappointing. There had once been a position known as general information officer in the Agriculture Department. It seemed to be a good match, and did not require expertise in agricultural matters. The field agents wished it still existed. However, with budget cuts and the population movement away from rural areas, the positions were slowly being eliminated. The last one in Texas had been eliminated in 1982.

He suggested that the Parks Department might offer an avenue to the area I was interested in. He outlined the steps necessary to obtain federal employment. He told me that, in addition to the civil service requirements, the only way to get a job was through direct contact with a local agency or their district office. He also gave me a good review of the federal pay system.

At this point it was becoming obvious that the information I was gathering was necessary, but not completely appropriate. If I wanted to gather information about specific jobs in a specific area, I needed to focus on the area. The parks idea seemed like another possible direction.

In the library, I discovered that the regional office serving my target area was in Santa Fe, New Mexico. I had already been looking at the possibility of traveling to the target area. This would help me obtain an internship, which I needed to complete my degree. It would also make possible some more targeted interviews. I set aside a five-day weekend for this trip. I wrote letters to department heads at the two schools located closest to Santa Fe, and to the regional office of the Parks Department, announcing when I would be there and expressing my desire for an interview to gain information as part of the work on my degree.

Once in my target area, the interviews took a different turn. Instead of an academic exercise, the information became more important and seemed more real. At Santa Fe, with surprisingly little delay, I was able to see an assistant to the director. Here I learned that the Parks Department had a classification that seemed to be a good match, paid a salary that would support us and could offer my wife a job if she decided to go back to work after the move.

I also discovered that, because of budget cuts and policy changes, the average time from initial application to full time employment was three to five years, and included intermediate steps of working part time for the federal government, or for a state park system. This information finally made me realize that it would be possible to find a job match that met my geographical requirements. Although the time involved was problematic, I had been given hope.

Enthusiastically, I proceeded to the first community college on my list. It was a moderately large institution located on a reservation. Although the department head was unavailable, I was able to interview one of the professors. I discovered they use graduate interns. However, the semester I was interested in was already booked up. I also learned that most of their jobs were filled by these interns, or by visiting lecturers sent by the Bureau of Indian Affairs. However, since the school was administered by a tribal council, all jobs were temporary until a qualified Indian was available. The interview also allowed me to gather general information about the area, get information about community organizations and get a referral to one.

At a United Way-type organization, I was able to get a listing of other similar organizations in much of my target area, a letter of introduction and the names of key people to contact. Because of the remoteness of the area, many of the jobs were filled by local inhabitants. However, they *normally used outsiders as directors of local offices, and for other positions, on a one-year basis. The duties were very closely aligned with my preferences and I was told I was well qualified for most of the agencies. However, the salary range was extremely low, and it would require that my wife work in order to live above the poverty level. I had, nevertheless, found another possibility and had a list of contacts.*

My next interview, the last of my planned stops, was at a very small community college that was also on an Indian reservation. Though my letter had been forwarded to personnel, I was able to get an interview with an instructor in my program area. After thirty minutes of general information gathering, he referred me to the person chairing the division, who would be more capable of answering some of my questions. He suggested I go directly to her office and see if she had time to see me. She had been involved with my inquiry about an internship and had also been informed about my proposed visit.

She saw me immediately, and with an almost instant rapport we began a session that lasted two hours. First, we discussed the history and focus of the college. Next, she turned her attention to me. Soon she was comfortable with me, my goals and the purpose of my visit. We all but finalized an internship agreement. Although they had never participated in one before, only the final arrangements with my university needed to be tied up.

The interview then changed focus and I found myself in a job interview for an immediate opening in their counseling department. I restated my immediate task of gathering information and stated my priority of completing my current graduate program. I was told that if the internship did work out we would be in a position to further evaluate each other. Unless she found out something very unexpected about me, she was prepared to consider me for a teaching position if one existed and a counseling position if a teaching slot was unavailable.

It finally dawned on me that I had stumbled onto some unexpected information. Counseling departments in small colleges in the area were hard to fill. Because of the low, but livable, salaries and the remoteness, most people applying for these positions were using them as stepping stones to higher paying jobs in larger cities. They were seeking experience and a reference. Even though the last teaching position had been applied for by fifty-four qualified applicants, she was willing to discuss the next available position with me in the hope of acquiring a permanent, qualified counselor, even on a part time basis.

With a short stop at one of the nearby social service agency offices, more of a courtesy call than an interview, I concluded my efforts and returned home.

The idea of having a dual role as teacher and counselor seems to fit all of my needs and skills. It also seems to be the best match for a job that will pay a livable income and be available in my target area. Accordingly, I have rewritten my resume with that joint role as my objective. I intend to pursue the internship in my target area so that I will be in a position to see if the area and teaching meet my expectations. I will also be in a geographical location that will facilitate contacting other schools in person to check out job availability. The two semesters of the internship should offer ample opportunity to do both informational and job interviewing.

Case Study 7-2

The library research/interviewing process essentially involves reviewing and clarifying possibilities. Like a fuzzy picture seen through the lens of an unfocused camera, several employment possibilities may seem vaguely attractive. Then, as more data is gathered, the picture sharpens. This case study is a good illustration of such focusing. Its author began with interest, training and past experience in the human service area. There are many roles in this broad work area, however. As he reads journals and talks to people, some possibilities are eliminated and others begin to look more interesting. Note how, because of previous work experience, he is easily able to make contact with knowledgeable informants, and to go immediately to the supervisory level. Do you think he could have learned as much if he were breaking into human service occupations for the first time? As he talks to people, it becomes obvious that he has much to offer. There are more opportunities than he expected. How common do you think this is? Would he have found as many possibilities open to him if he had not done extensive self-analysis first? (For his self-analysis paper, turn back to Case Study 5-2.)

Discovering the Demand

I believe that my life/work planning efforts have influenced the way I think about my future career in a very positive way. Prior to this work, my view was limited to a narrow focus on family therapy for families, groups or individuals who experience problems with chemical abuse or addiction. That narrow view has been broadened as I have come to realize that my interests, personality traits and skills are all vital ingredients that make up the person that I am now and the person I will be in the future.

I have become acutely aware of the degree of change that I have experienced, although my basic motivations have changed little. I seem to have three primary motivating forces in my life. They are family, interactions with the people around me and risk taking. These forces seem to be the essence of my personality.

Family has always been very important. It is even more important as I grow older and better understand how much my family and I provide nurturance and support to each other.

Who I am is also reinforced by the people around me; they constantly assure me that I am okay. I enjoy being needed and respected by those associates with whom I share a common core of experience, and a common bond of interests, goals, hopes and dreams. I am indeed a social animal.

My life is also stimulated by risk taking, my third major motivator. All my past accomplishments and successes have been a direct result of facing and attempting to overcome my fears. Risk-taking has generated personal growth.

One of my goals in life is to promote growth in others, in a climate that also makes it possible for me to grow and develop. In addition, I need to be financially successful, though I am not yet sure what that means.

So I examined my goals, combined with my basic motivational pattern and my interests, and I began to see that my job search could be much broader in scope. There were many possibilities: a variety of jobs in the human services area such as consultant, agent, lobbyist, labor negotiator, employee assistance program counselor or salesman. I now had a new viewpoint, and new avenues down which to direct my career search.

Research on the more traditional, popular jobs was basically very simple. Jobs that were less known and more recently developed were more difficult. The Occupational Outlook Handbook, Occupational Outlook Quarterly and other books and journals were helpful in researching occupations such as counselor, therapist and salesman, but many did not discuss jobs in Employee Assistance Programs or family therapy. For these, my major sources for job descriptions and salaries were professional journals and articles in popular magazines. EAP Digest, Airman, Air University Review, Alcohol Health and Research World, Alcoholism Digest Annual, International Journal of Family Counseling and Family Process are a few of the publications that I found useful.

While my research was fairly intensive, I learned very little about the actual jobs, nor could I get a sense of work environments, advancement possibilities or management policies. Soon it was clear that I had gotten all I could from library research. Now I had to find individuals in those fields whom I could question directly. Thus, the next step was to set up interviews.

I decided that I would use cold calls only as a last resort. They seemed to be very time consuming and possibly unproductive. I realized that my most valuable resource was my network of friends, associates and switchboard people. I am retired from the military, a certified alcoholism and drug abuse counselor and am completing a one-year internship in a psychiatric hospital, so my network is extensive.

Library research, and numerous discussions with my family and others made it clear to me that I should pay closer attention to the skills that I have already developed. When I retired as a military air traffic controller, I had somehow wrongly assumed that the past was behind me and that I had to learn totally new skills and ways of being. I did not realize that my basic motivations would not change, that my interests, personality traits and skills were still the core of my life. I became more aware of my past and present as I looked to the future.

Interviewing became my primary focus. I activated my network by letting switchboard people know what I was seeking, and by following up contacts I had previously established. The results were impressive. Interviews were simple to obtain. My greatest difficulty was restricting my interviews, eliminating those jobs that seemed less interesting or were financially unrewarding. I decided to interview one person in each of the following situations: employee assistance program, family therapy (private practice), inpatient chemical abuse program, military family support center and military social action program. In most cases, I interviewed the director of each program. I have often discussed these and similar jobs with the people who do them, and I was interested in how management viewed them. I felt excited and enthusiastic as I conducted each interview, especially when discussing positions which I had not considered before.

I learned from these meetings that I had been setting my goals too low. There were many jobs that suited my needs. Because of my unusual background and acquired skills, I was in demand and could be selective about the position I eventually accepted. I have learned that being male is an asset in human services occupations, where most professionals are women. This is particularly true in therapy, where a male role model is sometimes needed.

My age also contributes to a "professional image" of which I was unaware prior to these interviews. I was pleasantly surprised that my years of management experience, my military background, chemical dependence expertise and therapy training combined to make me sought after by employers.

I also found that private practice as a therapist would not meet my needs at this point in my development. I can possibly work as a consultant or supervisor in the future. For the present, my skills and desire to work closely with others require that I work within some organizational structure. I am therefore excluding private practice from my job search for the present. When I explore it in the future it will have to be within the framework of working with a group, not alone. I am also not willing to spend the massive amount of time needed to establish and market a private practice. Even though the possible rewards are great, I am not willing to take that much time from my family.

The area that I had not considered for employment, prior to these interviews, was the mili-

tary. I was aware of, and had worked for, people who filled civilian positions within the military human services areas, but had not felt qualified to consider them. Once again I found that my combination of history and skills opened up new areas of employment opportunity.

Because of twenty-five years in various positions in the armed forces, I understand the problems involved in working with military members and their families. I speak the language and have experienced similar difficulties. I understand and respect the value of the military system, and as a civilian can maintain the objectivity necessary to help families survive that system. From the directors of two programs I learned that competition for such positions is keen. I also learned about twenty-seven new facilities that will be opened within the next two years. These positions are available world-wide, some in countries and at bases where I have extensive experience.

I was most impressed by my interview with the director of a major international employee assistance program (EAP). As I interviewed him, I experienced that old familiar feeling of anticipation, of engaging a challenge yet unknown. I felt I was stepping out on the cutting edge of risk taking. Here was a job that would test and use my cumulative skills and talents. I was told that I fit the organization image perfectly, and that there were many different positions that I could fill. If I became bored I could simply change what I was doing, yet still remain in the field. I could also establish my own program in the future. EAPs are designed to reduce the impact of employee alcoholism, drug abuse and mental health problems, all areas in which I have varying degrees of experience and expertise. EAPs also offer me the opportunity to expand my skills into the employee wellness programs of the future.

I have made the decision to start out my new career in an EAP. In fact, I am negotiating with the director whom I interviewed for a part time position while I complete my degree. For the present, I want to remain in the Clear Lake/Houston area, so I will use my contacts to find a position there. The company I am negotiating with is eager to hire me. The difficulty is timing and the availability of a suitable position. I have alerted my network that I am seeking employment in an EAP and I am confident that I will find the job that suits me. I have also begun to study the professional literature of EAPs, and am exploring the design and organization of many local programs.

My "Plan B" is to seek employment as a civilian within the field of military human service. I now have access to the listings and availability of many of these positions. Most of all, I know that I am capable and qualified to fill them.

My "Plan C" is to remain in this area and do contract work in the field of chemical abuse and dependency, while continuing to search for jobs that I have not yet discovered. It is good to know that I am not locked into any career and that there are many, many possibilities that I have yet to explore. This work has helped me realize that I am limited only by my own restrictions and narrowness of thinking. I will be successful in future careers if I know my own strengths and weaknesses and aim for situations similar to those in which I have been successful in the past.

Case Study 7-3

Most of us think we have at least a general idea of what people with common job titles actually do all day. Most of us are wrong. The author of this paper discovered during her interviews that there were important aspects of every job she considered that surprised her. Community college counseling had more duties (and better pay) than expected. Continuing education was surprisingly insecure. Social work was difficult to do successfully. Teaching was pressured and teachers chronically short of time. What do you think of the author's strategy for dealing with the information she gathered? Is it reasonable to put off an occupational decision, go back to school and then learn from experience? Suppose for some reason that going back to school was not practical at this point; if you were a career counselor, what would you suggest then? Making a good career decision is not just a matter of deciding what to do *now*. Shrewd decisions also take into account how difficult or easy it will be to move on to the next position at a later time. Do you think the author of this paper is doing a good job of positioning herself for the future?

Mastering Social Work

I believe that I have identified those aspects of my personality and character which define my motivational core. I am a person who needs to use her abilities to help others. I enjoy learning new things that can be shared and put to work. Having meaningful work that uses my creative energies is important to me. Because I am an internally motivated person, I am best rewarded by the personal satisfaction of doing something very well, or helping someone reach his/her goals.

Everything that I have learned thus far convinces me that my degree choice (behavioral science) is a good one. Considering my interest in sharing what I have learned to help others, I decided to investigate careers in counseling, adult education and social work.

To prepare for interviewing, I began my investigation in the library. The Occupational Outlook Handbook *and* The American Almanac of Jobs and Salaries *provided good job descriptions and basic information on salaries and employment trends. I reviewed several professional journals to get a sense of the issues that are currently important in these fields. With this background, I felt prepared to undertake the interviews.*

My first appointment was made with a guidance counselor at a community college. I was impressed by the cheerfulness of the center in which her office was located. Because we were already acquainted, it was very easy to establish good rapport. She enthusiastically agreed to meet with me, and generously blocked out an hour for the interview. As a student, I had talked to guidance counselors a number of times and felt I had a pretty good idea of what the job entailed. I found out otherwise. She not only has the usual educational and personal counseling duties that I expected, but also a number of other obligations as well. She serves as the coordinator for handicapped services, does in-service training and plans, promotes and coordinates special school events and continuing education seminars.

This job is both challenging and personally rewarding to her, but it is definitely not a nine to five job. A person in this position must be willing to participate in school and community events. He/she must work some nights because of the nature of community college schedules. In addition, it is necessary to participate actively in professional associations and stay abreast of issues in the field by taking courses and seminars. One nice bonus that is part of her job is that she has the opportunity to travel, both to visit other col-

lege campuses in the state and also to attend seminars and conventions. She recently attended an important convention in Washington, D.C.

While her educational background is high school teaching and guidance counseling, she explained that it is possible to do this work with a master's degree in psychology or social work as well. All three backgrounds will prepare one to teach at this level or to do personal counseling.

This interview was especially helpful to me because she was willing to share personal information in two areas. First, she showed me her job description and her own personal goals and evaluations. I was able to get a sense of what some of the expectations of both a counselor and an employer might be. I was able to see how the work of people in these positions is evaluated and rewarded.

The second piece of helpful information was an explanation of how salaries are structured for counselors and professors in community college settings. I was most surprised to find out that her salary was at least $10,000 more than average for such positions. She explained that the tax base of her community college district was the determining factor, and that it was not unusual for professors and counselors to make more than their counterparts in local four-year colleges and universities.

This, of course, is the good news. The bad news is that the field is very competitive, and many of the positions that open up are filled by referral. She had been recruited from her high school position by a former fellow teacher.

It was not the least bit difficult for me to evaluate what I had learned in this interview. It was very apparent to me that this would be an ideal job. I would enjoy the counseling, planning and teaching. I liked the friendly and active environment. The interaction between staff and students appealed to me as well. Clearly, if this type of position became available in the future, I would readily seize it.

To investigate career possibilities in teaching adults, I decided to interview a dean of continuing education at another community college. He described various career options in the continuing education field. First, if you have expertise in any area, with or without degrees, it is possible to teach that subject as a continuing education

offering, so long as you can create a course and find a demand for it. At present I do not have sufficient expertise to do a program on my own, but I would like to keep this option open for the future.

He also discussed possible job opportunities administering adult education programs. Such positions are often available in large community college systems, and can be entered with a bachelor's degree. These positions rely more on planning skills than on academic credentials. The entry pay is very low, but these jobs are good training grounds for a future position as a program head.

Again, I was very fortunate. This person offered to share a number of publications and personal documents with me. He showed me the official description of his duties as head of continuing education. In addition, I received some professional publications related to adult education. One magazine contained a recent study of continuing education administrators and directors. It revealed some interesting trends in the field.

It was quickly evident that adult education is a stepchild in the field of education. Few directors of continuing education programs have any training in teaching adults. Most had more or less fallen into their positions. Few had planned to enter the field or had actively sought such positions. There was no consistent pattern of salaries or academic credentials. Both ranged from very low to very high.

This particular person brings impressive credentials to his career, and makes the third largest salary in the state for such a position. He has a doctorate in education and has taught in public schools. He has a wealth of experience and is particularly known for his special ability to plan and implement educational resources for teachers. As an employee at NASA, he was part of a team that developed programs for teaching space science in public schools. He was also responsible for developing cross-cultural studies for teachers during a racial integration crisis. He is an especially well-informed individual and a unique resource person in a number of areas.

He discussed the negative as well as the positive aspects of directing adult education programs. The job requires family sacrifices. He must work some nights and be very active and visible in community activities in order to identify community needs and have resources for teachers. There can be a great deal of pressure and frustration dealing with a tremendous amount of detail when planning courses and working with various faculty personalities. He told me that the whole field is currently in flux as a consequence of uncertain state funding. There is a move to make such programs self-supporting, but most people who take courses are unwilling to pay the actual costs of these programs. Until such issues are resolved, job security is uncertain.

I find the field of continuing education very interesting, but I do not think that the full time administrative option suits my personality. Still, I want to keep the teaching option open for consideration. My interests in both career and adult development lend themselves well to developing some interesting courses.

My third interview was a striking contrast to the previous two. I made an appointment to meet with a social service worker employed by a state agency. I was warmly greeted and felt welcome as I entered the department. However, I could not help but notice the conspicuous absence of smiles. The atmosphere was completely different from the community college setting. While everyone was friendly to me, I did not sense friendliness toward the clients or any staff enthusiasm for their work. The offices were small and very cluttered and worn looking. While this would not present an overwhelming problem to me, I was surprised to find that I was much affected by the environment. I believe that it is a consideration that I had previously underrated.

The interview went well, and I was able to obtain a great deal of information about working for the department. I first learned about the work that this woman does with the parents of families who receive aid for dependent children. She detailed the services available to such families. She described her program to help them find jobs by developing their job search skills. She warned that the greatest problem in dealing with this and other such programs is the apathy of the clients and their inability to keep appointments and complete training. It is, I'm sure, a frustrating aspect of all social work.

The aspect of this interview that was so valuable was that she explained the process of obtaining employment. We discussed how applications are processed for each job and how to fill them out correctly to meet the criteria for each position. She even invited two recently employed workers to participate in the interview so that I might have the most recent information on new testing procedures and get hints on the areas of the agency that had the most potential. I received an excellent briefing on the subject.

It is possible to enter social service positions with a bachelor's degree in any area. There is potential for promotion to a variety of positions, with good chances for advancement. Supervisory positions generally require a master of social work (M.S.W.) degree. Salaries are competitive with social service positions in the private sector. There are a number of good benefits. A bonus in working here is that it is possible to transfer to other locations in the state.

The price for all these benefits is the rigidity and red tape that is characteristic of all bureaucracies. The benefits might help one overlook some of the deficiencies of working for the state. Clearly, there are possibilities here to consider.

For my last two appointments I interviewed women who have M.S.W. degrees, but are using them in different ways. The first is in private practice, specializing in counseling for substance abuse. She conducts educational seminars and provides counseling for both individuals and groups. This interview turned out differently than I expected. While she was friendly and helpful, I was unable to get specific information about job possibilities and salaries from her. When asked about the potential in private counseling, she only volunteered that it depended on what you did and how many clients you had.

She did offer advice and information of a different kind that was valuable in its own way. She described the various ways to use the M.S.W.: counseling, planning, teaching and research. We talked about the importance of getting a good field placement in the training process. She stressed the importance of picking a good agency that will provide a quality learning environment, as opposed to picking a place because you think this might be the area in which you would like to *work. She indicated that one could avoid being forced to choose just one option, such as treatment or planning, by simply being willing to take additional course work.*

We talked about the personal satisfaction that comes from having a position that fits your needs and allows you to develop and use your abilities. She talked about the likelihood of moving in and out of various levels of social work, as new opportunities become available with increased experience. Clearly, the M.S.W. is a ticket into the field and opens up a whole realm of professional possibilities. While this interview did not produce concrete facts about salaries and positions, I gained a clear sense of how social work might fit into my future.

My interview with the second woman with an M.S.W. served as an inspiring finale. This person teaches psychology and sociology at a community college, does private counseling in a Christian counseling center and has served as a caseworker for the state. I had previously talked to her about her social work experience, and also had taken four of her behavioral science courses. She had already served as both a role model and a mentor. It was easy to conduct the interview in a very personal way. For the moment, I was most interested in her teaching role as an associate professor.

She described her transition from casework to the classroom. This particular position had been found through a referral. Her most difficult problems involve the preparation of new materials and the development of good test instruments. Her limited number of teaching methods courses may be part of these problems. She finds the shortage of time a major problem. The personal problems of her students and the demands of paper work compete for this limited resource.

She has found the community college a good place to provide counseling via the classroom. She also sees the classroom as a good vehicle for making social issues real for her students. She confirmed what I had already been told about salaries for professors in affluent community college districts. We discussed the fact that such positions are not readily available, and how important it is to maintain contacts within the colleges to find out about openings. She encouraged me to pursue my M.S.W. and believes that I will be able to find a good position either in social work or in teaching at a community college.

My interviews have accomplished more than I expected. They have confirmed a plan of action that I have been considering. In addition, I have made contacts in places where I might want to work in the future. Further, I obtained a number of referrals to people from whom I can get further information.

I now realize that all of the jobs I am seriously considering for my future career could be done with an M.S.W. Therefore, I plan to enter the graduate program in social work this fall. While I will choose the treatment option, I fully intend to take additional course work in planning. In addition, I will fit in teaching methods courses as time permits. It is my plan to do counseling in an agency for my first work experience, but I will be watching and asking questions about teaching and counseling opportunities in the community college setting. Should my plan fail, I will pursue a social service position with the state, using the bachelor's degree that I will complete in May.

When I started the interview process, I thought I would be finished asking questions after the final interview. In fact, this has been only a beginning. I now realize that my job opportunities are directly related to the number of questions I am willing to ask.

Eight. Interviewing People Before They Interview You

Some of the information you need in order to set career goals and successfully reach them can be found in the library. Much, however, cannot. There are many things you need to know that you can learn only from other people. Luckily, that is not difficult. Our consistent experience has been that, properly approached, most people are happy to give you an insider's view. They will tell you about their jobs, about developments in the industry and about the people and firms who could possibly hire you.

Do Your Homework First

There is a logical order to follow when gathering such information. You will do best if you learn as much as you can from printed materials first and then talk to people who can fill in the gaps. When interviewing, meet first with those who work at a job in which you are interested. After two or three of these discussions, meet the people who do the hiring. They will have a somewhat different perspective, which you will appreciate better because of your first interviews.

In addition to these two groups, look for outsiders who can give you other views of the industry which interests you and the major firms and people in it. Stock brokers, commercial bankers, employment agency counselors and those who work for executive search firms, market researchers, wholesalers who sell to the industry, insurance people, government regulators — anyone who deals with the industry regularly can give you useful insights. An outsider's perspective can be especially helpful in understanding the problems and opportunities an industry faces.

Save appointments with your most knowledgeable and highly placed informants until you are well into the interviewing process. That way you can ask them what they alone can tell you, instead of using their valuable time discussing what you can easily learn from others.

The Magic Words

How do you get people to talk to you? Mostly it's a matter of choosing them carefully, and approaching them properly. The magic words are: "I've got to make some important decisions and I would really appreciate some information." In the proper context, these words open doors.

When making the first contact, it's particularly helpful to mention the name of someone your informant knows personally. Make it clear that yours is not a random phone call. This is important in these days of constant "telemarketing" (telephone selling). Many salespeople call every firm in town, trying to sell their products. You have to make it clear that yours is a *personal* call.

Switchboard People Can Plug You In

Start with friends, or friends of friends. They will know some potential informants whom you can interview. Your next source of referrals is "switchboard people" who, by the nature of their positions, can easily connect you with those whom you want to meet. A rabbi, priest or minister will usually be happy to refer you to someone in the congregation who is a banker, or in sales, or computers, or advertising, or whatever you are researching. Your representative in the legislature knows many people, and will also be happy to give you some names. After all, you're a constituent and voter. Bankers, chamber of commerce directors and insurance people usually know the community well. Just ask yourself: among the people I know (even if only slightly), or can easily meet, who deals with a wide variety of individuals? Generate a list, go to see them and ask for referrals.

One sure source of information is the president or other officer of a professional or trade association. Such persons are both easy to approach and knowledgeable. After all, unfriendly social isolates don't get elected to leadership positions!

The first step, then, is to get referrals. What you read in the library will be helpful, but it will usually give you only a national picture. And printed materials are always somewhat out of date. What you need now is an up to date sense of what's happening in your part of the country.

Following Up Referrals

Begin phoning the people to whom you've been referred. Give your full name. Mention how you heard about them, or from whom you got their name. Let them know that you're at an important point in your life. You are gathering information on what job to seek next, or are trying to decide where to seek it (what industry, what size firm, etc.). You would really appreciate it if they would let you ask them some questions. Suggest a time when you could get together ("any morning this week"), but leave that decision to them.

They may offer to answer your questions on the phone. Sometimes that will work, but usually you will get much more out of an interview if you can do it in person. Be ready to describe the general areas you want to discuss, but keep suggesting times and days when you could meet them at their place of work. Most people will see you, and usually within a week or two. Others will be both busy and helpful, and it will take a month to fit you in. A few will say no, which is their privilege. Be gracious, and go on to the next call.

Initially, ask for 15 or 20 minutes, and be prepared to leave after that time. More often, however, you'll find that once people start talking they won't want to stop, and you may have trouble getting away. We have worked with hundreds of individuals doing such interviewing. Our experience is that people are quite generous and will share much valuable information with someone who asks, so long as that person is polite and properly prepared.

No one conversation will tell you everything you want to know. Some of the information given will turn out to be inaccurate. A series of interviews, however, should allow you to put together a clear picture of what a job demands, and how easy or difficult it would be for you to get an attractive job offer.

Now begin your own search by making a list of people to contact on the sheet provided in Exercise 8-1 on the next page.

There Is Much to Learn

What are you going to ask in these conversations? That will depend on the occupation or industry that you're investigating, of course. Generally, however, you will be asking questions about several important topics: the nature of the position (just what is this job really like?), potential for advancement (where can I go from here?), the availability of employment (how hard is it to get hired, and who makes the decisions?) and the personal reflections of your source (would you do it again?).

It is essential, before you meet with anyone, to identify clearly what you want to learn from them. Type out at least a few of the questions you want to ask. A well thought out first question is particularly helpful, since it will get the interview off to a good start.

The great advantage of interviewing knowledgeable people *before* you seek job interviews is that your discussions can focus entirely on *your* needs, rather than on those of the employer. There are many important issues you can easily bring up when you're doing preliminary information-gathering. It can be much more awkward to raise these same questions during a job interview. At that stage, you want to be free to focus on the *employer's* needs.

Job interviews are usually stressful. Each party wants to make a good impression, and each is afraid of making a mistake or being rejected. The preliminary information-gathering process is much more relaxed. You are only asking for assistance and advice, which people enjoy giving.

This is why it is essential to make clear to the person you're seeing that you are *not* looking for a job. You are gathering information so you can make an informed decision about what job to seek, and where to seek it.

Ben Greco draws an analogy between the library research/interviewing process and shopping. He describes how, early in his marriage, he would become irritated when his wife took an entire day to go on a shopping expedition, returning with only one or two purchases. Then one day, when they were shopping together, he pointed out what looked to him like a good clothing buy. She promptly informed him that the item's color, length and design were out of style, and that it was on sale elsewhere for a much lower price. He then realized that shopping isn't just buying; it's also gathering information. Buying comes later. Similarly, library research/interviewing is, in effect, "job shopping." Buying — applying for a job — comes later.

Questioning

If you're gathering information on a job you have never had, a good way to begin (perhaps jokingly admitting that it sounds like a dumb question) is by asking just what your informant really does all day. What is a

People to See for Information

Topic on Which Information Is Needed	People Who Would Know, or Who Can Refer Me to Those Who Would Know (List person, title, address and phone)
_____	_____
_____	_____
_____	_____
_____	_____
_____	_____
_____	_____
_____	_____
_____	_____
_____	_____
_____	_____
_____	_____
_____	_____
_____	_____
_____	_____
_____	_____
_____	_____
_____	_____
_____	_____
_____	_____

typical day like? As he or she answers, try to pick out how much of the day is spent with other people. Equally important, what kinds of relationships are involved: helping, directing, selling or what? How much time is devoted to data or ideas? How much is spent with machines or other physical objects? Is this a job done independently, or as part of a team?

Follow this up with a question about the type of person who is most successful in this job. What combination of skills and personality characteristics makes it easy to do well?

For most people, the best job is one which is complex enough to be challenging without being overwhelming. Research suggests that persons with complex, challenging jobs maintain their intellectual alertness and flexibility. Boring, unchallenging work can lead to a loss of these characteristics. There seems to be a law of "use it or lose it." Similarly, those whose jobs require them to be self-directed at work are more independent and self-directed in other areas of life.

In Liberia — By Tomorrow?

Try to get a sense of how much responsibility the job carries, and how much pressure it involves. Some jobs are cyclical, with heavy demands at certain times of the year (accountants at income tax time, for example, or retail jobs around Christmas). Get some idea of how many hours of work the job really takes, including work typically done at home or on weekends. Ask how much travel is involved each year, and whether it is common to be relocated from one town to another.

You want some idea of how much job security you would have. Some industries are cyclical, with large layoffs when the economy turns down. Certain jobs (typically staff positions) are the first to be eliminated when cash is short. It can save you a lot of grief to find this out ahead of time.

You also want to know whether people in this line of work commonly bring some previous experience (for example, working first as a reporter before doing public relations work). Similarly, find out how much ease of movement there is to similar jobs in other firms or industries.

All This and Pay Too?

You need to know typical starting salaries. Equally important, what income is common after five years of successful experience? It is essential to get this information, but you have to phrase the questions carefully. Many people are touchy about revealing their own salaries, and it is not polite to ask.

So be clear that you are *not* asking them what they earn. You only want to know typical *starting* salaries, and then the range of incomes earned by those with more experience. If your informant simply says salaries are "competitive," quote the salary data you found during your library research. Ask if these national figures are at least roughly on target for your area.

It's often best, by the way, to save this rather delicate topic until the end of the interview. Do not, however, skip it altogether. If you can't talk money while gathering information, you will have real problems talking salary during a job interview.

If the job seems attractive, remember to discuss typical fringe benefits and vacation time, whether it is common to have the use of a company car and so on. Getting this information now will save you from being overly concerned with it during a job interview later.

If you are investigating an occupation which is new to you, be sure you leave the interview knowing what your informant believes to be the best preparation for entering this occupation: the combination of natural talent, formal education, previous work experience, necessary licenses, association memberships or anything else that would be most likely to help someone enter the field and do well at it.

Think Ahead

Ask how much visibility is typical in the job you are investigating. Getting promoted often takes more than doing a job well. If you want to move on to more responsible positions, those who can help you do this have to know the quality of your work.

In some jobs, visibility is not a problem (television newscasting, to take an extreme example). In other jobs (some accounting positions, for instance) you might be doing excellent work, but no one beyond your immediate supervisor would be aware of it. So it's important to find out whether visibility in a given job will come largely from the work itself. If not, you may need to invest time and resources in active membership in professional associations, writing or other extra efforts.

In addition, ask about the typical tradeoffs involved in working for large or small firms. Large corporations often provide more training on the job. They also usually demand more specialization, however, and provide less opportunity for independent action. Pay, in large companies, depends on the level of formal education

Questions to Raise when Interviewing

1. Organizational location: whom do you supervise, to whom do you report? Where does this position fit on the organization chart?

2. What's a typical work day like? A typical week? What is the rhythm of the year?

3. What are the most difficult problems and decisions you face?

4. How much variety is there in your work? How much specialization?

5. Are any degrees or licenses required?

6. How did you get into this line of work?

7. If you were to leave this job, where could you go?

8. What is the supply/demand situation nationally? Locally? Are there unfilled positions, or a surplus of applicants?

9. How secure is employment?

10. Do you have any opportunity to earn outside income?

11. Would it be easy for you to move to another city?

12. After gaining some experience, is it possible to become self-employed?

13. Are there any civic or social obligations that go with this position?

14. Do you have any travel obligations?

15. How many hours a week do you typically work? Is it common to take work home?

16. What are the essential skills needed to do this job well?

17. What are the personality traits that help someone to be effective in this position?

18. What's the best and worst thing about this job?

19. Looking back, if you had it to do over again, is there anything you would do differently?

20. Are there any ways I could "try out" this line of work (summer employment, an internship, a part time job)?

21. What major changes do you see coming in your industry in the years ahead? How will they affect you?

22. What is a typical starting salary? What can someone expect to make after five or six years of experience?

23. How visible are you in this kind of work? How many people know if you are or are not doing well?

24. Is there anyone you can suggest (in a larger/smaller firm, in the public/private/ nonprofit sector, in a different industry) who would have a different perspective on this occupation?

more than it does in smaller firms. Because they are well-known and offer good wages and salaries, the number of applicants at major corporations is usually very high, so these positions are harder to obtain.

You'll also want to know what future developments your source sees coming, both in the occupation that interests you and in the entire industry. It is particularly important to know how much growth there is likely to be, and where. In addition, be sure to find out how many applicants typically compete for openings, and what factors carry the greatest weight when hiring decisions are made.

As you ask these questions, match the answers with what you have learned about your own skills and personality. Can you see yourself sitting in the chair of the person whom you're interviewing? Would you enjoy doing his or her job?

If the match is clearly good or obviously bad, you probably don't need to discuss it. If you're not sure, or if the match seems good in some ways but poor in others, try outlining your strongest skills quickly. Explain why you are interested in this occupation, and see what the person you are interviewing has to say. He or she may be able to suggest a related occupation which is a better match.

Personality Is Also Important

Any information you can get about specific employers will be helpful. Regardless of size, each firm has its own personality, its own corporate culture. Despite having exactly the same job title in the same size company, you could feel at home in one business and out of place in another.

The source of these differences is usually the person at the top, either now or in the past. The impact of Henry Ford on Ford Motor Company, for example, is still evident today, long after his death. The values and personality of both the founder of a firm, and the present leadership, tend to permeate the entire organization. So anything specific you can learn about local firms and their leadership will be useful.

If you have successfully established good rapport with your informant, you can ask such questions as: what are the best and worst things about this job? If you had to do it over again, would you still choose this occupation and industry? Is there anything you would do differently? Are there pitfalls that are particularly important to avoid, or actions that would give me a head start? If I decide to go into this occupation, is there anything I should do now (groups to join, magazines to begin reading regularly or whatever) to be properly positioned?

Moving On

Toward the end of the interview, be sure to ask for one or more referrals to "some other people it might be helpful for me to talk to, perhaps with a slightly different perspective." It is these referrals which keep your interviews going until you have a complete picture.

When interviewing, it can be useful to take a few notes. A legal pad in a folder that also has a pocket or clipboard can make this easier. A set of questions typed on a single page, placed in this pocket or clipboard, will give you something to glance at as you talk.

We have provided a list of questions for you to choose from in Exercise 8-2. If some of these questions are not appropriate for the position you're researching, just make up your own. Remember, though: like all conversations, an interview is somewhat unpredictable. It's best to "go with the flow" rather than mechanically asking one question after another.

The Medium Is the Message

You will learn a great deal about a job by careful observation as well as by asking questions. Take a close look at the work setting. Note how people dress. Observe how much work space there is, how it is furnished and arranged, whether it is noisy or crowded and so on. Get a sense of the interpersonal atmosphere (hurried or relaxed, tense or friendly), and the kinds of relationships people have (distant, competitive, cooperative). Do you see yourself working comfortably and productively in this environment?

Try to get a sense of the typical personality in this field. Working every day with a group of reporters is notably different from working regularly with a group of computer programmers. Ask yourself how you would fit in with the people in this industry.

Learning the People and the Language

You will notice that certain names and companies are frequently mentioned during your interviews. Be sure to make a note of them. You want to find out who the leaders are, and where things are happening. You're mapping the field, so to speak, and finding out who's who. Make a particular effort to visit these leading companies and meet some of these people.

Everyone you interview is a potential colleague. One indirect payoff of this process is that, if you do enter this occupation, you will have the advantage of knowing a variety of people in the business.

Another benefit is that you will find yourself becoming more comfortable discussing the job you're investigating, and the skills the job requires. You're learning the specialized language peculiar to the field. You're becoming familiar with its problems as well as its outlook for the future. All this is preparing you for the interview that will take place when (and if) you apply for available positions, or propose that one be created.

From Depth to Depth

Often an interview will raise questions which will take you back to the library. Then, when you've learned as much as you can there, it is time to discuss the matter again with a knowledgeable informant. The process takes you back and forth between what is available in writing and what you can learn only from people. As you do this, you will find yourself getting more from what you read, and asking more thorough and sophisticated questions when you interview.

At first your questions will be somewhat general. As you learn more, they will become more specific. You will find that, more and more, you are providing valuable information as well as seeking it. This is one sign you are successfully getting a handle on both the occupation and the industry you are exploring. You should shortly be able to make an intelligent decision about whether and where to seek employment.

Occasionally you will experience an unusual rapport with someone you interview. It's only natural, as you meet a variety of people, to run into a few whom you particularly like. If you do decide to seek a job in this occupation or industry, these will be the first people to contact about possible openings. If the attraction is mutual, you will have not only a good job but a congenial environment. It is also more likely that you will have a supervisor who will take a personal interest in you and your progress. You then have not only a job but a mentor.

Always send a thank you note to the person you interviewed. Sum up some significant things you learned, and let them know that it was a help to you and you appreciated it. Do this even if you don't think you learned much, or feel the interview went badly. Your perception may change, and the thank you note itself will help to make your informant's memory of the experience a favorable one. People remember your courtesy.

Handling Job Offers

What should you do if someone offers you a job during one of these interviews?

Obviously, that's a decision you will have to make depending on your individual situation. A job offer is a real compliment, and should always be treated as such. It is usually best to stick to your original plans, however. Thank the person, and tell them you're flattered by the offer and definitely would like to keep in touch. Point out, however, that you promised yourself two weeks (or four or six or the summer or whatever you decided) to learn about the field before seeking any specific position. Explain that it's an important decision, and you want to be sure you know what you're doing.

This answer respects the offer, but preserves your options and makes it plain that you were being truthful about seeking only information. But do promise that you will be back in touch, no matter what, to let them know what you've decided to do.

A spontaneous offer of employment, by the way, tells you something about the organization's management style. How comfortable would you be in a place where decisions are made this quickly? Is it possible you would be let go just as quickly?

To Sum It Up

Interviewing is a time-consuming activity. It is also a high-payoff activity. Even four or five meetings can bring you a great deal of useful information, as the case studies at the end of this chapter show. An experienced person changing careers, on the other hand, may easily have 40 or 50 interviews before making a final decision about what position to seek, and where.

This process could take several months. You, of course, may not need to do that much. But there are several solid reasons to invest as much time as necessary in the library research/interviewing process.

First, interviewing knowledgeable individuals gives you information about every aspect of the occupation you are considering. It allows you to discuss the skills needed, the openings coming up, how much competition you can expect and typical salaries and opportunities for advancement. It also gives you a chance to observe working environments, to come across people you like and to learn the language of the field. Done properly, interviewing will replace at least some of the chance element which is part of every job search with solid information.

124

Second, the process of interviewing people in order to gather information is excellent preparation for the traditional job interview. You will be much less nervous about employment interview discussions when you've just finished a series of relaxed conversations on the same topics. In addition, if asked why you chose to apply to a given company, you will have a clear and considered answer. Your questions will show how well informed you are. You will already be acquainted with some of the people who work in the field. You will know how to dress for the interview so that you seem like "one of us." When asked about salary you will have a good sense of what is reasonable and typical, a critical factor if you are going to negotiate effectively.

There is a third thing to consider. Especially if you are unemployed, you need to realize that being in a hurry to get a job can be perceived, during a job interview, as panic. This makes interviewers very uncomfortable, and can lead them to move on to other applicants. Excessive haste can, therefore, be counterproductive. Take your time and do it right.

Those Special Jobs

A final value of letting one interview lead to another is that it represents the only practical way to explore the many interesting nooks and crannies of our enormously diverse labor market. This is how you find jobs which fit an unusual combination of personal desires and characteristics. Two examples will help to illustrate this.

The first was the experience of a young man who had been a medic in the armed forces. He had genuinely enjoyed the work and was, apparently, a natural diagnostician. He had not yet finished his B.A., however, and medical school was not a practical option. Yet he wanted a well-paid job in the medical area. (He had a job as assistant manager of a retail store and hated it.)

As we discussed the situation, one suggestion was that he explore pharmaceutical sales. Another was to make an appointment with the administrator of a local hospital, outline his skills and experience and ask if there were any civilian possibilities that paralleled his military work.

He did this, and learned there was a position in the medical area called "physician's assistant." He obtained the name of one, and also found a doctor who employed a physician's assistant. He talked to each of them.

What he discovered was discouraging. The educational requirements for this position were higher than

he thought. Everything had to be done under the close supervision of an M.D., and fear of malpractice suits made some doctors hesitant about employing physician's assistants.

He continued to talk to people, each interview leading to another. Then someone told him about a local firm which determined whether an applicant for insurance was healthy enough to be a good risk.

The more he heard about this job, the more attractive it seemed. The administration of these tests did not lead to any prescription or treatment (the results being used only by the insurance company). Such work did not, therefore, have to be done under a doctor's supervision.

As it happened, his informant had heard about an opening at one of these firms. Finding someone familiar with the company, he learned more about them, and got some information on the person for whom he would be working. He then applied for the job, and got it. He not only doubled his salary, he loved the work. He did well at it, too, and quickly earned a raise.

Another person in the same group had considerable facility at foreign languages. She was an outgoing, funloving person who enjoyed parties and travel, and had worked at an American embassy in Europe. The thought of a routine job was distasteful to her.

A discussion of her interests, skills and personality did not suggest anything which really seemed to fit her needs. Her hobby, however, was genealogies, so she began her interviewing with a local genealogical group. This led her to an interview with a practicing genealogist. She was surprised to learn that she could earn a living this way. In fact, the person she interviewed was very friendly, said he had more work than he could handle and offered to refer clients to her.

She really wasn't interested in doing genealogies full time, so she did not accept the offer. She continued interviewing, however, and discovered a travel agency which specialized in genealogical tours. She began talking to them about a job traveling with these groups. Her language skills would be valuable; she could easily help the group members use European records centers to trace back their ancestries. Of course, all her travel expenses would be paid, in addition to her salary. She would have time to sight-see on her own, and an occasional party would not be unknown....

Not everyone's search for appropriate employment brings them to such uncommon jobs. We do, however, live in an extraordinarily complex society, with far more occupational possibilities than most of us realize. Only by talking to people familiar with different sectors of the labor market can we discover the full range of options open to us.

Decision Time

When the facts are in, it is decision time. For some people, the decision really makes itself. Some job possibilities are so exciting there's really no question about which position to seek.

In other cases the decision is more difficult. The decision tree introduced in Chapter Five can assist in sorting out what you've learned, and helping clarify your priorities. Having done this, there is also a real value in talking the issues through with others whom you trust.

Then, once you've thought things through as clearly as you can, there is something to be said for just going with how you feel. Somehow, when you find the right place, you know it.

As a practical matter, it is wise to adopt both a "Plan A" and a "Plan B." "Plan A" is what you most want. "Plan B" is a fallback: an acceptable if less exciting alternative which is easier to obtain. The uncertainties of life and the labor market being what they are, a good "Plan B" is like a parachute. You may not need it, but if you do it can keep you from falling too far too fast. A colored parachute is particularly recommended.

CASE STUDIES

Case Study 8-1

There are a number of things worth noting in this case study. First, although the information the author found in the library suggested a rather bleak picture for M.A.-level therapists, people working in the field were much more positive. How often do you think this kind of discrepancy occurs? Therapy can be done in a variety of settings. Non-profit agencies, for-profit hospitals, government institutions and those in private practice all provide therapeutic services. Each setting has its own pressures. Budget cuts can be a problem in state agencies. The need for constant marketing is part of having a private practice. Tensions between a desire to provide service and the need to make a profit trouble for-profit institutions. Notice how the author's organizing and problem-solving skills, which otherwise would suggest an administrative position, are channeled by her interest in therapy into direct work with patients. (To compare this paper with her initial self-analysis, re-read Case Study 4-1.) Therapy, for her, is where the

excitement and the action are to be found. With experience, however, part time administration remains an attractive option. How well do you think she did at conducting her interviews? Did they provide useful information? Open up new possibilities? Confirm her decision to work in family therapy?

Seeking a Setting for Therapy

The experience of defining my skills, interests, and personality traits has given me a new sense of self and a clearer view of where I would be most effective and satisfied.

I am an excellent organizer. I like managing and supervision, although I wouldn't want to work exclusively in that capacity. I am very people-oriented, good at communicating and have a natural talent for identifying with others. I enjoy challenges and like to problem-solve, especially on a personal level. My primary interest is in the area of mental health. I have an ongoing curiosity about the "whys" and "hows" of human behavior. Another interest is physical fitness, which I see as closely connected to effective mental functioning.

As Barbara Sher suggests in Wishcraft, *I have examined my motivations and emotions to discover my "personal touchstone." For me, this is the creative fulfillment that comes from helping other people. I am able to confront problems and figure out appropriate ways of handling them. I use my communication skills to provide workable options for problem situations. My motivational pattern leads me to find satisfaction in being a facilitator of positive change.*

My library research turned up some interesting information regarding job possibilities and perspectives. The Occupational Outlook Handbook, *compiled by the U.S. Department of Labor, projected a rather grim future for M.A.-level therapists. There apparently will not be enough job openings to accommodate the growing number of applicants. The* National Register of Health Services in Psychology *listed only those practitioners who voluntarily submitted their names and specialties. Even though it did not include all providers, this publication could be helpful when constructing a list of people to contact during a job search.*

I found the most pertinent information in the Directory of Community Resources and Services put out by the United Way. This publication listed a large number of social service agencies located in the area, along with the names of their directors. It is an excellent source for locating persons who could provide information about job possibilities.

While the library search was helpful in gaining insight into the makeup of the job market, it did not provide any clues as to the nature of the various job environments or about the requirements of a given position. To obtain this information, I had to go directly to those who are currently practicing in the field.

Since I am now pursuing an M.A. in behavioral sciences and have made the decision to work in the field of family therapy, I focused my interviews on three areas in which this kind of therapy is practiced: the private sector, institutions, and agencies. In each of these areas, I selected individuals whom I felt could provide some perspective about the environment in which they work, and who would discuss the pros and cons of their own positions.

My first interview was with an M.A.-level family therapist who has been in private practice for about five years. She had worked at several agencies in the past. I found it interesting that she had not planned to practice privately. She saw clients for some time under the supervision of another practitioner and was quite content with that arrangement. It provided many contacts and a firm support system. When this professional moved away, however, she no longer had a place to see clients. So, of necessity, she had to set up her own office.

She pointed out that, as a private therapist, a person must essentially create his or her own professional space. This entails much more than opening an office and waiting for clients to appear. A therapist must constantly nurture the business by maintaining visibility and following up on referrals. She commented that she finds it difficult to "sell" herself as a therapist by contacting doctors and other professionals in the community. She prefers that people come to know about her on a more casual, non-therapeutic basis. She teaches occasionally, frequently gives workshops or seminars and involves herself in a variety of community projects. Her discussion about maintaining visibility inspired me to think about the various methods I might use to become known in the community. It seems to be a major issue when one is working independently.

I interviewed another M.A.-level practitioner who is in the process of relocating to a private suite with one other therapist. He stressed the importance of being creative and flexible in private practice. If the client caseload is low, for example, one can exercise the option of contracting with institutions, agencies and psychiatrists on a part time basis. Again, the ability to "sell" oneself and maintain visibility appear to be critical to success. He advised me to participate actively in professional organizations in order to meet and be known by others in the field.

Both of these private practitioners are able to structure work time so that they see clients three or four days (and evenings) a week. They use the other days to relax or involve themselves in some other activity. I was rather surprised at this, since I had always assumed that in private practice one's availability to clients would always be the top priority.

Both feel that is it imperative to have a support network of colleagues with whom to discuss client management problems. Self-discipline was stressed in both interviews. Being successful in private practice involves keeping up with referrals, constantly making new contacts and structuring "off" time so that it is personally productive in some way. (Relaxing is considered to be personally productive!) The only negative aspect mentioned was the unpredictability of income.

Much of what was discussed in these two interviews was not new to me, although I now have a much clearer picture of what it would be like to practice on my own. A high level of motivation and personal organization is essential. It is not a position that should be undertaken by the novice, since experience must be gained and networks built before attempting to sustain oneself on an independent basis. It is, however, a possibility for the future.

I talked with three individuals who work within an agency setting. The first is an administrator for the children's division of a state-funded facility. She holds an M.S.W. and has worked previously as a private therapist and an agency social worker. In her current position, she is primarily responsible for budgeting and program development. She does consult with staff therapists about difficulties they are having with client families, although she has no direct involvement with clients. She finds that her close association with skilled professional therapists is quite stimulating and rewarding in itself. Her biggest problem is trying to maintain the necessary programs with a less-than-adequate budget.

As I listened to this woman explain the functions and goals of the organization, I sensed the importance of the work that is being done with the children and their parents or caretakers. Most clients are lower-income and, in a very real sense, this facility provides their only hope for finding effective solutions to their problems. She said that most are sent by schools or other authorities, and are frequently viewed as "hard-core" problems. Her position as an administrator is vital, and her sense of accomplishment within these parameters is strong.

As she discussed her job routine, however, I felt that it would be very difficult for me to fit into this type of position. The sense of excitement just isn't there. Most of her day is spent in meetings or doing paperwork, such as reports and budgets. Even though I enjoy organizing, managing and supervising, I would not want to exclude the hands-on excitement and challenge that comes from practicing therapy.

At this administrator's suggestion, I interviewed a staff therapist within the agency who has an M.A. in counseling. Here is where I found the sense of excitement — the action.

Therapist caseloads are quite high — about thirty families per week. The staff therapist explained that the family systems are typically disorganized and chaotic, and it is her task to teach organization and structure so that there is a framework in which to resolve difficulties. There tends to be considerable stress in this job, and she feels very strongly that anyone in this position must learn to leave concerns about clients at the office. She also commented that the support network of M.A.- and Ph.D.-level professionals within the facility is strong and accessible, and she attributes much of her success to this factor.

I felt genuinely comfortable with this woman, partly because she is a warm person and partly because I identified strongly with the kind of

therapeutic effort in which she is involved. She thinks that this particular facility provides excellent training and supervision for a beginning therapist. I will strongly consider this agency as a possible place of employment after graduation.

My next interview was with a woman who is co-owner of a private agency. Her job is roughly divided into three parts. She is, at the same time, administrator, supervisor and therapist. I was quite impressed by her flexibility, and particularly by the balance that is needed to perform the various functions of this position. She uses her organizational and problem-solving skills to maintain and expand the business. For example, she is currently setting up a network program with United Way which will make therapeutic services available to lower-income clients. As clinical director, she uses management and supervisory skills. At the same time, she has her own caseload and works directly with clients.

It seemed to me that this position offers the best of all worlds. I asked her if there was anything she didn't like about her job. Basically, she is very content. She did acknowledge, however, that there is continuing pressure from her responsibility to keep the business afloat. She admitted that much of her stress is self-created. She frequently takes on more than she can comfortably handle.

The down-side of this position seems to be similar to that of the private practitioner. There is always some uncertainty about future income, and this concern is even more prevalent in a depressed economy.

I came away with a good understanding of what is required to be successful in such a position. One must be a self-starter and enjoy challenge. The ability to problem-solve at both the administrative and therapeutic levels is essential. One must be willing to work with professionals to create new channels for client contact, and be involved in outside projects to maintain visibility. As I stated about private practice, this is no place for the beginning therapist. It is, however, the kind of position that I would very much enjoy at some point in the future.

The last part of my search for information was directed to the institutional setting. I interviewed the project coordinator for the (substance abuse) adolescent unit of a local hospital. Basi-

cally, she is responsible for maintaining an efficient, well functioning unit, and she coordinates the nursing and therapy staffs to that end. A good deal of her time is spent in staff meetings that deal primarily with case reviews and program planning. She also provides supervision for staff therapists and therapy interns. While she does have some degree of interaction with patients and families, she does not work as a therapist, except in a supervisory capacity. She likes the variety that her job offers, but views it as a stepping stone to a position dealing with outpatient therapy.

The negative aspects of this position seem to be quite formidable. While I would enjoy the organizational and supervisory duties, I would want to be more involved in direct therapy with patients and their families. There are also environmental disadvantages. As is probably true of any institution, there is a political undertow that tends to create a lot of unnecessary pettiness and competitiveness among the staff. The hospital program can function as a viable treatment center, or as a holding tank, depending on the policy of a particular management. She did not want to elaborate on this subject, but I sensed that she is both ethically and personally concerned about the therapeutic effectiveness of the current program. I was not at all surprised by this statement, for I have heard similar concerns expressed by staff members at other hospital treatment facilities.

I would not completely rule out an institutional setting as a possibility for future employment. At this point, however, it does not seem like my best option. I would have to gather information about the management policies of any proposed establishment, and talk with staff personnel, before making such a decision.

It was very encouraging to learn that all the personnel I interviewed are content with their choice of a counseling career at the M.A. level. Most are not planning to obtain a doctorate. They all agreed that there would be significant professional and financial advantages to having a Ph.D., but none thought that the additional training would necessarily make them better therapists.

They all also stated in one way or another that the personal rewards of practicing therapy

were well worth the effort although, in some cases, their incomes were somewhat less than satisfactory. All felt that if they became dissatisfied with their present positions, moving within the therapeutic community would be little or no problem.

These interviews have been extremely helpful in giving me a perspective about what a variety of working environments are like, and how one functions in different kinds of positions. I was able to visualize myself in each of these settings, and to get an idea of how comfortable I would be. I have a much better understanding of the skills and personality traits required for each position, and this information will help me in determining the steps necessary to achieve my own career goals.

On the basis of what I have gathered, I am even more convinced that I have chosen a path that is right for me. I am at least a year away from actively looking for work. I previously looked forward to my future job search with a certain amount of reservation. The process of learning how to approach the job market has dispelled many of my fears. I am now actually looking forward to the adventure of searching for the position that is right for me.

Case Study 8-2

This case study is a good illustration of how one step leads to another in the library research/interviewing process. Based on her skills, personality and interests, the author identified a series of attractive occupations in adult education and tourism. Preliminary library work provided essential facts about duties, salaries and so on. She then spoke to people who held several of the positions which attracted her. These initial choices seemed appropriate. None of the people to whom she spoke had positions which were unappealing. One job, however, looked like a particularly good fit. This has become her employment goal. From the information given, do you agree that a position coordinating staff and instructional development in a college setting is a realistic choice, and one she will find satisfying? Notice how easily she penetrated a network of people, specialized newspapers, annual meetings and professional association officers that, before these interviews, she didn't know existed. How did she "break in?" Is it always this easy? What part do you think preparation played in obtaining this information? Note also what happened when she talked to several individuals about her vocational goals. Each person had a different perspective, and therefore each gave her different referrals, or brought up new and useful information.

College Coordination

My interests are in the general area of adult education. I want to work with people in either helping, service or teaching/learning settings, meet new people and travel. Some of my personality traits are tactfulness, honesty, enthusiasm, an easy-going manner, flexibility, a sense of humor, patience, persistence, perseverance, orderliness in business matters, integrity, resourcefulness, creativity and self-motivation in teaching/ learning areas. My strongest skills are: my ability to work with adults in an easy-going, yet authoritative manner; my ability to organize people, things and printed materials; my writing ability in the area of developing learning/teaching materials; my leadership skills; and my ability to handle work which requires paying attention to detail.

I decided to research jobs involving adult education and the travel/tourism industry. Some of the specific job titles I considered were coordinator of staff and instructional development, community college classroom instructor, travel agent, visitor development specialist, conference service program director and audio-visual services specialist. I thought these jobs would be good matches for my interests, personality traits and skills because they all involve performing a service for, helping or teaching adults. They would also draw on most of the personality traits I seem to exhibit most often. They are all in areas that are growing and that offer the opportunity to continue learning new things and meeting new people. They all require paying attention to detail in some way, and almost all involve coordination of people, things and printed materials.

Working as a coordinator of staff and instructional development, community college teacher, conference service program director or audio-visual services specialist would make excellent use of my adult education skills, my people skills and my organizational ability, as well

as my personality traits of creativity, orderliness, resourcefulness and self-motivation in learning/ teaching areas. These jobs have many characteristics that fit what I like to do and am comfortable doing.

The library resources I used were the Harris County Business Guide, *the* Occupational Outlook Handbook, The American Almanac of Jobs and Salaries, Where to Find Business Information *and the* Encyclopedia of Business Information Sources. *I found the* Occupational Outlook Handbook *and* The American Almanac of Jobs and Salaries *to be the two most useful books. They both gave me general overview information on the travel/ tourism and education fields and the salary ranges in each field. These books gave me an idea of what job titles to look for and ask about during my interview phase. The* Harris County Business Guide *was helpful in locating travel industry businesses, helping me determine what part of town they were located in, and knowing who the owner, president or chief officer in charge might be.*

The other two sources I found extremely useful were the research librarian and the Business Yellow Pages. *I found it helpful to call the places where I wanted an interview, in order to confirm the names of the people in charge. Twice I found that the person listed in my information source as being in charge was no longer with the company or organization.*

Another informational resource I found helpful were promotional bulletins put out by companies or college systems, such as course catalogues and annual reports. I obtained these either by going to the company and asking for a copy or through the research librarian. My reading made me familiar with the general trends and salary ranges and gave me a basic idea of what these industries had to offer.

This research did not give me, however, all the knowledge I needed about the wide variety of opportunities available in these fields. Reading only scratched the surface. It did help me to ask more intelligent and pointed questions about the areas I was investigating. But to understand what really goes on in a job you need to talk to someone who does it every day.

Mainly I found that the printed information did not answer questions about how specialized or how diversified jobs are. It also did not tell me about employment opportunities for women and minorities. The research in these fields did make me less nervous, especially after the first interview, because I discovered that I had enough knowledge to be conversant about the occupational field. As I got into the interviews I found them very enjoyable.

Four of my interviews were with people in college settings who deal with various aspects of adult education. I first talked to the director of a branch of a large community college. He had previously headed a division on the main campus. That division is now called the Staff and Instructional Development Division. I found out from him what the requirements are to be an instructor in the system, and that they hire quite a few part time instructors. This would be a good way to try out the field and also get some college teaching experience. I found out that in the academic areas you need to have a master's degree to teach. He told me how he got his present job and what he does. He also told me about his previous job, and suggested I talk to the man who took his place.

I did, and the discussion was probably the most helpful and informative of my interviews. He told me about what he does, and what the staff he supervises does. I found here the kind of job I really want to pursue. The job title is Coordinator of Staff and Instructional Development. He also suggested that I look for similar positions under the titles Faculty Developer and Instructional Developer. He showed me a copy of The Chronicle of Higher Education, which is a newspaper that advertises jobs in education. He told me I might get some leads from it on jobs in this field.

During our conversation I was informed that there is little career mobility within the college from this position unless you are promoted to management, and then you no longer do adult education kinds of activities. He also told me that people enter these jobs with varied backgrounds and degrees. However, he says that what he currently looks for when hiring is a person in a somewhat related area with a master's degree, and some experience or working knowledge of computers and audio-visual equipment. He also looks for high aptitude for teaching and learning.

He told me of two organizations that I might want to look into: the National Council of Staff, Program, and Organizational Development for two-year colleges, and the Association for Educational Communications and Technology. He says that increased use of the computer and closed-circuit television in education are trends for the future. He gave me the names of four other people I might want to contact in this field. They are the head of the National Institute of Staff and Organizational Development in the School of Education at the largest university in the state; the head of Human Resources and Staff Development at a major corporation; the woman who heads the Staff Development Department at another local county college; and the director of Audio-Visual Services at a large local university.

I later interviewed this latter person, and it was quite helpful. He told me about his job, what his staff does and the kinds of people he looks for when he hires. He suggested that if I wanted to know what was going on in the field and how it can be applied to education, I should contact an organization called the International Television Association. They sponsor brief training programs that I could attend. He told me that a good way to find out what jobs are open and available in the field would be to attend the National Audio-Visual Association conference. I found out that there is almost no career mobility in his division, but that the jobs are relatively secure. He suggested I contact the audio-visual coordinator at my university for a view of how this kind of division operates in a smaller institution.

My third interview was with a woman at the continuing education center of a major university. She is the Conference Service Program Director. Her job is to coordinate and set up training classes that involve computers. She is responsible for course content and the competency of the instructors. Her duties also include budgeting and setting up class schedules, generally a semester in advance. She suggested that I might be interested in a new group called the Houston Data Processing Group. Her job is a good place to learn about management and computers.

My fourth interview was with an employee of the Convention and Visitors Council. She is the Public Relations Specialist. From her I learned quite a bit about how tourism is promoted and *also about how companies and industries are encouraged to hold their conventions here. I learned how she got her job and the kind of background she had to enter this field. She was an English major in college, and her job just before joining the Council was as a personnel counselor in an employment agency. This job is really her first experience in public relations. I decided from our talk that tourism is an area I would probably be very happy working in. She referred me to two other people in her organization who can tell me abut specific job areas, one in convention sales and the other one in visitor development.*

I really like this way of obtaining information. You get a feel for the work environment. You get to see the pace of the organization. You also gain far more practical information than through reading and research. I also found that interviewing several people in a field is even more helpful than just talking to one. With several you get an idea of how diverse or limited the field is. It really helped me to have a list of questions prepared ahead of time to refer to during the interviews. It helped me stay on target and lessened my anxiety level.

The interviewing process got much easier after my second experience. The people I interviewed really enjoyed talking about themselves and their jobs. They all seemed well pleased with their present positions. They have been on their jobs from three months to seven years. Most of them got where they are, not so much by design, but by being in the right place in the organization at the right time, or knowing someone who knew of the job opening and told them about it.

On the basis of the information I've gathered, I intend to seek a job in a college setting where I will be responsible for coordinating activities for staff and instructional development.

Case Study 8-3

This case study provides a nice illustration of how self-understanding can evolve as one position after another is examined. Teaching and training, by their nature, demand an interest in both the subject and the people to be taught. All of us have had teachers who were primarily interested in their fields, and others whose first concern was their students. The author of this paper is clearly at the people-oriented end of the

scale. During the interviewing, her initial interest in training expands into an interest in doing both organizational development *and* training. Then a setting has to be found. Such work can be done in a corporation, a small business, a non-profit institution or a government agency. There were sources of referral all around (co-workers, friends, fellow graduate students). People doing organizational development and training in a variety of settings were located and interviewed. Do you think the process is as easy as the author makes it appear? Note how she plans to use the possibilities of her present job to develop new skills, which she will then use in a new job. Do you think this is a practical strategy? More generally, how easy is it to develop new skills on the job? Is this something at which you should aim? What do you think of more schooling as a "Plan B?" Are there any faster approaches?

Training and Development

Over the last few months I have learned a tremendous amount about myself and what motivates me. For the first time I learned I have a basic motivational pattern. I have also learned that it is possible to have a job in which you can do what you love and what you do best. One of the best things I have gained from this effort is the ability to express what I want and what I do well.

I would like to be involved in teaching or training, something I have enjoyed throughout my life. In the last couple of years I have gotten really interested in teaching adults. I need to learn new things, and have variety in what I do. I have good communication skills, and work well with detailed data and numbers. The security of a regular salary is important to me, but I also like the freedom of flexible hours. Within those flexible hours I need scheduled deadlines, however, because I am a terrific procrastinator. I also enjoy the excitement of a little travel periodically.

Two factors repeatedly surfaced in this self-examination process. First, I love to work with people. The best part of my current job is interacting with my peers, and supervising my department. I have been very unhappy in past jobs where this interaction was missing.

The second factor is my love for books, and an environment in which books are important tools. I have always worked in libraries and loved the academic environment.

After taking a step back to look at what I do well and what excites me, I started to plan which jobs to research. The best possibility seemed to be working as a trainer responsible for teaching newly developed software to computer users. This job would use my detail skills and my teaching skills. It would allow regular interaction with other adults, and also give me variety in an environment where learning is valued. Next, I decided to broaden my investigation to include training in general. This would use many of the same skills and interests.

First I went to the library. I found it much easier to research the job of trainer; narrowing it to a computer trainer left me at a dead end. There was information on computer programmers, computer operators and computer repair people, but nothing on training.

I consulted The American Almanac of Jobs and Salaries and the Occupational Outlook Handbook. I learned that what a trainer does depends greatly on the size of the organization. In smaller places you may have a number of personnel duties as well. In larger corporations you may do only training. Salaries ranged from the low-20s to the mid-30s, but were much lower for Texas state government jobs.

Training was included with personnel work in these sources. Later I found that to be the case in most organizations. I also found some information on a couple of professional organizations, including the American Society for Training and Development, and some other sources from which to seek further information. Where to Find Business Information and the Encyclopedia of Business Sources were helpful for this. The educational requirements for trainers ranged from some college to a completed degree. Future employment needs look hopeful, but very competitive.

The information I gained in the library gave me a background to build on, but I lacked a feel for what it is really like to have a training job. I could see that the job would be very different in a corporation, a non-profit organization or a government agency. I also suspected that the educational requirements were higher than those stated in my sources, and I wanted to verify this. In addition, I had heard the phrase "organizational development" tossed around at work, and wanted to find out more about it.

My first interview was with a person who does all of this — training, personnel work and organizational development. She is the Director of Organizational Development at a local professional library. I have worked with her for three years. She is interested in career development, so this interview was really a joy. She helped clarify the difference between training and organizational development, and gave me lots of good information. She suggested some course work, gave me some hints on what mistakes to avoid and encouraged me to pursue my interests. She also cautioned me about the problems of doing organizational development in one's own organization, and talked some about consulting. I left the interview realizing we had talked very little about training, but with an excitement about organizational development, and a new direction for my thinking.

In my next interview, I investigated the possibility of being a software trainer. The variety in this work sounded attractive, but I soon realized that I would enjoy learning the software only if I could use it as a tool, and not just for the sake of teaching it. I also realized that I was not especially interested in the computer course work that might be involved. When I left the office, I was sure that I had misunderstood something about myself all along. I am good with detail and have always worked with it, but what is really important to me is working with people. I find people much more interesting than machines.

My next interview was born out of a conversation with my best friend. I am beginning to recognize what a resource people are! She mentioned a trainer who worked in her organization and told me she would mention that I might call. Certain aspects of this training position appealed to me, but again I realized that I wanted something more than just training. The trainer works in a large organization, and this is her only responsibility. She confirmed my thoughts on needing a master's degree. Interestingly enough, however, she said it often did not matter what field the degree is in. Salaries were in line with what I had found in the library. A Training Specialist II ranged from $20,000 to $24,000. Her salary as a III was higher. Near the end of the interview she mentioned a lack of interaction with others as a disadvantage of her job. A red flag went up before me, and I decided I should probably steer clear of very large organizations.

Next, I talked to two other referrals from my first interview. The first once worked for a university, organizing and delivering management training. He is now with another local university. This interview was very different from the others because I was not talking to him about his job. He was suggested as a good person from whom to obtain advice on how to get started in the field. The most important information he gave me was about organizational development. I got very clear on what might be involved, and he reinforced the warning about doing it internally.

The second thing I realized in this interview was related to what I enjoy in my interactions with other people. I enjoy teaching, but I enjoy a real two-way communication, a sharing even more. Organizational development involved much more of this two-way communication than training, which is traditionally more one-way.

The last important advice I got from him was on how to break into the field. He suggested I begin transitioning from my present position, so that those credentials would allow me to make a smoother move into another sector if I chose to switch. He suggested I start by involving myself in some training or personnel activities.

My second referral proved to be my most exciting discussion. The consulting firm where I interviewed is very involved in the dynamics of human interaction, both in their training sessions and in the organizational development work they do. My source said the way to get involved in organizational development is to start doing general training work and then broaden into organizational development. She said most small firms do not care about degrees, but are very interested in management experience. She also said one of the hardest transitions for her was to stop talking non-profit talk and start talking business in order to convince management that her firm had something valuable to sell them.

She, like myself, comes from a non-profit background. Her salary estimate was in the range I expected, mid-20s to 30K with some management experience. She warned me of stiff competition because of lay-offs over the last couple of years. She encouraged me to plan my move carefully, and gave me hints on preparing for the shift.

She is responsible for hiring new people in this organization. The president gives the final approval, but she said they have a very good working relationship and he trusts her judgment. I found her advice on how to get started particularly valuable because she has hiring responsibility. She suggested I attend other people's programs as often as I can. Like many others, she told me to join the American Society for Training and Development so that I could become known and make contacts. She also suggested that I apprentice myself to some established trainers for two purposes: the exposure and the learning experience. I believe I have made a valuable contact and intend to keep in touch.

Finally, I talked to a referral from a fellow graduate student. This interview was valuable because it was my first in a for-profit setting where training is not the main goal of the organization, but rather a means to reach that goal more efficiently. My source is the only trainer, so he uses a number of outside consultants or people employed in other divisions of the plant for many of his training sessions. I got a real sense that he is isolated. He, too, mentioned the competition due to lay-offs, but was not as positive about future prospects in this part of the country.

He said the best place to look for training jobs right now is in the northeast, where training is making a comeback. When I talked about salary he said the pay was higher in private industry than in the public sector, but that it was difficult to give me a figure. He said at least a college degree and probably an M.A. (in any field), and some previous supervisory experience, were necessary. I left his plant, after turning in my visitor's badge and signing out, feeling like a released prisoner. I don't think this industry is the place for me!

Evaluating what I learned in my interviews, I am very excited about the prospect of working in a private consulting firm where I could be involved in both training and organizational development. I would be able to maintain close ties with peers in the organization and have contact with other adults in the training sessions.

During the Christmas holidays, I intend to create a step by step plan so that I can schedule *my efforts and watch my progress. I am taking a three-and-a-half day management seminar in February. I have approached a colleague and proposed doing some training sessions with her. Her response was positive. I am trying to set up an interview with the president of the consulting firm. He has been out of town, so I will do this next month. I sent away for some information on the American Society for Training and Development, and will send in my membership dues when it arrives.*

The best thing that has come from this is the prospect of a new job where I work. A colleague (the first person I interviewed) told me she intends to leave sometime within the next year, and will try to lay the groundwork for me to move into her re-designed job. Because of changes in the organization, she believes the job will evolve into being an assistant to one of the administrators. The duties will include some personnel tasks and some training responsibilities — a perfect stepping stone into the field. The present administrator was my mentor when I moved into my current position, so we already have a good working relationship. From this position I could gain enough experience to make the transition to a consulting firm.

"Plan B" comes into action if this possibility falls through. I can still do all the other things I talked about above, and can also extend the classwork I intend to take anyway into a degree in human resources management. By the time I finish this degree I will have around five years of supervisory experience to add to my credentials.

Case Study 8-4

The author of this case study has a strong interest in health and fitness, and a desire to work with and teach adults. Because adult fitness is a new field, there was little of value in the standard reference books in the library. Magazines and journals, on the other hand, provided useful information. To learn more about the many settings in which adult fitness programs are now offered, interviews were sought with people who work in a variety of locations: a university, a small business, county government and a major corporation. These interviews lead to a realization that some aspects of the work are constant (the rhythm of demand, the many talented people trying to find jobs in this field). Other

concerns are limited to the private sector (worries about liability, the need for constant marketing, job insecurity). Difficulties during the first two interviews quickly gave way to more even exchanges. Why? How can you handle an informant who gives primarily "yes" and "no" answers? The author is soon able to share what has been learned during the early interviews with those she sees later. This helps establish an easy rapport. What does this suggest about the people whom you should interview first, and those whom you should see only after you have more information? There seems to be no problem getting referrals to others. Her attraction to the field becomes stronger as she learns more. Despite the many challenges this kind of work presents, she is deeply impressed by the people she meets, and wants to join them. Given the competition for this kind of job, and the insecurity of these positions, do you think this is a realistic decision?

A Healthy Interest in Private Enterprise

Since my interests lie in the area of exercise and nutrition, I decided to interview people in the field of fitness. My personality is ideally suited to teaching, both in one-on-one and group situations. I have the skill to impart knowledge with clarity and (some) humor. I understand what motivates people and am able to transfer my own enthusiasm to others. I genuinely care about people and desire to help them benefit from my knowledge and skills. Finally, I need to be in control of my time and I like to make the decisions. From all of this, I decided that the three areas that might best fit my need to teach fitness would be either a classroom situation (in a university setting), a corporation of some kind or running my own business.

I interviewed a university professor, to discuss classroom teaching; a woman who owns and manages a fitness center, to discuss running one's own business in this particular industry; a company fitness consultant, to find out what the position entails and to discuss the advantages and disadvantages of working within a corporate structure; a research assistant at an aerobic center, to discuss fitness testing and personalized programs; and finally, the project coordinator for a public health district to learn about developing one's own program and what is involved in creating and marketing a fitness package.

Before beginning my interviews, I went to the library and reviewed several reference books. I found little information relevant to my job choices, perhaps because the field of fitness management is relatively new. There is, as yet, little data available.

I looked through the Physical Fitness/Sports Medicine Index *and found some very interesting articles, but came across nothing that gave specifics on the industry itself. Then I went to a local bookstore and browsed through various health magazines. In one,* American Health, *I read an informative article about the "business" of exercise physiology. The article mentioned salary ranges for different jobs in the fitness industry, and discussed degree requirements.*

I decided at this point to go ahead with my interviews, to ask people in the business where to go for the facts. In almost every interview, I was given the names of at least two other people or places to contact, and the lines were kept open for me to return if I needed more information.

I started out dreading my first interview, and yet was actually sorry to see the last one end. I certainly became more relaxed as I gained experience at what I was doing and became more knowledgeable. My questions became less outline-oriented and more me-specific. The last three interviews were almost (though I hesitate to use the word) cozy. We were two informed people talking about a subject and a field that interested both of us. Time limits on my part were forgotten and, on theirs, graciously ignored.

My first interview was with the Director of Recreational Sports at a local university, and it was by far the stiffest. I adhered to my prepared questions exactly and, as a result, got little elaboration, mostly just "yes" or "no" answers. I was quite intimidated. I did, however, get two referrals and made a definite decision that I did not want to return to classroom teaching.

My next discussion was with the owner of a fitness center. She was quite articulate. We obviously shared many of the same life goals. Her commitment to helping other people benefit from her center came across strongly. She detailed the struggles she had been through and the success she had earned. One piece of information that surprised me is that there are definite fitness "seasons." There is, it seems, a heavy demand after

Christmas — she called it the "resolution rush" — and again in the spring (bathing suit season) and once again in September, mostly, she said, from mothers whose kids are back in school and who are ready to do something for themselves.

Strangely enough, I heard about this same cycle from all those with whom I talked. Even the factory workers discussed in the interview with a fitness consultant followed this pattern — heavy after Christmas, again in the early spring and then again in the fall. June, July and August, because of family travel, hot weather and school vacations, are the slowest months of the year.

We talked at great length about the risks of self-employment, and also about the rewards. She is highly gratified by the financial success of her venture, but her biggest satisfaction comes from her customers' positive feedback.

My third interview was with the fitness consultant for a major corporation. He has been on the job for just under a year, and was informative and forthcoming. He spent long hours developing the program, but is now finding the hours required on the job more flexible. He finds great satisfaction in his work and definitely considers it a good training ground for other things, such as self-employment or acting as a consultant to more than one company. He has recently been getting more exposure to other potential employers. The major advantage of his work is that this is a brand new field, and he can set his own limits.

A research assistant at an aerobic center in a nearby city was most informative concerning the actual state of the fitness industry. The center is considered by many the mecca of the exercise world. It is here that much of the research on exercise is carried on. Every day is a new learning experience in this environment. The work load is great and the pace hectic.

Her actual work consists of administering stress and fitness tests and assessing nutrition levels. She collects and evaluates the information and then writes exercise prescriptions based on the data. This past year, she has been giving workshops and making sales calls on companies interested in a personalized aerobic lifestyle program. We talked mostly about the skills involved in her kind of work: verbal, analytical, physical and decision making. All of which, I was pleased

136

to note, correspond with my own.

My final interview was with the Special Programs Health Promoter for a county public health district. She is working under a federal grant to promote fitness programs in the area. Her job includes doing need assessment research, setting up and leading exercise programs, giving nutrition seminars, determining employee fitness levels and gathering data. Many of her research materials, as well as assessment and release forms, are adapted from the "Heart at Work" kit put out by the American Heart Association. This kit is a health package that I have been involved with for the past year. I have presented it to businesses in my area.

The emphasis of her job has shifted from designing the program to implementing it, and finally to marketing it more effectively. I noticed a similar phenomenon with several people I interviewed. All stressed the importance of learning how to market a program. They believe that marketing is, or has become, the focal point of their jobs.

Like the others, she finds her work creatively stimulating and a solid training ground for other career possibilities. Many people working in this field seem ready to move on, not necessarily higher on their particular ladder, but out to other challenging areas. They all consider the field crowded with talent, with few positions available. Although the market for fitness will increase, there will be so many fitness programs available that only the really good ones — those that are research-based and comprehensive — will survive. They feel, as I do, that there will always be a market for excellence.

Two other features of this type of work were referred to during the course of these interviews. One is the liability factor, something I had not considered. Signed release forms are often used. The aerobic center follows the policy of always having a doctor present when testing is done in the field rather than at the center. The question of liability is a serious concern for many corporations and is probably the biggest factor in the decision not to implement on-site exercise programs and/or facilities. For those in business for themselves, the risk of liability adds high insurance premiums to the other uncertainties of private enterprise.

The second factor, also a disadvantage in this line of work, is the fact that these jobs offer little or no security. Positions with non-profit organizations are dependent on the economy. A fitness consultant's job is also, to a great extent, dependent upon a health budget. Fitness is still often seen as a "fringe" and if the ax comes down, these jobs will be among the first to go.

The people I interviewed, however, talked about their jobs with energy and enthusiasm. A real sense of satisfaction was evident. They all spoke of how their jobs helped them to stay fit and to be aware of their bodies. Their commitment to health has become a way of life, and their work seems to have stimulated each to extend his or her life goals. They are finding themselves challenged to do more and to do it more effectively.

I gained much knowledge from these interviews, theoretical as well as practical. I was given the names and phone numbers of other people to contact, as well as the addresses of several journals, a newsletter and a foundation on exercise physiology. I now have several avenues to more information which I shall certainly pursue. I intend to remain in contact with at least two of those I interviewed for help when and if I need it.

My goal now is to start my own health and fitness business. There will be much to learn and do before I am ready. What I have learned from these interviews will, I believe, point me in the right direction.

The information I garnered during these discussions, and the techniques I learned for obtaining information, have been invaluable to me. I fully intend to continue practicing these skills by calling on those people whose names I have been given. The more knowledge I have about myself and about the workings of this industry, the better qualified and equipped I will be for the path I finally choose to take.

Appendix 8-1: The Right Resume for these Times

The resume is a short document which relates what you have to offer an employer to the demands of a particular position. At some point in the information gathering process it will become clear what job you will probably be seeking. At this point you need to review what you have learned about yourself, and about the job, and *draft* a resume. You can show this draft to some of the people you interview, and ask for their comments. Be sure, however, to make it clear that it is just a draft, and do not leave it with them. You are still learning, not applying for a job.

Many people place great importance on having the *right* resume. While you certainly want an appropriate one, it is a mistake to make your resume the focal point of your job search activities. It is personal contact, not pieces of paper, that will play the major role in helping you find employment.

A good resume is unquestionably a useful tool when looking for work. It provides a brief written summary of your qualifications for people who have not yet met you or had a chance to discuss these things with you personally. You want that written summary to make a good impression. There are several common resume formats, and it is important that you choose one which fits both your background and the position you are seeking.

Useful though they are, resumes are not magic documents, and they are certainly not worth agonizing over. Although there are many services which will write your resume for a fee, we urge you to write your own. They are not that complicated, and it is not worth the money to pay someone to do it. We will show you various resume formats and styles, and provide step by step directions.

You don't have to have a resume to get either an interview or a job offer. If you are looking for a position that pays by the hour, or a salaried clerical job, you can often be hired after discussing your skills and experience verbally. If you are dealing with a large firm, this information will usually be collected on a job application form.

If you are looking for a professional or managerial position, however, a resume will usually be expected. First of all, even after an excellent interview with the person to whom you would report, he or she will usually have to discuss your application with other executives. They are used to seeing a resume. It helps them to review your background quickly. Not having a resume would suggest that you are either not very serious about your application, or are a person who cannot be counted on to do things correctly.

The reason a resume exists is to provide concise data about you and your experience. It is obviously to your advantage to present this information in such a way that the relationship between your qualifications and the demands of the job is as clear and convincing as possible.

In thinking about your resume, remember that it is one part of your overall marketing strategy. It should serve as a supplement to your program of making personal contacts. A resume is to a job seeker what a business card is to the employee of a company. It gives the essential facts and, at the same time, communicates something "qualitative" about you.

Test this out for yourself. Look carefully at a few business cards. Notice the print, the quality of the paper, the color of the paper, the logo or graphics, the person's title, the address of the office. What impression do you have of the individual and the company after first looking at the card?

Because it is more a marketing tool than a detailed historical document, the resume need not contain everything an employer may want to know. In fact, the opposite is true. The resume should stimulate interest in you. It should arouse curiosity in the reader, without giving all of the answers. The idea is to make the person want to talk with you, i.e., have you in for an interview.

Your resume should communicate quickly. Most people don't read resumes. They skim them. Do not assume that your resume will receive more than 30 seconds of attention. What is not absorbed in that time will be missed. Be very careful, therefore, to avoid writing anything which is too wordy or intricate. If the first appearance of a resume is intimidating, it may not be read at all. Many of our suggestions about preparing your resume are intended to give you an edge in being sure what you write is read and remembered.

What Will a Resume Do for You?

You want a resume which fits today's competitive labor market. An employer wants something about you in writing that shows what you have to offer. You want to meet the employer's desire in a way that increases his or her interest in meeting you and learning more about you.

A typical "Ho-Hum, Just Like All the Rest" resume is written in job description style. This style emphasizes your past titles and job duties without ever telling the reader what you actually did, or how well you did it. There is nothing about your achievements, competence or worth to the company. In today's labor market, this isn't enough. It makes more sense to go back to the accomplishment statements you developed earlier, and to write a resume that will catch the eye of the reader and suggest that you are someone worth talking to.

A resume, in other words, can help to increase someone's interest in possibly hiring you. What a resume will not do, unfortunately, is get you a job. A good resume will enhance your chances, but it will not substitute for the personal contacts and impressions that lead to successful interviews and good job offers. It would be easier if we could just write something so impressive that the employer would then offer a job without further ado. Unfortunately, that is not how things work.

General Guidelines for Resume Construction

Before getting into the details of resume construction, there are some general guidelines that should be made explicit. We want you to produce a resume which is:

- *Short.* It should be no more than two pages long. Some employers prefer two pages rather than one because this gives a little more detail; others feel strongly that one page is enough. Our advice is to keep it at one page if you can. If you do go on to a second page, try not to fill it. If you have more than twenty years of work experience, of course, your employment history and accomplishments will usually require two pages.
- *Impressive.* The resume should be typed or photocopied on high quality bond paper. If photocopied, the reproduction should look good. Use only white or very lightly tinted paper.

Printing is neither necessary nor desirable, unless you are in a graphics or visual arts profession. Printing suggests that large numbers of your resumes are littering the landscape, and can be found in every office in town.
- *Attractive.* The resume should be visually appealing. Leave quite a bit of white space. Margins should be even.
- *Easily Skimmed.* The resume should be designed to be read quickly and easily, with key points at the beginning.
- *Honest.* The resume should contain only the truth. There should be no false statements or inaccuracies.

Choosing a Format for Your Resume

There are several ways that resumes can be arranged. In this section we will review the major approaches. These are the chronological, functional, targeted, creative and letter resumes; the curriculum vitae; and the portfolio. The most common formats by far are the chronological and the functional, so we will emphasize these.

The Chronological Format

A chronological resume presents your job history in reverse chronological order, starting with your most recent position. It summarizes your skills and accomplishments under each job listed, with the major focus on activities of the past five years.

This approach is the most accepted, and therefore the "safest" way for you to write your resume. It is the traditional, conservative style. We suggest you use this format when dealing with a major corporation or financial institution. It is a format which can also work well if your most recent position carried an impressive or highly descriptive title, and you were responsible for significant accomplishments during the time you held that title. Finally, this format, since it tends to emphasize your movement from one position to another, can make it obvious that you have experienced a steady increase in responsibility and job titles. If you have had such a clear career progression, this is the way to show it.

On the other hand, a traditional resume will not work well for you if you are:
- Changing to a new occupation or industry, so that there is a big difference between your past job titles and what you want to do now.

DENNIS F. BURK
311 Avenue H.
Bellaire, Texas   77099
Phone: (713) 981-3171

OBJECTIVE

Public Relations and Corporate Communications

SUMMARY

Six years of achievement in corporate communications including shareholder communication, public affairs, speech writing and corporate image. Industry experience includes electronics and a high-technology research and development company.

EXPERIENCE

WONDER CORPORATION TECHNOLOGY CENTER, Houston, Texas   1982-1986

Director of Information and Public Affairs

o Managed a four person staff responsible for internal and external communications.

o Created successful corporate publicity campaign; supervised communication program for first public stock offering.

o Co-authored approximately four articles per year with technical staff; all were published in professional journals.

o Originated a 350-employee community involvement volunteer program which received awards from municipal and state agencies for public service contribution.

o Cited by National Aeronautics and Space Administration for scripting a public television documentary on the Apollo-Soyuz Test Project.

o Researched and wrote position papers on the space program for Senator John Wilkens during his 1984 re-election campaign.

o Edited company newsletter which became famous in the industry for useful technical information presented with humor; newsletter won the Communication Digest Annual "Straight Talk Award" for outstanding external communication for four consecutive years.

U.S. ELECTRIC COMPANY   1980-1982

Information Specialist

o Co-Authored The Final Frontier with James Harding, CEO of U. S. Electric. This book, about the future of NASA, sold over 45,000 copies.

o Wrote speeches for corporate executives' appearances at professional association national conventions and senate hearings.

o Wrote and edited over $40 million worth of successful electronics proposals to NASA.

EDUCATION, MILITARY AND PROFESSIONAL

o Colonel, United States Air Force, 1977-1980

o University of Virginia, M.A., Communications, 1977

o Virginia Military Institute, B.A., Journalism, 1975

RICHARD P. BATES, CPA
943 Coleridge
Dallas, Texas 77290

Home: (214) 867-8443   Office: (214) 771-1235

OBJECTIVE

Financial administration position with specialization in project management requiring
leadership, organizational and financial problem-solving capabilities.

SUMMARY

Eight years of financial accomplishment in such areas as financial reporting systems, cash
flow management and auditing in the insurance, manufacturing and public accounting
industries.

EXPERIENCE

RIVERSIDE INSURANCE CORPORATION, Santa Fe, New Mexico   1979-1986

Assistant Director of Corporate Audit

o Introduced a deposit system that reduced float on weekly insurance payments, increasing
   interest income $100,000 annually.

o Initiated an operational audit routine to ensure management that directives were
   implemented.

TERRY INDUSTRIES, Carrolton, Wyoming   1976-1978

Senior Financial Auditor

o Computerized accounts receivable department improving average collection time on
   payments of invoices by 20%.

o Modernized accounts payable, resulting in a cost savings of $75,000 per year in
   discounts taken.

o Implemented procedures to audit credit limits for customers; negotiated payment
   schedules with past due customers, resulting in no loss when several former customers
   declared bankruptcy.

Assistant Financial Auditor

o Changed inventory system to LIFO resulting in $750,000 savings.

o Developed computerized inventory control system which provided accurate cost and asset
   information, which was also a valuable sales tool.

o Introduced a computerized cash flow auditing system, making possible improved financial
   forecasting activities.

ROBERTS CUMMINGS, Casper, Wyoming   1973-1976

Staff Auditor

o Analyzed accounting records for firms in a variety of industries; concentrated on
   auditing operational systems.

o Developed and supervised staff auditing training program for junior members which
   contributed to promotions for four out of six members in less than two years.

EDUCATION

B.B.A., Accounting, University of Wyoming, (Cheyenne, Wyoming), 1973

SANDRA L. BRILL
943 Westover Terrace
Bainbridge, Ohio 45800

Home: (112) 465-7923   Office: (112) 868-8881

OBJECTIVE

Secretary to senior executive who needs to make each moment count, with opportunity to
manage the executive's business schedule.

SUMMARY

Eight years of accomplishment in streamlining the schedules of top-level executives, and
producing an office environment that works smoothly, freeing the executive to pursue his
or her own goals.

WORK HISTORY

GRANITE GENERAL INSURANCE CORPORATION, Cleveland, Ohio   1980-1986

Executive Secretary to Vice President, Operations

o Created a system for scheduling regular visits by managers, supervisors and workers who
   reported to the Vice President. Result: more complete communication exchange in
   approximately one-third less time.

o Designed and implemented a system for scheduling regular teleconferences among office
   managers in 63 branch locations.

o Diplomatically handled important phone calls, thereby decreasing demand on the Vice
   President's time.

o Developed and maintained a business calendar that worked for the Vice President.

o Planned itineraries and arranged frequent nationwide trips which lasted for several
   weeks and included over 50 locations visited per trip; kept traveling time to a minimum.

o Planned and produced business meetings in which the Vice President met with other
   industry leaders; consistently praised for efficiency, hospitality and service.

o Planned logistics and coordinated semi-annual seminars in which the Vice President gave
   presentations to other executives, the CEO and the Board of Directors.

o Supervised a staff of three, including a receptionist and two secretaries who
   consistently produced projects within time constraints.

CLEVELAND HOSPITAL CENTER, Cleveland, Ohio   1977-1980

Executive Secretary to Chief Hospital Administrator

o Acted as liaison between diverse groups such as community representatives, medical
   staff, administrative staff and patients. Evaluated urgency of communication and
   negotiated meeting schedules to meet the needs of all groups.

o Coordinated logistics for workshops among branches of medical services.

o Devised and maintained personal and business schedule and calendar for the
   Administrator, resulting in no missed meetings in the two years of my tenure.

o Supervised an office clerk who maintained workable office filing systems.

PERSONAL

Married, no children. Interests include golf, racquetball and art.

- Just beginning, with little or no employment history.
- Seeking work in a creative or artistic field.
- Trying to minimize attention to your last job, or to emphasize what you did in an earlier position.
- Trying to deemphasize how often you have changed jobs because you fear being seen as a "job hopper."
- Trying to minimize your age, because you see yourself as either too young or too old to be taken seriously by employers.
- Trying to minimize the fact that you have not been promoted very often.

The advantage of the chronological resume is thus also its weakness. It is a widely used and accepted format. That means that it will not be seen as inappropriate. It also means that it is likely to be lost in the stack with all the others. The fundamental question therefore is: will this format bring out your strengths, or will it conceal them? The answer to this question should determine whether this is the approach for you, or whether you are better off using something else.

The Functional Format

The functional format is so named because it places more emphasis on what you can do — the functions you can perform, and perform unusually well — than on the job titles you have had. The essence of a functional resume is its emphasis on your skills and accomplishments. These accomplishments are grouped to bring out their consistency and quality, without concern for the job title you held at the time. Your employment history is usually added at the end, but in a very summary form.

The advantages of the functional resume are:

- *Its focus.* This format allows you to highlight your strengths. It lets you demonstrate your transferable skills, and show clearly that the same abilities have been used in a variety of settings. Most important, it allows you to pull these accomplishments from a variety of past jobs and focus them on the tasks of a position you have not held before.
- *Succinctness.* The functional resume presents important information in a very concise way. This is particularly useful if you want to keep everything on one page.
- *De-emphasis on employment history.* This is helpful if you have changed jobs frequently. It is also appropriate if the firms where you

worked are not well known, have poor reputations or are irrelevant to the industry you are trying to enter. Similarly, lapses in employment, demotions, terminations or the lack of a logical progression in your employment history are less obvious in this format.
- *Readability.* A functional resume shows some creativity, and is easy to skim quickly.

These advantages are also disadvantages, depending on who receives the resume and on the situation. Older executives and personnel professionals, particularly, attach a stigma to the functional resume. They assume anyone with such a resume has something to hide. Employment agencies also dislike this format, since it makes their job of documenting your work history more difficult. Some executives discount any accomplishments unless they know the company you were with at the time. Others don't like this approach because it is different, and they don't like *anything* that is unconventional.

This is probably the point to mention that one of us (Wegmann) for years had his students take various resumes to employers to see whether they thought them appropriate. What happened over and over was that the same resume, shown to employers in the same industry, would draw widely varying responses. One employer would say a given resume was great, another that it was all wrong. Tastes in resumes apparently vary as widely as tastes in everything else. Hence there is no perfect resume. Responses to a resume are as much a function of who sees it as of how it is constructed.

The Targeted Resume

The targeted resume is written for a specific job opening. This approach allows you to demonstrate how well you fit a particular position. To do this, you need to get either an interview or a great deal of information about the job before giving the firm your resume. This may not be particularly difficult, especially in the city in which you live. When you *are* asked for a resume (usually to show to someone whom you have not yet met), you then tailor it to what you have learned. You can now emphasize what you know the firm is looking for, and come across as particularly well matched to the position in question.

Gathering enough information about the job before you apply, or arranging an interview without a resume, will occasionally be difficult when dealing with major corporations. You don't want them to think you

CAROLYN S. CHOI
17237 Ravenwood
Mobile, Alabama 36524
Home: (205) 646-7233
Work: (205) 999-2864

OBJECTIVE

Project Engineering position with small to medium sized chemical company

SUMMARY

Five years of project engineering in chemical plants on projects ranging from $50,000 plant upgrade to $7 million dollar casting plant project.

ACCOMPLISHMENTS

Project Development

o Developed equipment specifications and physical layout for $7 million casting plant project resulting in 37% productivity increase during first year of operation.

o Developed schematic for upgrading plant power generation process, including cooling towers and auxiliary equipment.

Equipment Specification

o Specified boilers, heat exchangers, pumps and tanks for plant modification.

o Specified baghouse filters, dust collecting systems, pumps and agitators for 13 highly successful renovation projects.

o Specified quality control parameters for construction of cooling systems.

Process and Instrument Diagrams

o Recommended process and instrument diagram for casting plant; adopted with resulting cost savings of $1.2 million.

o Identified potential problems in process specifications and suggested alternative processes; result: several successful projects with no start-up problems.

o Prepared diagrams for plant's power generation project; result: improved system reliability.

Project Management and Design Engineering

o Developed schedule, manpower projection and cost control systems resulting in $750,000 cost savings over two year period.

o Prepared contracts and design parameters for project administration and construction.

WORK HISTORY

INTERNATIONAL CHEMICAL, Mobile, Alabama   1982-1986
    Lead Mechanical Engineer
WORTHAM CHEMICAL, Detroit, Michigan   1981-1982
    Project Engineer
WORTHAM CHEMICAL, EASTERN, Atlantic City, New Jersey   1977-1981
    Assistant Design Engineer

EDUCATION

Masters of Mechanical Engineering, 1981, Detroit City University, Detroit, Michigan.

Bachelor of Science, Mechanical Engineering, 1976, New Jersey City College, Atlantic City, New Jersey.

Registered Professional Engineer in Michigan.

144

DWIGHT M. CHILDS
7919 Stratford Dr.
St. Louis, MO 63292
Home: (314) 668-1910
Office: (314) 973-0120

OBJECTIVE

Financial management position in a medium to large corporation.

SUMMARY

Over eight years experience in the financial operations of a forty million dollar retail corporation. Experience includes accounting, control, debt management, financial planning and tax accounting.

ACCOMPLISHMENTS

FINANCIAL

o Analyzed variances between budget and expenditures and predicted a $1 million spending overage six months in advance, allowing corrective action.

o Did cash flow forecasts to enable senior management to evaluate business plans.

o Evaluated bank borrowing lines to minimize cost and plan debt programs.

o Directed borrowing program in excess of five million dollars; achieved economical interest rate and needed cash flexibility.

o Managed daily bank balances to avoid excess balances and increase interest income.

ACCOUNTING AND CONTROL

o Conceived and implemented changes in pension plan funding, reducing annual costs by $400,000.

o Managed accounting, accounts payable, payroll and data processing departments totaling 20 employees.

o Initiated new billing procedures which improved average collection time by 4 days.

o Absorbed the accounting functions of an acquired business, eliminating duplication and reducing overhead.

o Developed new credit procedures resulting in a 40% reduction in bad debt write-offs.

TAXES

o Successfully challenged a disallowance by the Internal Revenue Service of $35,000.

o Participated in a federal income tax audit, successfully substantiating report.

o Managed state and local tax reporting without penalties.

BUSINESS EXPERIENCE

National Jewelry Corporation

Assistant to Controller	1984-1986
Tax Manager	1981-1984
Cost Accountant	1979-1981

EDUCATION

Certified Public Accountant
B.B.A., University of California-Santa Barbara, Accounting, 1979

PERSONAL

Married - Four children

Interests - Fishing, gardening, writing

PHILLIP R. OSBORNE
82361 Emerson
Los Angeles, California 93714
(213) 317-7102 (Home)
(213) 526-3798 (Office)

OBJECTIVE

Human Resource Manager of a medium to large company

SUMMARY

Over 20 years experience in Human Resource administration; specialized experience in employee relations and compensation management in manufacturing plant setting.

ACCOMPLISHMENTS

Employee Relations

o Negotiated labor agreements for two plant locations within budget and without work interruption.

o Won 22 of 25 arbitration cases in unionized manufacturing plant. Resolved most grievances before they reached arbitration.

o Established alcohol and drug abuse programs.

o Clarified sick leave policies and added incentives that reduced absenteeism 16% at no additional expense.

o Designed and organized retirement seminars for employees approaching retirement age.

o Wrote and implemented affirmative action plans which produced placement rates of 22% per year and enabled the company to win $18 million in government contracts.

Compensation

o Directed an evaluation of all positions in 3000 employee firm.

o Developed a compensation system including new performance evaluation methods and standards; now used corporate-wide.

o Designed and implemented a system to record and correlate merit dollars, pay ranges and performance and to allocate annual merit budget based on correlations.

Acquisition Compensation Studies

o Reviewed 400 sales, manufacturing and staff positions at acquired subsidiary for redundancy.

o Analyzed compensation of subsidiary personnel; successfully integrated subsidiary into corporate system.

BUSINESS EXPERIENCE

Hot Chop Manufacturing Corporation

Manager of Employee Relations	1974-1985
Assistant Manager, Performance Evaluation	1967-1974
Compensation Specialist	1964-1967
Customer Service Coordinator	1958-1964

don't have one; you just don't want to give it to them until later. And, of course, you have to be willing to redo your resume each time you deal seriously with a new firm. A word processor helps.

The Creative Resume

This type of resume is, by definition, one which is quite untypical, and does not fit any of the categories discussed so far. Something like this is appropriate if you are in an artistic or other profession where it makes sense to demonstrate your creative abilities. One of us (Chapman) has a friend who is a public relations and media consultant, and does very innovative work. Her resume is written in the form of a press release that describes her skills and experience.

The Letter Resume

The letter resume simply puts the information from a resume into the form of a letter. It has the advantage of being more personalized, and more obviously addressed to a particular reader. It can also be written in a way that makes it less obvious, at least at first glance, that you are looking for a job. This can be an advantage, since secretaries often send any letter with a resume directly to the personnel office, so that the person to whom it is addressed never sees it.

The fundamental question is whether sending letter resumes to a large number of executives is likely to bring any response. It is our observation that this approach seems to be more acceptable, and to have better results, in very large metropolitan areas, but not elsewhere. If you live in or around New York, Chicago or Los Angeles, therefore, this can be an effective approach. In smaller cities, however, it is much less likely to make the kind of impression that will stimulate a favorable response.

The Curriculum Vitae

This form of resume is appropriate if you are looking for an academic or professional position (that is, for a job as a professor, research chemist or something of this sort). This resume is notably longer than the other forms, since it lists publications, professional papers presented, courses taught, professional references and so on. Academicians and researchers want this information; business people do not. If you are open to a position in either a business or academic setting, it would be wise for you to have two different resumes.

The Portfolio

For those working in creative fields such as art, design, photography, advertising and other areas where it is possible to present examples of what you have done, the portfolio is an appropriate resume substitute. Here you present some printed information which emphasizes where and with whom you studied, the dates and locations when your work has been displayed, references to any current displays or usage of your creations and so on. Then photographs of your work illustrate what you have done. This portfolio may literally be a large leather-bound container full of photos and illustrations.

Employment Data Sheets

If you are seeking a non-professional job and will be filling out a variety of job application forms, it can be helpful to prepare an employment data sheet. This one page summary contains your social security number, past employers and dates of employment, names and phone numbers of past supervisors, any licenses or certifications held and so on. If you pick up application forms at one or two personnel offices it will quickly become evident that most of them ask for essentially the same information. It's a great time-saver to have this data typed out on one or two sheets. You can copy what you need quickly and accurately onto any necessary forms. You *will* have to copy it, though. Personnel workers know where to look for the information they want on their own forms, and don't want to hunt through your version to find something. This may seem picky, but there's no use making life difficult for personnel people, since they probably have a stack of applications and can easily throw yours away if it's not done properly.

Writing Your Resume

Although there are several resume formats, each is largely made up of the same information arranged in a different order. We will, therefore, walk you through some important guidelines for each part of the chronological resume. When appropriate, you can adapt these directions to whichever other format you are using.

The Heading

Your name, address and phone number(s) go at the top of the resume. There is no need to put the word

"Resume" at the top of the page. The most common form for the heading has your name centered on top, and a line for each item that follows. It looks like this:

```
              Elliot Johnson
             2987 Hanson Drive
              Tucson, AZ 89341
               (831) 863-9825
            (831) 530-7329 (Home)
```

Notice that this form gives your home address, and then both your business (or daytime) phone and your home phone. You can vary this depending on where you want to receive mail, and where you are free to take phone calls. Avoid post office box addresses, though; they make some employers suspicious.

The above heading is in a conventional style, and has a pleasing appearance. However, it takes up four or five lines on the page, which uses up more space than you may want to invest, especially if you are trying to keep everything on one page. An alternative format puts this information on three lines by splitting the heading:

```
Elliot Johnson                   (831) 863-9825
2987 Hanson Drive          (831) 530-7329 (Home)
Tucson, AZ 89341
```

Either of these two headings, or any reasonable variant, will work; choose whatever fits your situation.

The Objective Statement

The objective statement is a short phrase or sentence describing the position you are seeking. It should be clear, concise and specific. Avoid industry jargon and technical terms if possible; some of the people who see your resume (personnel people or higher executives, for example) may not have technical backgrounds.

The objective statement is important, and should be written with care. If you have trouble with it, try to make the problem explicit. One possibility is that you are not completely clear about what you want. In that case you need to clarify your goals.

If you have decided that either of two positions would be acceptable, you will usually need a separate resume for each. If you want to work at an occupation which is found in two quite different industries, you might also be wise to prepare different resumes. Suppose you are a computer programmer with administrative experience, for example, applying for openings at both software houses and petrochemical firms. These industries are sufficiently different that they may use someone with your skills in different ways. Similarly, their needs might lead you to emphasize different training and experience.

Summary Statement

This section provides a summary of your qualifications for the job. If the reader is skimming quickly, and reads only your objective and summary statements, he or she should learn what you want and what you have to offer. It is crucial, therefore, that this summary statement clearly relate your strongest skills to the job you are seeking.

In one or two sentences, you have to communicate your work history, your skills and accomplishments and your prior experience (the industries where you have worked, and the jobs you have held). A good model is to fill in the blanks on a statement of this sort:

"Over _____ years of experience in the _____ [describe your past activities, such as sales, manufacturing, distribution or whatever] of _____ [describe the product or industry]. Demonstrated skills in _____ , _____ and _____ .

After the reader looks at your objective, he or she knows what you want. The next logical question is whether you are really qualified to do that job. The summary statement should argue that the answer is yes. It also needs to answer the question, "What are this person's strengths?" Finally, it should motivate the reader to take your application seriously enough to read the rest of the resume.

Business Experience

Here you summarize your work history. Employers want to know if you have any experience at the job you are seeking. This is a perfectly reasonable concern. Someone who has done the job before is more likely to "hit the ground running." An experienced person has usually developed efficient ways to get things done, and should be able to avoid common mistakes. An inexperienced person, on the other hand, must be trained, will not at first be very productive and will have much to learn from experience (often at the employer's expense).

Your work history includes the names of the firms where you have worked, the city where the firm (or branch office) was located, the job title and the dates of employment.

Here are some guidelines to follow when organizing this information:

- List your work assignments in reverse order, giving the most recent first. Put down the company name (include the parent corporation if there was one), location, job title and dates. For example:

```
-- Montgomery Ward (Mobil Corp.), Chicago, IL
   Buyer (Men's Clothing), 1982-1987.
```
or
```
SEARS ROEBUCK AND COMPANY        1978- 1982
Chicago, Illinois
Buyer (Children's Apparel)
```

- If your job title is not completely descriptive, put explanatory information in parentheses.
- If your firm used an unusual job title not found at other companies, put a more common title or explanation in parentheses.
- Avoid using initials unless they are the official company name. For example, not everyone would know that DEC stands for Digital Equipment Corporation.
- If you held a long series of job titles over a period of several years, be explicit about the most recent ones and cover the older titles with a summary phrase. "Various sales and supervisory positions," for example.

If you are using the chronological format, accomplishment statements should follow each job title. Concentrate on your most recent positions, since employers will be most interested in what you have produced lately.

Accomplishment Statements

Accomplishment statements are critical in a resume. They are the evidence for what you can do, and do unusually well. They are the difference between 20 years of experience and one year of experience repeated 20 times. They provide evidence that you really did something in prior jobs besides putting in time and warming a seat.

The wise and effective use of accomplishment statements is what makes a good resume. Here is where you demonstrate what the company is likely to get for its money if you are hired. In today's competitive labor market, there are other candidates who have the same degrees and work experience as you do. What you must stress, therefore, is your ability to get things done.

If you have contributed to the success of past employers, it is a reasonable assumption that you will contribute to the success of your next employer. Anyone who is considering offering you a job wants to know what results you are likely to produce, and the only convincing evidence you can offer to address this concern is what you have produced in the past.

You need, therefore, to return to Chapter Four and review the list of accomplishments you wrote up in Exercise 4-1. Look carefully for activities that are clearly relevant to what will be required in the job you are now seeking.

Condense what you did into one sentence, and keep that sentence as short as you can. Remember: you are not trying to tell the reader everything, only enough of the story to convince him or her you are someone who should be seen in person. Get some help from a friend if you need it, and re-write these sentences until they are succinct, clear, fact-filled and interesting.

Here are some guidelines to follow:

- Start with one or more action verbs that accurately convey the significance and magnitude of what you did. For example, "Designed, implemented and successfully operated" suggests a more important role than "Installed."
- Then summarize what happened as a result of your action. Give the results, known in the trade as "the bottom line": improved sales, expansion to new markets, more production with fewer expenses or whatever.
- If at all possible, include a numerical measurement of what you produced (percents, dollars or numbers of new customers).
- Prepare 10 or 15 accomplishment statements before doing your resume. Then carefully choose the ones you actually want to use. Put your best ones first (by best we refer both to the quality of what you produced, and also to what is most clearly relevant to the job you are now seeking).
- Do your best to hold the length of any accomplishment statement to no more than two typed lines.
- Avoid technical jargon; write so anyone can read and understand what you did.

- Avoid abbreviations, especially those common in your old firm but possibly meaningless to anyone else.
- Do not put down anything that might be seen as proprietary data (that is, information to which your old firm has a legal and exclusive right). Former CIA operatives face a similar restriction on descriptions of their activities.
- Do not exaggerate or embellish. If other employers happen to know your old boss and call to ask about your participation in some successful activity, they should get the same impression they got from your resume.
- If the accomplishment was really the result of a group effort, make this clear. But make your contribution to that effort equally clear. Employers are very interested in what you have done successfully as part of a team effort, both as a team member and a team leader.

There are a wide variety of accomplishment statements in the sample resumes. Review these before writing your own.

Education

The part of the resume that describes your formal education should be brief. Use one line for each college degree you earned. Here are some guidelines to follow when writing this section:

- The most recent degree should be listed first.
- Give the name of the institution which awarded the degree, the degree itself (B.A., M.B.A. or whatever), the major area of study and the date of graduation. If the institution is not well known, list the city in which it is located. For example: Yale University, M.A., Economics, 1963; Appalachian State University (Boone, NC), B.A., Economics, 1961.
- List *completed* degrees only. Include professional licenses and certificates (to provide psychological services, operate a public radio station, teach, act as an engineer or whatever) where applicable.
- Omit training programs unless they are directly related to the job you are seeking, and were long and significant enough to be taken seriously. A graduate course at a major university might meet this requirement; a one-day training seminar would not.

We recommend that you omit this section entirely if you do not have a college degree. If you are developing a data sheet to use in filling out job application forms, however, you should include information about the high schools you attended, and any other schooling you have taken, even if the entire program was not completed. Most job application forms will ask for this information, with dates.

Because of recent publicity about individuals whose resumes listed degrees which they never received, a number of businesses now routinely verify any degrees claimed. It is essential, therefore, that everything in this part of your resume be clear and accurate. If the employer suspects you are fudging here, everything else you say will also be called into question.

The education section is ordinarily placed toward the end of the resume. This is because employers ordinarily care much more about your recent work experience than about your formal education. There are exceptions, however. If you have a Harvard M.B.A., or are a recent college graduate with little work experience, it might be to your advantage to move the education section toward the front.

Personal Data

This is an optional section, but it can be to your advantage to include it. Any information that gives the reader an image of you as an active, interesting, successful person can make a good impression. In a targeted resume, anything that you have in common with the person who hires is also worth listing.

Choose what you put in this section with care. You have no legal or ethical responsibility to say anything about your family, age, religion, race, height, weight, hobbies or anything else of this nature. It is, in fact, illegal for the employer to ask about many of these topics, since they could be the basis for discrimination. So, if you choose to include a personal section in your resume, be sure to select only those facts which you believe will demonstrate to the employer that you are the kind of active, enthusiastic, energetic person who would do particularly well at the job in question.

References

References should not be listed on your resume. Instead, prepare a list of references and put it on a separate sheet to use when the discussion with an employer gets serious, and a reference list is specifically requested. We recommend you use the same type and quality of paper for this list as you used for the resume.

A Final Note

If you have never done one, writing a resume requires a certain amount of work. Since this entire book deals with life-time adult survival skills, think of your resume as the first draft of an evolving document. As the years go by you will hold new jobs, develop new skills, acquire experience and become more productive. Your resume will evolve accordingly. If you can write it on a word processor, so much the better. Update it once or twice a year, so it is ready whenever needed.

SECTION IV.

ARRANGING INTERVIEWS

Introduction to Section IV

An intelligent, informed decision about what position to seek, and where to seek it, is based on a careful consideration of what you do best, and what employers need. If you have gathered this information, and balanced your needs against those of employers, you have now cleared the first major hurdle. You have identified a job which you could do well, and for which there is demand. Now your goal is to be offered that job.

This takes you into the search phase. You have decided what you want. Now you have to get it. This is "sweaty palms" time. It's also the time when all you've done so far really starts to pay off.

To generate a job offer, you must successfully complete two final steps. First, you have to arrange meetings with those who hire. Second, you have to tell them clearly and convincingly what you do well, so they offer you the position you want.

This section will review the various ways to obtain employment interviews. Section V will then discuss how to handle those interviews effectively, negotiate the details of a job offer and get off to a good start in your new position.

As you prepare to seek employment interviews, your first challenge is deciding how to go about it. As a practical matter, you can adopt one or more of the following methods: (1) use a personal approach; ask for appointments with employers whom you know, or to whom you can be introduced; (2) be methodical; approach one employer after another, not knowing which have openings, until you find something; or (3) use a person or institution which gathers lists of openings, such as the want ads, an employment agency or a school placement office.

Each of these methods is widely used, and each can lead to an interview. If you took a survey of the American workforce, asking people how they got their present jobs, you would find that roughly a third of them used each method. However — and this is the key point — there is a relationship between the search method used and the quality of job obtained. On average, the best jobs are obtained by using personal approaches, the second best by methodically approaching one employer after another and the worst through intermediaries. What you get depends on how you get it.

Things, in other words, are not as they seem. In a logical world, the reasonable procedure would be to go someplace where employers and the unemployed are routinely brought together. It is essential to understand that that's not what happens, and for good reason.

Employers are more concerned about whom to hire than most of us realize. Many employers have hired people who stole from them, or who could not get along with their customers and other employees, or who came in late or not at all or who disappeared one day without notice, leaving them in the lurch. Once burned, twice wary. Employers hire nervously. A bad hiring decision can ruin a business. This is especially true in a small or medium sized firm, which is where so many employment opportunities are found today. Hard though it is to believe, an employer may actually be more uncomfortable and uncertain than you are during a job interview.

At the heart of planning a successful job search, therefore, is the ability to look at things from the employer's point of view. When there is an opening to be filled, the employer's major worry is not how to locate a large group of applicants. In these days of high unemployment, that's easy enough. What the employer really wants is a few good applicants who can be trusted, and about whom something is know. Like the Marines, employers just want a few good people.

But that's not what an employer gets from a want ad. What an ad typically produces is a deluge of applications from unknown people of uncertain ability. Many people will answer an ad even when they are not even close to having the qualifications the job demands. In addition, those who are out of work are often strongly tempted to lie (or at least greatly exaggerate) on their resumes and in job interviews. To compound the problem, people given as references fear lawsuits and are therefore hesitant to reveal anything negative about a former employee. As a result, it can be difficult to distinguish the suitable applicants from the inadequate. The employer therefore proceeds warily.

Remember: the most desirable positions are those in which you do significant work. It is precisely when filling these positions that the employer can really get hurt if the wrong person is hired. Hence, if at all possible, good jobs are filled by promotion. Present employees are much better known than new applicants. However, if no current employee is able to handle the opening, the next most attractive route is to hire through personal recommendations and referrals. Failing this, an employer can hire an individual who came in on his or her own initiative and made a good impression.

Brokers and intermediaries are largely used as a last resort. Employers tend to turn to them when there is a problem. Sometimes the problem is that the job is distasteful and ill paid. In other cases the position demands exceptionally high levels of skill and experience, so that only a small number of people can fill it. There are, of course, exceptions. College placement offices, for example, handle many very desirable positions. On the whole, though, intermediaries handle the leftover jobs.

Things are thus not as they seem. What looks like the obvious way to discover what jobs are available turns out to be both inadequate and incomplete. Want ads and other intermediaries give a distorted picture of the positions which are open at any given time. Most employers, after all, are not required to tell anyone they have a job to fill. As a result, there is no central register of openings, no one place you can go to review all available jobs, or even a high proportion of them.

Under these conditions, what do you do? The answer to that is obvious: you keep on reading this book. What is most important, as you begin your job search efforts, is that you act in a way which has the highest probability of getting you a good position, and getting it within a reasonable period of time.

Nine. It's Not Who You Know, It's Who You Meet

This chapter deals with the hiring method preferred by both employers and those seeking employment: the informal, word of mouth approach. There are good reasons for this preference. When a friend recommends you for a position, especially if it is at the place where he or she works, both you and the employer go into the interview with trustworthy information about each other. More knowledge leads to better decisions. Large corporations have discovered that new hires referred to them by other employees stay longer than those hired in other ways.

The higher a position's pay and responsibility, the more likely it will be filled by an "insider" rather than through an advertisement or public notice. There are exceptions, of course. The law requires that certain jobs be publicly advertised, particularly those in government agencies or funded with government money. Even then, however, the candidate who is known by the supervisor or is recommended by someone of stature is more likely to be hired than an unknown who replies to a published notice.

It would be natural to assume that referral to such openings is available only to those with "connections." This turns out not to be true. In a study of professionals who had recently changed jobs, Mark Granovetter discovered an important pattern. Although many learned about their new positions through personal contacts, most of those contacts were people whom they didn't know very well. Often the informants were met by chance, had not been seen for months and had never been particularly close friends. Yet these chance meetings provided the information which led to a new job. Granovetter was so struck by this pattern that he called it "the strength of weak ties."

The important point, then, is that you do not have to be rich or well-connected. Anyone who works at it can penetrate the informal networks found in any industry, and obtain information about available openings. You go from person to person, meeting new people and learning what you need to know. You can do this whether or not you have a large group of well-connected friends and relatives to draw on. You did this when interviewing people to get the information you needed to decide what job to seek. You can do it

again to get the referrals which will lead to employment interviews.

The Referral Interview

It is essential to have a clear idea of what you will be doing in these meetings. Your goal is to discover where a specific job opening can be found or created, and who to see about it. You want referrals to people who are looking for, or at least could use, someone with your skills.

It is these owners, managers and executives who have the power to hire, and also the knowledge and influence to refer you effectively to others. Their names will open doors, and get you through secretaries. As an individual rises in a corporation or agency, he or she spends more time outside the organization. Such persons are, as a result, more likely to be aware of openings in both their own and other settings.

Your goal, then, is to meet with employers to talk about job possibilities. You are not necessarily applying for a job, since there may not be one available. You are explaining what job you have decided to seek, and asking for advice and information as you try to find an opening.

There is a real ambiguity here. The situation is much like meeting a single person at a cocktail party. He or she is introduced, and is attractive. The conversation goes well. But you don't know whether this new acquaintance is equally attracted to you. Nor do you know if he or she is romantically involved with someone else. So you play it by ear. You may eventually end up with a nice conversation, a social acquaintance, a date or a spouse, depending on how things go.

The same ambiguity is present at the beginning of a referral interview. You present yourself and your goals. Then, depending on the impression you make and the present needs of the executive, one of a number of outcomes may develop. Handling this exchange takes a certain subtlety and tolerance for ambiguity. But then, so do most good jobs.

Referral interviews are usually short: often 15 to 20 minutes, and rarely more than half an hour. They are with those who have the power to hire for the job you want, or with others who can lead you to these people. Sometimes they are with executives who are a level or two above the person to whom you would report if hired. In other cases they are with those who can introduce you to people you want to meet, and brief you on the firms in which you are interested.

This does not imply that you should not be talking to other people about your job search activities. As you meet friends and acquaintances, use the opportunity to give them a quick summary of what you want. Close with a cheerful, "Call me if you run across anything I should know about, will you?" You never know who might be aware of a good job possibility.

Your formal meetings, however, will usually be with carefully chosen individuals who are in a position to be of most help. It is important that you give some thought to what is happening in these meetings. More than anything else, you need to let the person you're seeing get to know you. Your major concern must be making a favorable impression. Unless you do, no highly placed person is going to risk his or her reputation by referring you to someone else. Only after establishing trust and rapport can you successfully ask for information and advice on how to find the position you want.

Good general managers are highly skilled at building relationships and exchanging information and favors. In this regard, you are an amateur dealing with a professional. The reason a good manager is able to get things done is that he or she understands how to meet the needs of others, build trust and ask the right person in the right way for help when needed.

Nothing will happen until the executive to whom you're speaking is convinced you are serious, capable and trustworthy. If so, he or she will be happy to consider you for an opening or refer you to others who might be able to use you. Indeed, you can probably judge the impression you've made by the referrals that result. No referral or a suggestion you join an organization or do further reading usually suggests you were judged not yet qualified for what you're seeking. Referral to someone at a lower level is more positive. If an executive sends you to his or her peers, you really went over well.

Obtaining the Referral Interview

You arrange referral interviews the same way you obtained informational interviews: you ask for them, using the name of someone whom the executive knows. Because you are dealing with persons at a higher level of responsibility, however, this will fre-

quently take more persistence. Managers are often protected by zealous secretaries who turn away anyone who might take up his or her time. You need to develop some skill at convincing secretaries to put your call through, or better yet give you an appointment with the person you want to see.

This will be easier if your request is properly prepared. First, list the people you want to meet. They will often be at or near the top of the corporations, agencies or organizations in which you are interested. In large organizations, they will be one to three levels above the position you want. Then look for someone who will recommend you to each of these people.

Review everyone you met when you were interviewing for information, everyone you know socially, the alumni list from your school or college and so on. Go back to the switchboard people (your priest, minister or rabbi; your banker; the heads of any professional organizations in the field) who helped "plug you in" when you were gathering information. Let them know what you learned, the decisions you've made and the job you are now seeking.

If you keep at it, you can usually find a referral source whom you know, even if only slightly. Remember, the whole idea is to use *weak* ties effectively. Stick with it until you find someone whose name would be recognized by each person you want to see.

Then, once you have a referral, write a note to the person you want to meet. Explain why you want to get together, and that you will be phoning shortly. A sample letter is on the next page.

Allow a day or two for the letter to be delivered. Then phone for an appointment. Explain to the secretary that you have recently written Mr. Makemoney on the recommendation of Mike Gregarious, so he is expecting you to call. Ask the secretary to either give you an appointment, or let you talk to him so you can ask personally for a time when you could meet.

Sometimes it is better to get together outside of work. Breakfast or luncheon meetings can be good settings in which to get the information and referrals you need. A professional meeting, a charity event or any other situation where you can arrange to be introduced by a mutual acquaintance will also give you a chance to explain your situation and ask for assistance.

Why Should They Help?

Referral interviewing can be a slow process. You will hit some dead ends. Some people will be far more helpful

John H. Makemoney
Multiplicative Enterprises
St. Louis, MO 63137

Dear Mr. Makemoney:

In a recent conversation with Mike Gregarious,
the president of St. Louis Financial Facil-
itators, your name came up as someone I needed
to meet.

I've recently come to St. Louis from Arkansas
after finishing my degree in finance at Little-
town State. I asked Mike about the opportunities here in St. Louis. Finance has always
been an intense interest of mine, and I am
trying to learn as much as I can about the St.
Louis financial community, since this is where
I want to live and work.

Mike graciously answered as many of my questions as he could, and then suggested that you
were one of the most informed people in this
area. He said you could undoubtedly provide me
with an excellent overview, and could easily
answer some of the questions he couldn't.

I will phone your office in a day or two to see
if you could spare 15 or 20 minutes. After all
Mike said about you, I'm really looking forward
to meeting you in person.

Sincerely,

George H. Jobseeker

than others. It's like fishing. Some days you hit, some days you don't. You just have to have faith that the fish are there. When you get to the right place at the right time, the match will occur.

Why should these individuals want to help you? They may simply be good and friendly people. In addition, however, it is the nature of managerial positions that they are filled by people who build networks of contacts with whom they cooperate, and from whom they receive invaluable information and assistance.

Those who hold lower level jobs in an organization are often primarily concerned with technical matters: how to run a machine, or keep the accounting straight, or the forms in order. As you go higher, however, people spend their time differently. They deal with the people problems. They coordinate, settle interpersonal conflicts and try to get the right person in the right job. It is in the self-interest of managers and executives to meet qualified newcomers (and old-timers, for that matter) in their fields. The ability to put people in touch with each other, and to build credits by helping others do the same, is at the heart of their jobs.

That doesn't mean you can just come in and ask one of these executives for a job. There may not be a position open. Nor can they predict whether someone they suggest you see will want to hire you. Further, there is a natural tendency to resent being asked to do something one is unable to do. The whole art of referral interviewing, therefore, is to let these executives get to know you and what you have to offer. You should never put them on the spot by directly asking for a job. When you made the appointment, you didn't ask for a job interview; you asked for information.

The referral interview does give the decision-maker an opportunity to "window-shop." He or she can get a sense of what you're like, and what you have to offer, with no obligation to offer you employment. What happens next is up to him or her. Explain who you are and what you're doing, ask for information and advice and then let the conversation go where it will.

People who are at high levels in any field receive a great deal of information. In most cases, you will get solidly based advice from them. Once someone has given you suggestions, his or her good judgment is at stake. It becomes important, at least in some small way, that this advice work out well. There is also a natural curiosity to find out what happened to you, and therefore a willingness to keep in touch. You now have another member for your contact network. It may take dozens of these interviews but, done effectively, the effort can lead to a wealth of information about job possibilities.

Newly Created Positions

Sometimes, if you make a good impression and there either happens to be an open position, or the executive has been thinking about creating one, you will be told there is a chance of being hired. You are now in a preliminary job interview. Your goal is to continue to make a good impression, and to be invited back for a second interview.

A newly created position is a major goal of your efforts. All managers and executives face problems. They are also aware of opportunities. Often these problems and opportunities have not been addressed because of other pressing demands. If, however, the right person comes along, an opening can be created and the new hire turned loose to get something done.

Part of being in the right place at the right time is finding a problem or opportunity that you want to address, and an employer who sees things the same way. Referral interviewing is a search for such a match.

Obviously, you won't hit this situation every time. More commonly, you will present yourself, ask advice and talk about the field. Try hard to be sure your source learns something of value from you in the course of the conversation. If you make a good impression, the person to whom you are speaking will name others with whom you might profitably speak. Write down their names and ask permission to mention the source of the referral.

If no names or ideas come up spontaneously by the end of the conversation, bring the subject up yourself. Do it gently, however. You are asking a great favor. By letting you use his or her name, an executive is implicitly endorsing you and your goals. It is no small thing for someone to give you access to a personal network of contacts which is a critical factor in his or her own success.

If you really have not made that strong an impression, you may not be given a referral; alternatively, you may be sent to someone of no importance, who will be of little or no help. (If this happens consistently, you need to pull back and take a look at what you're doing. Either your goals or your self-presentation need to be reconsidered.)

In these meetings, as in any thoughtful exchange, there is a real value to responsive, intelligent listening. You want to present relevant facts about yourself, but most of all you want to share the thoughts of an experienced and knowledgeable person. If you are told something you don't understand, ask for clarification. If you hear something inconsistent with what you have read or been told, politely ask about the discrepancy. The more thoughtful and involved the exchange, the better the impression you are going to make.

Businesses Large and Small

When seeking referral interviews, do not limit yourself to the larger firms. Major corporations are very visible. Just as they get more job applications, their executives also get more requests for referral interviews. Hence you will find many of them resistant. They don't mind doing this occasionally, but they can't spare the time to do it too often.

In smaller firms, however, such requests are much less common. Yet the owners often have some fine contacts and much information about the field. They can offer you good leads. There are many job opportunities in small businesses, often with more freedom than can be found in most large, highly structured corporations. It makes sense to invest some time learning about these opportunities.

Go after the large corporations if you wish; just don't do so exclusively. Even if you think that's where you want to work, you may find it hard to get in directly. Take your time, and look for people with close connections to the appropriate executives. Someone you contact in a smaller business, perhaps a supplier to a major corporation, may provide you with the key referral.

Look for a Subtle Shift in Perspective

How do you know, in a referral interview, when the person to whom you're speaking is seriously considering you for a job (either an opening or a newly-created position)? You can't always tell for sure, but there are certain signs. Among these are: an intense probing of your ideas; talking at length about the company's problems; introducing you to others in the office; bringing up a position different from the one you are seeking; or letting the interview go beyond half an hour. Knowing when an executive to whom you're speaking is beginning to seriously consider you for a position with his or her firm is a matter of judgment. It is often not easy to tell.

If the employer does make it clear that hiring you is a real possibility, you need to know if he or she wants to move into a job interview now or, as is more common, wants to schedule another meeting at a later date. To find out, you can say something like, "This sounds like something I would be very interested in. Should we discuss it now, or would you rather set up a time when we can get together again?"

If you are not sure that the employer is considering you for a position, but have some indications in this direction, try something like, "I'm interested in what you've been saying. Would you like me to put some ideas on paper about how your firm could exploit this opportunity, and how I could contribute? I could send it to you to look over, and then call and set up a time when we could talk about it." This won't guarantee you a job, but if you get a positive response it means that at your next interview you will definitely be talking about the possibility of one.

It is possible that, for an entry level job, you could be offered a position on the spot. This is uncommon, however, and will rarely happen if a more advanced position is involved.

After the Interview

After the referral interview is over, be sure to send a thank you letter. In this letter, mention one or two significant things you learned. Express your appreciation for the information and advice you received. If you were referred to others, be specific about how you are going to follow up on the referral.

Send a thank you letter even if the interview didn't seem to go well. You never know how your informant experienced things, and the letter itself may change his or her perception.

Use personal letterhead stationery with your address and phone number printed on it. Many executives will set your letter aside. If they come across a job possibility later, they will pull it out and phone or write you. You want them to be able to find you easily.

If you forgot to mention something during the interview, put it in the letter. If you think you gave a wrong impression, correct it in the letter. When the interview did go well, let the person know how much you appreciated the exchange. Do not hesitate to mention that you intend to call if a need for more information develops during your search efforts.

Keep a list of everyone to whom you speak. If you are meeting the top people in your field and making good impressions on them, job interviews will develop. When they do, you will need information on specific firms and people. Much of that information will come from your contact network. It can be invaluable to speak to the right person just before a job interview. He or she may know quite a bit about the person who will be interviewing you, or the company or agency where you are being considered.

Do It

On the next page is a sheet to use as you begin seeking referral interviews. You may already know some of the managers and executives you need to see. More often, you will need to contact others who know them, to get an introduction. List the people you need to contact, and then go see them.

Once you get into the process it will become self-generating. The top people in any field know each other, and can easily refer you around. Although it takes time to get the process started, it also develops its own momentum. For a month or two after you've taken a new job, you will continue to get calls about employment possibilities.

Referral Interview List

Person to Be Seen   Persons Who Might Know Them

_____   _____

_____   _____

_____   _____

_____   _____

_____   _____

_____   _____

_____   _____

_____   _____

_____   _____

_____   _____

_____   _____

_____   _____

_____   _____

_____   _____

_____   _____

_____   _____

_____   _____

_____   _____

_____   _____

_____   _____

Ten. Obtaining Job Interviews: The Cold Call

One of the themes of this book is that a job search is, to a large extent, an information search. One of the most important pieces of information, and the most most difficult to obtain, is *where* job openings can be found.

About 30% of the country's jobs come open in any given year. If you are in a helicopter, looking down on the city in which you live, you can be sure there are unfilled jobs down there *somewhere*. The problem is that you don't have any idea where.

To find an employer who needs you, you can try to penetrate the informal networks where knowledge about openings exists, as the last chapter recommended. Or you can go directly to an employer and ask if there are any openings, which is the process this chapter will discuss.

What we are talking about is known to sales people as "cold calling." It is also called the "direct approach" method. The approach to an employer is "cold" because you have no idea whether there is an opening and no referral by someone the employer knows. You go from one employer to another, hoping to run across something, and trying to make a favorable impression.

The Numbers Game

You are involved in a "numbers game." If you approach enough employers, you will eventually come across an opening and obtain an interview for it. The more common the job sought, the more quickly an opening can usually be found. Also, the more specific your skills and the higher the demand for them, the easier it will be to get an interview.

What you are doing, in effect, is taking a sample. If four out of every 100 businesses have job openings of the type you want on any given day, and you contact 100 businesses a week for several weeks, you should find around four openings a week, at least on average. This sample need not be random. In fact, it makes more sense to set up criteria of size, location and so on, and approach the most attractive firms first.

There is nothing novel about trying to find work this way. People have been looking for work by "hitting the bricks" for many, many years. It is a riskier search method than using referrals, because you usually know much less about what a firm is like. For many jobs, however, it may be faster. You have to make your own decision about how to handle this tradeoff.

As a personal experience, directly approaching one employer after another can be pretty discouraging. If four employers out of 100 have an opening, you not only have to deal with the four places which have the openings, but with the 96 that don't. This can be a time-consuming and tiring process. Not all of these 96 will be friendly and helpful. For someone who is sensitive to rejection, constantly approaching strangers who say no can be distasteful and even devastating. Studies find it is unusual for most unemployed people to contact more than two or three employers a week. At that rate, of course, it can take a long time to find an opening, and even longer to find one where the job is offered and accepted.

Recall the degree to which new job creation is concentrated in small and medium sized businesses. To every employer, but especially to the small employer, hiring is a very personal process. The quality of person hired can make or break the business. Hence a preference for people who are personally recommended. In addition, given their small size, the odds are against you at any one place. You have to approach a large number of small employers to find an appropriate opening.

Make a Proposal

If you have had a series of referral interviews, some of the employers to whom you've spoken will call you back. Others will tell colleagues about you. You may get a call from someone you don't even know to explore a possibility, because he or she heard about you from someone to whom you spoke earlier.

You need not leave all the initiative in the hands of employers. Depending on the skills and experience you have to offer, you can re-approach those you met (particularly the ones to whom you were most attracted), and make a proposal. Outline what you would like to do for them, and the results you could produce. Alternatively, you can do some research on other employers you have not yet met, and approach them with proposals. If you make several, and if they are well thought out and meet real needs, you should have a good chance for a positive response.

The "Numbers Game," Mail Version

You may be in a situation where you have not done much referral interviewing. The type of job you want may not lend itself to proposal-making. Or you may be applying for a job from a distance, without being able to travel frequently to your target area. What then?

One effective approach is to make a marketing trip. Choose a city in which you would like to live, and where demand for your occupation is good. Then contact employers, using the fact that you will be in town for only a short time as a good reason for granting an appointment. The fact that you are coming from somewhere else can give you remarkable leverage in arranging interviews.

One workable approach when dealing with employers at a distance is to mail your resume ahead to a carefully chosen group of firms. Names and addresses can be obtained from the sources discussed in Chapter Seven. The letter should give some of your strengths. It must make it clear that the employer has something to gain by seeing you. Mention that you will be in town shortly, and will phone to see about getting together. Perhaps you can make this trip during your vacation time. The letter to the fictional Mr. Runsit is a sample of such a letter.

Upon arrival in town, begin calling the employers to whom you've written. Even if only one in twenty agrees to see you, you will have several interviews. You may, of course, get a much better or a much worse response, depending on your skills, the impact of your letter and the supply/demand relationship in the city's labor market.

Another approach is to phone ahead. Sometimes "I'm calling long distance" or "I'm going to be in town in two weeks" gets people's attention, and helps to get an interview.

The "Numbers Game," Phone Version

Depending on the kind of job you are seeking, you may be able to find openings through a telephone survey. Phoning is more effective than writing letters. It is certainly the preferable first approach if you are seeking work in your own city. It can also work well in setting up appointments from a distance. It is the method of choice for reaching small and medium sized employers, since it lets your fingers do the driving.

Because of their size, openings at any one small

```
Thomas P. Runsit
Supervisor, Sales Department
Absorbent Towel, Inc.
Parsippany, NJ 07054

Dear Mr. Runsit:

As a sales representative for Conglomerate
Clothing, I have had the opportunity to market
a wide range of clothing items, including
towels and bath accessories. Over the last five
years my sales record has consistently advanced
at least 20% each year.

Part of this success has come from carefully
researching potential new markets. I have been
trying several new ideas in the towel area with
considerable success, and would like to
specialize in this area of marketing.

For family reasons, relocation to New Jersey
would be desirable. We will be spending the
week of September 2-7 on vacation in your area.
I will phone you shortly after arrival to see
if we could get together. I look forward to
meeting you and sharing ideas on how to
approach some interesting new markets.


        Sincerely,


        Robert L. Jobseeker
```

business will not come up that frequently. You may, in fact, want to avoid calling those with only two or three employees. Many of these are family businesses which are unlikely to hire you. On the other hand, a large proportion of new jobs are being created in firms with fewer than 20 employees. It is not difficult to phone 30 or more small and medium sized businesses over a couple of hours, and one or more in this group should be willing to see you.

One government study found that over 70% of all businesses, regardless of size, had at least one opening during a six month period. So openings do exist. It's mostly a matter of chance whether you happen to call the right business at the right time.

If you have access to a local business directory, you can phone and immediately ask for the owner or manager by name. If not, use the Yellow Pages. When you reach a business, ask to speak to the manager (unless the person who usually hires for the kind of job you want typically has a different title, in which case you ask for that person). Be sure to get the manager's name, and write it down. If he or she is not in, call back later and, this time, ask for him or her directly. If he or she is in, it's better to have the name as you begin the conversation.

Be sure to give your name also, and immediately explain who you are. It is an essential part of the psychology of telephone communication that two people who know each other's names, and address each other by name, take the conversation more seriously.

Once you reach the person who does the hiring, mention the job you are seeking and one or two of your qualifications. You don't want to be interviewed over the phone, but you do want to come across as a qualified candidate. Ask if there is a time when you could stop by in person. If there is an opening, or even a good possibility of one, there is a good chance you will be invited to come in and discuss it.

Even if there is no opening, and no apparent probability of one soon, keep a record of the people you talk to. You can call the same list again in a month or so. Given the high degree of turnover in the American labor market, an opening may well come up unexpectedly in the weeks ahead in at least one of these places.

This method of surveying small and medium sized employers is tedious, since most will reply that they have no openings. It is also more difficult than it used to be. Many people today are selling things by phone, often to the irritation of employers, who are frequently interrupted when they are trying to get some work done.

However, it does work. Properly used, telemarketing is a very effective sales tool. Your results will be particularly good if you come across well on the phone, and can make your call stand out from the others.

Phoning methodically for an hour or two will usually produce at least one job interview, and sometimes several. Those who have kept records when using this method find an average of roughly one interview granted per 20 or 30 calls. This will vary, of course, depending on the job being sought, the local employment situation, how comfortably you deal with strangers and your telephone skills. Once an interview is granted, of course, you will have to move quickly to learn all you can about the employer before the interview.

Phoning Major Corporations

Although phoning works well with small employers, the situation when contacting large corporations is more complicated. Unlike small firms, where the owner or manager hires directly, major corporations typically have personnel departments. Here hiring is usually a three-step process.

The personnel department first receives written job applications. Personnel officials, when reviewing these applications, are particularly interested in a person's work history. They react negatively to frequent changes of employer, and unexplained gaps in the applicant's work history (was the person in prison? in an institution? living off someone else?). They look for successful experience at the same job as the one that's open. They tend to be unreceptive to career changers.

Personnel interviewers then meet with the applicants who look best on paper. Two or three of those who seem fully qualified are sent on to the department head, who decides which one will be hired.

At the first two of these steps (application form and personnel interview) you can be "screened out." Since there are typically many applicants, anything negative usually leads to rejection. Only at the third step (interview by the supervisor) can you be hired.

Studies show that personnel departments often do not know of all available openings. Indeed, even in medium sized companies there may be no one individual who does. The best approach when dealing with large firms, therefore, is to begin by obtaining the name of the person for whom you would be working. Think of the large corporation as a collection of small, semi-independent parts. You want to go directly to the person in charge of the section where someone with your skills would work. Call the switchboard or some other office in the corporation, and ask for his or her name and phone number.

Then phone that person. Explain your interest in a position, and give one or two quick qualifications. Ask if you can come over and meet with him or her. If so, fine. If told there are no openings, request a meeting anyway. In a large company, openings often occur with some regularity. You want to be considered for the next available possibility. It can be worth the effort to meet the person in charge even if nothing is immediately available.

Because managers are busy, they may not be willing to see applicants who have not gone through the personnel office first. Some will refer you to the personnel department despite your best efforts to avoid this.

In that case, try hard to find out if there are any openings now, or are likely to be in the near future. You need this information to decide whether it is worth your time to go to the personnel office and fill out the application forms.

Do *not* simply phone personnel and ask if they are "taking applications." Many offices routinely have the unemployed fill out applications even though no suitable jobs are available, and there is little likelihood that any will be in the near future (when there is a list of employees on layoff who must be called back before anyone new can be hired, for example). Leaving a form on file without talking to someone is often a waste of time. Making a good impression in person can give you a head start on the next opening; having a form on file with hundreds of others is much less likely to bring an interview.

Remember: people hire people. Paper is far less likely to get you a job than personal contact. One way or another, you've got to get into direct contact with those who have the authority to hire, or at least with the personnel people who can pass you on with a favorable recommendation.

Job Application Forms

If you decide to fill out a job application, be sure to do so properly. Read the directions slowly and carefully. Carry an employment data sheet with the information (dates of past jobs, social security number, schools attended and dates of attendance) that such forms routinely require. Use this to fill out the form accurately and completely the first time. Do not leave any part of the form blank. If some part does not apply to you, write "N/A" for "Not Applicable." For salary requirements write "open" or "negotiable."

Do not put anything negative in writing. If you have a criminal record, or health problems that might affect your job performance, just write "will discuss in interview." Bring the problem up before beginning the interview. Indicate why you think you can do the job anyway, and ask whether the person would be willing to consider you. Most employers will, if you handle it this way.

Be sure to make good use of the part of the form where you can add "any other pertinent information." Use this section to sell yourself; do not leave it blank. Put down your strongest skills and some concrete accomplishments.

Remember: the application form is a screening device. It is used to select those applicants in whom the company will invest the time needed for an initial interview. Put down as much positive information about

yourself as you can, and avoid anything negative. Be neat, careful and complete. Give them no excuse to screen you out.

The "Numbers Game," in Person

If you decide to visit a personnel office without phoning first, do so with two goals. First, you need to find out whether the firm is hiring in your area of interest, or is likely to do so. Second, you want the name of an interviewer and a definite time when you can speak to that person.

You may be told there are openings, but that no one is interviewed until applications have been reviewed. Just say that you will be happy to fill out the application. You have some questions, however. Ask to speak to someone for just a few minutes after your application is complete. Ask for the name of an interviewer and a time when you could see him or her.

What you are trying to avoid is the situation where you walk in, fill out an application, give it to the receptionist and then leave. Again: paper is much less likely to get you hired than personal contact. You may get a job by filling out forms. You are more likely to get one, however, by dealing directly with those who hire, or at least those who can pass you on to the appropriate manager.

Applying to large firms involves more red tape than speaking directly to small employers. On the other hand, there are some distinct advantages to working for major corporations. They often have higher pay, more training opportunities, better fringe benefits and more secure employment. Because of this, and because they are so visible, there is a high level of competition for their openings.

The Persistent Shall Inherit the Job

Persistence is often the key to being hired by a large firm. Once you have the name of a specific person (preferably the department head, but at least someone in personnel), keep calling back. Be friendly, and keep expressing your interest. Large companies get many applicants, the bulk of whom show up once and are never heard from again. You need to behave differently. You have to make an effort to get them to notice you. You have to convince them that you really want to work for them.

Remember the old rule of selling: the sale doesn't start until the customer says no. There's no substitute for persistence and assertiveness. You will wait interminably, or be lost in the shuffle, unless you make a focused effort to get the information you need and get to know the people who can move your application along.

It is also possible, of course, to visit small employers in person. This makes sense in a small town. In a large city, however, the time this takes makes the phone more practical. You can spend many weeks (and a lot of gasoline money) looking for job openings in person. It's usually better to phone until you have an interview.

On the other hand, even in a major city, it is not unreasonable to visit employers personally if you are seeking an unusual job found in only a small number of locations. If you do this, and the person you want to see is not available immediately, you can ask for an appointment and return later.

Going in person also makes sense when jobs which exist in large numbers are concentrated in specific areas of town. Suppose you want a secretarial or clerical job, for example. It is quite possible to pick a downtown skyscraper, begin on the top floor, and go from one office to the next looking for an opening. You should have a job, or at least an interview, before you get to the ground floor.

Government Jobs

Government jobs have their own special characteristics, and require some adjustments to the strategies described above. It usually takes longer to obtain a government job than it does to get one in private industry. There is often more red tape, and a very slow decision making process.

As a consequence, there are two general rules for success when seeking a government job. First, start early. If, for example, you want to work for the federal government after June graduation, start filling out the forms in November. It will take that long to get through all the paperwork and get you on the list of qualified candidates. Being on this list is usually necessary before you can be interviewed for a specific position. State and local governments may be able to process an application more quickly, but don't count on it.

What you need to understand, however, is that carefully completing all those forms will not in itself get you hired. Hence the second rule: after you have all your documents on file, go on your own initiative to talk with those who make the hiring decisions.

They probably won't be able to offer you a position immediately. If you make a good impression, however, and your name turns up on the list of the qualified candidates from whom they can choose, they will naturally give you preference over someone whom they don't know. You cared enough to come in on your own to see them. The others are just names on a piece of paper. Again: the paperwork is essential, but you can't depend on it to get a job offer, or even an interview. There is still no substitute for personal contact.

A Word on Secretaries

Secretaries can be a great help to you as you seek job interviews. They can also cause you endless frustration. Experience suggests a few general rules which should help to avoid problems.

The most important rule is simply to pay attention to secretaries, and be nice to them. Be sure to get their names, and to address them by name. Don't depend on memory. Jot down each name along with that of the employer. Similarly, be sure to give the secretary your name. Don't be afraid to take a few minutes to chat with them. They like to be treated as the important parts of the organization which they are. In effect, they frequently decide whether you get an interview. And, if you do, their opinion is often asked about whether you should be hired.

Pay particular attention to secretaries and receptionists in personnel offices. They may be the ones who will do your reference checks, and it can help if they see you in a positive way.

The great secretarial stopper when you are trying to get through to the boss is, "And what is this in reference to?" If you say you are seeking employment, the secretary will typically refer you to the personnel department, which is just what you are trying to avoid. Hence you need an answer which is true, but which will also get you through to the person you're trying to reach.

One approach is to say you want to talk over something of mutual interest. Or you can say it's about a personal matter. If you have written ahead of time, you can try answering that you have been corresponding with the boss, and that he or she is expecting your call.

A particularly effective approach is to ask a complex or technical question the secretary can't answer, or a delicate one it would be unwise to answer. The natural reaction is then to put you through to the boss, who *can* handle the matter.

If you still can't get through, call another office and find out the hours of work. Then try calling 15 minutes before work begins in the morning, or after it ends in the late afternoon, or during the lunch hour. The odds are good that these are times when the secretary has not yet arrived, or has left, although the boss is there. With the secretary gone, he or she will usually pick up the phone personally, and you've gotten through.

If none of these approaches work, and this is a person you really want to see, you will simply have to use more creative methods. One person who couldn't get past a secretary decided to hang around the building entrance, as if reading the directory. He got on an elevator with someone from the office, struck up a conversation on the way up, and walked with him past the secretary, still talking. A gutsy approach, but it worked.

It's Tough but it Works

The first essential step in getting a job is seeing the person with the authority to hire. If you have had the time to do thorough informational and referral interviewing, this may be relatively painless. You will often be dealing with people whom you already know, or with those to whom you have been referred or recommended. This is much more comfortable than calling someone you don't know in an attempt to find a job opening.

If you decide to approach employers without referrals, then the next stage is more challenging. It's not that what you need to do is difficult to understand, or doesn't work. The problem — and the opportunity — is that the United States has a complex labor market consisting of thousands of independent firms and agencies. It's a difficult task to find the employer who needs you.

Just as statisticians have developed mathematical formulas which allow scientists to describe and predict random events, career counselors have developed means to penetrate this decentralized labor market. Although these methods work well enough, they do require you to approach many people who will say no to you. In theory, this shouldn't make any difference, as long as some say yes. In practice, however, it's hard not to become depressed and discouraged after the first dozen no's. You will inevitably feel that either there are no jobs out there, or nobody will ever offer one to you. The no's all feel like personal rejections.

Tom Jackson has an accurate picture of what any job search looks like:

NO NO NO NO NO NO NO NO NO
NO NO NO NO NO NO NO NO NO
NO NO NO NO NO NO NO NO YES

He suggests you begin your search for work by simply assuming there are a certain number of no's between you and the job you want. You have to get them all out of the way before you get a yes, which is a job offer you accept.

From this point of view, a day on which you are told no 30 times is better than a day on which you are told no only 15 times. More no's are out of the way, and you are closer to your yes.

It's a clever way to put it, but the insecurity and feelings of failure are still painful. After even a short string of no's, the temptation to have a beer, watch something on TV and forget the whole thing can be overwhelming. Studies of people looking for work find that few spend more than a couple of hours a day at their job search efforts. It's just not the kind of activity that most people, on their own, find easy to sustain.

There's also a trap here. The approach that seems safest (writing letters and sending resumes) is also often the least effective. The methods with a higher payoff (going to employers by phone or in person) also produce more personal rejection.

Build a Support Group

Realistically, then, it helps to have a support group. You need some assistance in handling this constant rejection. If you meet regularly with one or two other people who are looking for work, you can exchange ideas and leads. You'll probably be seeking different kinds of jobs. It is likely that each of you will run across possibilities of interest to the others. You can trade stories about your experiences. You'll find that many of your feelings are shared. You can provide each other with mutual support in this challenging effort.

To use such a group effectively, make a commitment at each meeting to reach specific goals during the coming week. You will make a certain number of phone calls, go to see a list of people personally and so on. When the week has passed, report what you did, and what happened. Then discuss how things are going, and set goals for the next week. This can speed up your job search process significantly. It will help motivate a steady effort and assist you in getting things done.

Appendix 10-1
Dealing with Difficult References

References are a key factor in determining whether a good interview eventually becomes a good job offer. A negative reference will often disqualify even a very attractive candidate. Consequently you need to take the whole matter of references very seriously.

It is not necessary that a reference say *anything* bad about you in order to raise doubts in an employer's mind. An obvious lack of enthusiasm, a vague response lacking in any detail or even a refusal to say anything at all can knock you out of consideration for a good position. Remember: employers hire nervously.

You need, therefore, to choose your references with great care. You should also prepare both the references and those who will be contacting them for this important exchange. You can't be there when they talk to each other, but you want to influence the exchange as much as you can.

What Is Negative Reference?

A negative reference is one which leads the employer to question your suitability for the job you want. This can occur in a variety of ways. The most obvious is when someone is contacted and says unflattering things about you: that you are technically out of date, are moody and difficult to work with, have trouble completing projects on time, were suspected of stealing from the company or would not be rehired.

Less obvious but often equally damaging is the reference who seems uncomfortable saying anything about you, does not appear to know you very well even though you worked together, cannot think of anything significant you accomplished, cannot articulate your strengths or speaks of you with an obvious lack of enthusiasm. When giving a reference, what is *not* said is often as important as what is said. Also quite important is whether your references are consistent in what they report.

How to Approach References

Keep in mind that some of the people who will be asked about you will not be on your reference list. An employer will typically request that you supply references, and

will contact some or all of them. A wise employer, however, will also try to find people familiar with your work whom you did *not* list, to get a more complete picture. If there is someone who logically should be on your list but is missing (your last boss, for example), an experienced employer will be *sure* to get in touch with that person. It is therefore in your best interest to work with everyone whom you suspect might be contacted, even if you don't put their names on your reference list, and really hope they aren't approached.

Your first step, then, is to develop a list of probable and possible references. We suggest that you take a sheet of paper and make a list of everyone who is likely to be called as a reference, whether you give their names to an employer or not. Beside each name list any incidents or reasons that might lead this person not to recommend you if contacted by a potential employer.

One person may be someone with whom you had a major disagreement that is still unresolved. Another may be an individual you never trusted, or with whom you were in a power struggle, or whom you hurt in some way, or who gave you a low performance rating or even fired you. List as many people and problems as you can. Then come back after a day or two and review the names, to see if you forgot anyone. Ask your spouse, or a good friend or former colleague, to go over what you have and see if anyone or anything is missing.

Having done this, rate each person on the list. Give an A to someone who would give you an enthusiastic endorsement, a B if you think the reaction would be positive but not totally so and a C to anyone who presents a minor but definite problem. Reserve the D rating for any person whom you definitely expect to be negative. The D group will be your biggest challenge.

You have to be careful when assigning these ratings. It is easy to assume that someone thinks highly of you when this is not the case. It is not unusual for talented people to lose good job offers because of negative references from people whom they thought would speak highly of them, but who in fact were unenthusiastic. Here again, friends and colleagues may be honest enough to tell you what someone really thinks of you and your work, even though that person never confronted you with direct criticism.

Handling the Difficult Reference

Now that you have identified the trouble spots, what are you going to do about them? What most people do is ignore the problem, and hope it will not hurt them. We think this is a mistake, and suggest a more active approach.

The best thing to do is to go directly to anyone who might provide a negative reference, and try to resolve whatever problems you have had with him or her. If you go into this conversation with the intent of resolving the conflict (rather than convincing the other person you were right all along!) you can usually work things out. Candor and straight talk, and a desire to let bygones be bygones, usually become mutual. After all, you may end up being a reference for the other person at some point. It is to your mutual advantage to resolve your problems.

If the possible negative reference was your last boss, we suggest that you prepare a sample reference statement around which to begin negotiations. This statement is a summary of the answers you would like given to questions usually asked of references. It covers such sensitive topics as:

- What are your strengths and weaknesses as an employee?
- How skilled are you technically? How current are you? What is your level of managerial skill?
- Why did you leave your last job?
- Would you be rehired if you reapplied at this firm? Why or why not?
- What were some of your significant accomplishments?
- How long did you work at your last job? At the job before that?
- Can you be counted on to produce results in a timely manner? What conditions make you unproductive?

The advantage of presenting your last employer with proposed answers to these questions is that you are much more likely to raise the important issues, and to leave the discussion knowing what will be said about you. Your goal is to get agreement on answers that are honest, and that both you and your last boss can live with.

You may not like everything your former boss feels has to be said about you. At least, however, you now know in detail *what* will be said, and you can talk to your potential new employer about it *before* that employer does the reference checks. You can forewarn him or her about any possible problems, and explain why they occurred. It is important to do this in a calm and mature manner that acknowledges the problems without making them seem like current issues of any great concern.

What is critical is not the negatives in what a former employer may say about you, but rather that they are expected and consistent with what *you* have said. It is the surprising and the inconsistent which will give you far more problems, and this is what you are avoiding.

Making Up Your Reference List

Ordinarily, your reference list should contain three to five names. It is common practice to include one personal reference; the others should be business references. If at all possible, include your last employer or supervisor. This person will be contacted anyway, and leaving him or her off the list is a red flag. It immediately suggests problems.

In selecting the remaining names, try to find people who have known you well over a period of several years. Look for someone who can be trusted to speak enthusiastically about you, and who is good at reacting quickly and well to unexpected questions. A person who can counteract any negative information is particularly helpful. If you can find someone with these characteristics who already knows the reference checker, that is a big plus. Be careful to avoid anyone with a tendency toward sarcasm. The last thing you want is someone insulting a potential employer.

It will be very helpful if you develop a reference statement, similar to that discussed above, for each of your references. You do not, of course, want them to read it verbatim. But if you discuss the issues on this list with them ahead of time, they are much more likely to say essentially the same thing as the other references when asked about you. This consistency will play a major role in convincing a potential employer that he or she has an accurate picture of what you are like.

How References Are Checked

There are numerous legal problems with reference checking. Anyone who says anything negative about you is potentially subject to a lawsuit. As a result, written references are almost worthless. No one is his right mind puts anything negative on paper.

Fearing lawsuits, most firms have adopted policies that severely limit the information provided during a reference check. Many will give no evaluative data at all about a former employee. They will provide the dates of employment and job title, but no more. They forbid any manager from giving a reference on behalf of the company.

This creates a situation where the manager can speak only for himself or herself, and only in an informal way. Some managers will do this; others won't. If they do, it will be verbally, not in writing. This is why most reference checks are done over the phone.

Since the call from a reference checker typically comes somewhat unexpectedly, when the manager is busy with other things, there is often little or no time to think through what it would be best to say about you. This is why we recommend that you talk about what you want said ahead of time, thus preparing your references for the call.

It should be clear from this discussion that a "letter of reference" from a past employer, addressed "To Whom It May Concern" and supplied by you, is of little value. However well meant, it will not be taken seriously by most employers. Except in special circumstances, we do not suggest that you ask for or use such letters.

Reference checking by government agencies is sometimes more formal. Rules and regulations may require that a certain number of letters of reference be obtained and filed. You can be sure of two things. First of all, the regulations will be observed. Second, any supervisor smart enough to be worth working for will also use informal channels to check you out. So get the letters, but do not neglect the other suggestions in this appendix.

Eleven. Want Ads and Agencies: Helping Least When Needed Most

In this chapter we will review the people and institutions, called labor market intermediaries, which try to bring together employers and those seeking employment. The want ads are the most obvious, and the most used. Roughly one out of every seven jobs is filled through them. Private employment agencies fill about one job in twenty, as does the United States Employment Service (also called the Job Service). Other intermediaries work with smaller numbers.

The first thing you need to know is that there are no intermediaries which serve the entire labor market. Few people with college degrees are helped by the Job Service. Blue collar workers almost never find jobs through employment agencies. You will rarely see a notice for a government position in the want ads. It is essential, therefore, that you determine which intermediaries, if any, typically deal with the industry and occupation in which you are interested.

The second thing you need to know is how intermediaries work. Intermediaries primarily serve employers, not those seeking employment. The unemployed come and go. It is the employer whose business is needed year after year. In general, intermediaries do not exist to find you a job. They exist to fill the jobs that employers want filled. The people who work for an intermediary are usually much more sensitive to the needs and desires of the client company than they are to you.

The third and most important thing you need to understand is why an employer is using an intermediary at all. Firms usually have two streams of applicants from which they can choose new employees: those who are referred to them by others (particularly by their present employees), and those who come in on their own initiative. The fact that a company uses an intermediary suggests that these two groups are insufficient to fill the available openings. It is important to know why. What is it that is causing the company to have difficulty filling these positions? There may be a perfectly reasonable answer, but you need to know what it is.

One important topic to bring up when doing preliminary, informational interviewing, therefore, is whether intermediaries are helpful in obtaining a particular kind of position. You need to understand both the strengths and limitations of the intermediaries who serve the occupations of interest to you. You will then be able to use them knowledgeably whenever it is convenient and appropriate.

This chapter will give you some basic facts on each of the major labor market intermediaries available to someone seeking employment. You will then need t find out on your own how these general patterns apply to your city, industry and occupation.

Do You Want a Want Ad Job?

The most obvious and commonly used list of job openings is, of course, the want ads. They appear daily in most local and national newspapers. There have been several studies of the openings which do, and do not, appear in these notices.

One survey of employers in two major cities found that only a small percentage made any use of the want ads. Most (76% in one city and 85% in the other) had not hired anyone through the want ads during the past year. Certain industries, such as finance, insurance and real estate, were particularly unlikely to advertise their openings.

The want ads seemed most successful as a way to hire clerical workers. Large firms in both cities were more likely to use the ads than were small firms. The study's general conclusion was that the want ads presented a distorted picture of the local labor market. Some jobs were consistently underrepresented and others overrepresented.

A larger effort, funded by the Department of Labor, examined both the daily and Sunday want ads in 12 sections of the country. Only 31% of these ads listed local openings not previously advertised. The rest of the want ad section contained ads by private employment agencies (19%), jobs outside of the area (12%), openings advertised previously (33%) and various attempts to sell something (6%).

Jobs characterized by the government as "low-pay, low-status" constituted less than 15% of the jobs in the cities studied. However, 25% of the openings listed in the want ads fell into this category.

The Sunday want ads have a particularly high proportion of jobs located in other cities. They also contain a higher proportion of professional, clerical and sales openings. The daily papers have a higher proportion of ads for service workers (domestic and restaurant jobs, for example). Despite the larger size of the Sunday newspaper, more ads make their first appearance in the daily editions, since there are six of these a week.

One important characteristic of most want ads is that they give very few details about what the advertised position really involves. When responding to a "blind" ad you do not even know who placed it, since only a box number is listed. Some of these ads may not even represent real jobs. A company may need salary data, or be testing the labor market to see how easy it is to hire certain workers before bidding on a contract.

Traps for the Unwary

Be cautious of advertised positions which have no salary because income is based solely on commission. Although some of these apparent opportunities may be legitimate, they can also be traps for the unwary. Similarly, "management trainee" positions may really be low paying clerical and sales jobs with, at best, a hypothetical possibility for promotion. Try to contact some employees informally before accepting such an offer, to learn more about the position and the employer. It is easy for an employer to exaggerate the promotion possibilities a job offers. On average, professionals who obtain jobs through the want ads have been found to be disproportionately underemployed.

When unemployment goes down, the number of ads goes up, and vice versa. The reason for this is not difficult to understand. As unemployment increases, employers have more and more people coming to them looking for work. At the same time, business is decreasing and they need fewer workers. Under these conditions, there is little likelihood that most employers will need to advertise an opening. The want ads, therefore, are least likely to help you precisely when you most need them.

Even when unemployment is not unusually high, any advertised opening will come to the attention of a large number of people. Almost any ad will draw dozens of responses. An ad in a national publication such as the *Wall Street Journal* will draw between 500 and 1000 resumes, even if high levels of skill and experience are demanded.

There is, therefore, an inevitable tradeoff between using informal methods of finding employment and answering advertisements. Searching informally means dealing with many employers who do not need your services. Answering ads, on the other hand, means being only one of a large number of applicants. The former is tedious and frustrating; the latter involves facing fierce competition.

The most reasonable way to use the want ads is skimming them daily. Because they list only a small fraction of the available jobs, you should never become discouraged if you find nothing of interest. If an opening looks attractive, of course, you can pursue it. If you find nothing appropriate, however, set the ads aside and continue using other search methods.

Employment Agencies: Myth and Reality

A high proportion of the classified ads in most daily and Sunday papers are placed, not by employers, but by employment agencies. To interpret these ads properly you need a clear idea of how these agencies work.

First, there is a difference between agencies which work for companies on retainer, and those which are paid on a contingency basis. A firm working on retainer has been hired to locate a highly qualified applicant (a computer engineer, for example) for a particular opening. The agency will be paid whether or not someone is hired, and ordinarily the opening will be listed with no other agency. If you have the qualifications for the job in question, they will be happy to see you. If you don't, they will have no interest at all in talking to you.

A contingency firm, on the other hand, may or may not know of any specific openings of a particular kind. They are trying to find openings, meet skilled people, and arrange matches. They will be paid only if a company hires someone they send for an interview. This is not an easy task, so reputable firms tend to specialize. By specializing, they can become more thoroughly acquainted with the needs of a limited set of corporations. They can also get to know some of the talented people who can fill the type of position in which they are interested. The important question for you is whether any of these contingency firms specialize in the kind of job you want.

We recommend that you be wary of contingency firms that do not specialize. There is a real danger that they have no more knowledge about your job market than you do. They may send your resume to every firm in town, hoping to interest someone. If, on your own, you make a personal contact at one of these corporations and obtain a job offer, the agency may claim a fee is owed them on the basis of that mailed resume. Since these fees are quite substantial (at least 10% of a year's salary, and often much more) some employers will withdraw a job offer rather than pay it.

There are also agencies which charge you, rather than the employer, a fee for trying to find you a job. We strongly recommend that you be very cautious about dealing with these agencies, and do so only after investigating them carefully.

Finally, there are a small group of firms (usually called executive search firms) which specialize in filling upper level management positions. The people with whom they work are very highly paid, and are only a minute proportion of the labor market. If you are curious about these search firms, there is a reference in the Notes to a good book on the topic.

When You Walk into an Agency, What Are You Getting Into?

Employment agencies come in all sizes and shapes. There are nationwide firms which, by telephone and computer, have access to job openings in most major U.S. cities. There are large firms with offices spread throughout a given city. There are one-person agencies with little more than a telephone and a small office.

Working for an employment agency is often a high pressured and demanding experience. There is a premium on speed. Many unemployed individuals list themselves with several agencies, just as some employers will list their openings in a variety of places. The agency's clients, in the meantime, are also applying to employers on their own.

Most agencies pay their counselors only on a commission basis. Counselors have to place people quickly to generate income. There is a high turnover rate in many employment agencies because of the pressures created by these demands. As a result, there's a good chance that if you use an agency you will be dealing with someone who is new at the business.

At first glance, it might seem to your benefit to have the agency so dependent on placing you quickly. It's not that simple. This situation can generate pressures which can work *against* your best interests. For one thing, employment agencies must work with those for whom jobs can be found easily. It is more profitable to place a secretary each day for a month than it is to find a position for a $60,000 executive after two month's work.

As a result, employment agencies usually prefer clients who have both job-specific skills and experience at the job they seek. Those seeking new career directions, on the other hand, are much less welcome. Finding them employment takes too much time.

If you go to an employment agency with an M.A. in accounting and five years of experience as an accountant, and want help finding a job in accounting, they will be more than happy to work with you. There is a good chance for a quick placement, and an equally quick commission. Suppose, on the other hand, that you have a B.A. in history and some graduate work in dance. You are not sure exactly what you want but feel a need for a position requiring both independence and creativity. The agency's reaction, at best, is likely to be: "Can you type?" Indeed, you may be told you are unemployable.

That isn't true. It is true, however, that it is rarely worth the agency's time to work with such a person. It is not that he or she cannot get a job, and a good one. The problem is the considerable effort needed to define the job and then obtain it. The percentage of salary the agency will receive just doesn't make it worth their while. Employment agencies are for people who are changing employers, not for those changing careers.

You might never guess that, however, from the ads which agencies place in the paper. To find enough easily placeable clients with whom to work, employment agencies must induce a large number of qualified applicants to register with them. From this pool of applicants they can then select those for whom jobs can be found most easily. Remember: employment agencies are commission businesses, and they make money by placing as many clients as possible as quickly as possible.

To draw in applicants, agencies advertise their best and most attractive job listings. (Unethical agencies will make up nonexistent, attractive-sounding jobs if they do not have enough good ones to advertise.) These advertisements bring in a stream of applicants. The most easily placed are selected. The rest are told there are no openings for which they are suitable, and quickly sent on their way.

The applicants who happen to match jobs which employers have listed with the agency are given a quick briefing on what the employer wants, and sent to interview. Agencies, however, usually have far more qualified applicants than openings. The counselor, therefore, gets on the phone and begins calling employer after employer, trying to find one who will interview a well-qualified candidate. Researchers who have spoken to owners of employment agencies estimate that as many as 70% of their placements come from jobs which are discovered this way. Only a minority of clients are matched with job openings which were first listed with the agency. Agencies, like individuals, find jobs primarily through direct contact with employers.

So What Do You Do?

If you decide to visit an agency, avoid Mondays. The rush of people answering Sunday's ads must be processed, and it's easy to get lost in the crowd. Read any contract *very* carefully before signing it. Be careful of application forms which also turn out to be contracts. Don't sign unless you understand the implications of what you are agreeing to.

Equally important, do not sign anything unless you trust the judgment, expertise and integrity of the person with whom you are working. An agency, no matter how good its general reputation, will only be as good for you as that person.

Once you have entered into a relationship with an agency counselor, it is essential to communicate fully and regularly. Keep him or her up to date on your job search activities. Counselors deal with many clients; if kept informed they can do more for you.

The most reasonable way to use an employment agency is as a partial substitute for referral interviewing. A good counselor will not send a client to a job interview unless he or she has first met with the employer to review the job's requirements. An experienced counselor, having dealt with employers over a period of years, will have a good idea of what they want. If you have experience in a high-demand occupation, you can go to an employment agency and explain the kind of situation you are seeking. You can specify the type of person for whom you want to work, and the working conditions and location you want.

An established agency knows local employers and can direct you to what you seek. This will be done best by an agency which specializes in your field, or at least by a specialized counselor within a full service organization.

An interview with the head of an appropriate professional association might bring you similar information about local employers. However, another advan-

tage the employment agency can offer is discretion. Perhaps you don't want your present employer to know you're thinking of leaving. An agency can check around for openings without revealing your name, or doing anything to start any gossip which could get back to your present employer. Be aware, though, that your new employer may offer you a lower salary because of the large fee which must be paid to the agency.

Be Realistic

You need to be realistic about what an agency can do for you. Most jobs can be filled by employers with people who come to them looking for work. Employers turn to agencies largely for jobs which are difficult to fill. As a result, agencies can only fill about one of every five openings which employers send them. If you have the unusual skills needed for many of these jobs, you probably don't need an agency.

There are exceptions. Some medium sized businesses will use an agency to fill all their openings. This saves them the cost of opening a personnel office. Generally, though, agencies are trying to fill openings where qualified applicants are in short supply.

Agencies become particularly ineffective when the economy turns down. During a recession, with few openings available and many applicants seeking work, most employers do not need to use employment agencies. Some completely shut down. Others radically scale back their operations. An employment agency, like the want ads, will be of least help to you when you most need assistance.

Even in good times, there are problems. Over the years, consumers have consistently voiced several complaints about employment agencies. Among the most common are: (1) bait and switch advertising (the great job in the ads always turns out to be filled; however, there is this other job, not as desirable...); (2) downgrading applicant skills to obtain quick placements (this can involve telling a client that what he or she really wants is not possible, and then sending him or her to interview for a secretarial or clerical position); and (3) financial abuses, such as the failure to refund fees when a job ends through no fault of the applicant, or transferring the applicant's fee obligation to a finance company without his or her prior knowledge or consent.

One of us (Wegmann), in a fit of uncertainty about obtaining tenure at the university, once visited an employment agency that specialized in professional positions. This was a good many years ago, before he began studying labor market operations. The young man with whom he had an appointment looked over Bob's resume. There was a long silence. He presumably noted Bob's four college degrees, including a *summa cum laude* B.A. and a Ph.D.; past experience as a high school math teacher, college professor and staff member for a United States Senate Subcommittee; the successful conduct of a citywide election campaign for the board of education; and present employment as a university professor.

The young man looked at him sadly, and said, "Bob, I'm not sure there's anything you can do." There was another long pause. "Personnel, maybe." End of interview.

Bob clearly didn't understand how this agency operated. His ignorance was typical. Schools and colleges don't teach how the labor market operates. Like the airline stewardesses mentioned in the introduction to Section I, Bob was unaware of even the most basic facts about employment agencies, such as their disinterest in people changing career direction.

As should be clear by now, going to an employment agency not realizing the small proportion of job openings to which they have access, or how they operate, or how they make their money, can be very dangerous to your level of self-esteem. There *are* ethical employment agencies, and they can be of help to you under certain conditions. It is to your advantage, however, to be an informed and cautious user of their services.

Who Is Served by the Employment Service?

Unlike a private employment agency, the United States Employment Service (or Job Service) does not charge a fee to either the employer or the applicant. Every state has such an agency, though the name varies from state to state. It may be called the Employment Commission, Department of Economic Security, Employment Development Department or some similar title. The people who work for this agency are state employees. The cost of the agency's operation is paid by the federal government. Part of the unemployment tax paid by every employer goes for this purpose, since the agency also administers unemployment compensation benefits.

Reference has already been made to a study of the want ads funded by the United States Department of Labor. This study, subtitled "A Bifocal View of the Labor Market," contrasted the openings advertised in the want ads with those listed with the employment service.

The employment service is stronger (has a higher proportion of job listings) in small towns and areas with low populations. Most sites studied, however, were centered around major cities. In nearly all of them, there were more new openings in the daily want ads than you could find in a daily visit to the local employment service office. Because of employment service budget cuts which have occurred since this study, this is even more true today.

Employment service lists, like the want ads, do not have a cross section of a city's openings. The proportion of jobs classified as "low-pay, low-status" in the dozen metropolitan areas studied was less than 15%. However, almost 40% of the new openings listed with local employment service offices fell into this category.

Although the probability that there is a job you want on these lists may not be great, visiting an employment service office can still be worthwhile. You will probably have to spend some time standing in line, but bear with it. Your goal is to make a good impression on one of the interviewers. An experienced employment service interviewer will know the local labor market. He or she may be able to give you some good ideas about where to apply. Once you have made this contact, you can then keep in touch by phone as you go about your job search. If you are clear about what you want and have realistic goals, an interviewer may be willing to phone employers whom he or she knows, trying to find you an opening.

Whether you want to use your local employment service office is a matter for you to decide. Use it when and where you think it will help. Like any other intermediary, they can't get you a job, but they may help you get an interview.

Who Will Be Placed by the Placement Office?

Most colleges and universities have an office of career planning and placement. More and more of these offices serve alumni as well as graduating students. Although it is usually only the larger corporations which can afford to send a recruiter for on-campus interviews, smaller employers do phone in job openings. There is no question that these placement offices can arrange employment interviews for some very desirable positions.

If you graduated from a community college, four year college or university, or even if you took only one course, you should stop by to see the school's placement director. Mention your goals, ask his or her advice and then phone back occasionally to keep in touch.

During your campus visit, stop by the alumni office and pick up a directory. Graduates from your institution, even if you've never met, have an immediate relationship to you. They can be sources of immensely useful information. In addition, before any job interview, check your alumni directory. Check to see whether anyone among the group who will be interviewing you also attended your institution. Sometimes you may find the son or daughter of an executive on the alumni list. If so, you've got a natural opening to establish rapport at the beginning of the interview. Those who graduated from a given school, or who sent their children there, often prefer to hire applicants who went to the same institution.

Civil Service Offices

You will usually find that openings with federal, state or local government are routed through a central personnel office. This is not always true, and you should check, but the law usually requires government offices to hire through centralized personnel procedures. Many city telephone directories now have a "Blue Pages" section for government phone numbers. You can find civil service offices listed there. The federal civil service is now called the Office of Personnel Management. State and local titles for these offices will vary, but the first place to look is under personnel. If that doesn't work, try the general information number.

If your skills and temperament match a government job, such employment can have real advantages. These positions are usually secure, barring major budget cuts. Fringe benefits are often good, and promotion opportunities come up regularly once you are in the system. Since government employment is declining as a proportion of total employment, however, you should expect considerable competition. There is also a good deal of paperwork, and the decision-making process is often slow. Hiring freezes, budget cuts, managerial changes and other problems typical of government agencies can stop the hiring process at almost any point. If there is anywhere that Murphy's Law applies, it is here: if anything can go wrong, it probably will. A "Plan B" is essential.

You'll probably run into some typical government insanity when applying for these positions. You'll also, however, make contact with well-run offices and agencies, and some fine people. Prevailing myths to the contrary, many necessary government services are provided efficiently and cost-effectively.

The Temporary Help Agency

A quick glance at your local Yellow Pages will reveal a long list of temporary help agencies. (They may, however, be listed under E, not T: "Employment Contractors — Temporary Help.") At one time, these services were almost exclusively for secretaries. Today they place people in jobs ranging from computer programing to acting as foreign language interpreters. Temporary help agencies can sometimes be of real use to you, for several reasons.

First, you can use them as a way to bring in some cash for survival during a period when you are doing informational or referral interviewing, or while waiting for a job which is slow to come through (a government position, for example). Openings listed with temporary help agencies can last from half a day to several months at a given location. Some agencies in major cities offer surprisingly flexible schedules. If you want to work only afternoons, or only three days a week, they can match you with an employer who needs someone for those hours.

Second, working through a temporary help agency can introduce you to a variety of working environments. This can help you decide what you want to do and where you want to do it. Such work also provides an opportunity to meet people whom you can later approach to learn more about an industry, or a specific firm. It's a good way to get a foot in the door.

This process works in both directions. It is common for companies to contract for temporary help and then, either immediately or at some later time, offer permanent positions to those workers who did a particularly good job. Just as working at temporary jobs helps you to look over a variety of employers, hiring temporaries helps employers to look over a variety of potential employees. The employer's contract with the temporary help agency usually provides that a fee be paid to the agency if a permanent job is offered the temporary worker within a set time period.

The temporary help market has grown enormously in recent years, and the use of these agencies is becoming more and more common. It is even possible to earn your living this way. Although being a "permanent temporary" is a logical contradiction, it is a practical possibility. Some agencies provide pension and health benefits to those who work for them on a steady basis.

If these agencies can help you during your job search, directly or indirectly, it makes sense to use them.

Other Possibilities and Dangers

In any major city, there are a variety of individuals who provide individual counseling on what occupation to pursue, or how to find the position you want. There are firms that charge thousands of dollars for these services, and there are agencies that charge little or nothing. The quality of what they offer varies as widely as the price, though without any apparent connection. If you think you need such a service, be sure to talk to at least two or three people who have used the one you are considering recently, to see if they were satisfied.

The want ads, private employment agencies, the Job Service and school placement offices are the major institutions which bring together employers and those seeking employment. Some community and neighborhood organizations provide similar services to their membership or geographic area. For blue collar work, there may be union hiring halls which place union members on certain jobs. There are government agencies and voluntary organizations which serve specific age and ethnic groups. As always, you have to talk to people, and see if any of these groups are likely to help you.

A variety of professional associations provide their members with help in finding employment. This is one of many good reasons to seek out the heads of such organizations. Because some professional jobs are normally sought in a national market, these lists can be a great help. They pull together openings from all over the country.

Alice in Jobland

If ever there was a situation with great need but little satisfaction, it is the area of labor market lists and intermediaries. All are incomplete and imperfect. Because many of the most desirable positions are filled by personal referral, the jobs on any list of openings are disproportionately full of the less attractive positions. Both employers and the unemployed use intermediaries largely when they can't get what they want using more informal methods. It is inevitable that an organization which tries to match the hardest to place workers with the hardest to fill jobs is going to have difficulties.

In addition, no labor market intermediary can get you a job. At best, they can help you get an interview. None will ever put you in touch with even a fraction of the total set of available jobs. However, one might lead you to just the position you're seeking. None should be relied on exclusively. Each, nonetheless, might be an important part of a particular job search. Their ability to help, unfortunately, declines during economic downturns, when you most need them.

The public announcement of an opening makes it known to a large group of unemployed persons, which intensifies the competition. Many applicants focus on the small proportion of jobs which are openly advertised. After finding again and again that these openings are either already filled, or not what they seemed, many of these people become frustrated. "There must be a better way," they cry. There *are* better ways, as we have seen, though they are neither quick nor painless.

So what do you do? It all depends on your age, skills and past experience, and above all on the type of job you're seeking. Your best bet is to review the available intermediaries, and then use only those which are appropriate for your situation.

SECTION V.

INTERVIEWING

Introduction to Section V

The interview is when it all comes together. There are a few instances in which people are hired without being interviewed, just as there are a few mail order brides who are married without being dated. Normally, however, what happens in the employment interview has more to do with who is hired than anything else.

In a large corporation there may be an intermediate step. Here, the personnel department conducts screening interviews, narrowing down the group of apparently qualified candidates. Should you have such an interview, you want to be judged qualified. Your goal is to avoid being screened out. This is not the time to ask detailed questions about the job. Personnel interviewers may have no experience with the position you want. It doesn't make sense to embarrass them by asking questions they can't answer.

Nor do you have to convince a personnel interviewer that you are the best candidate. That decision, after all, will be made by the supervisor. Your aim is to be sure you are seen as fully qualified. Equally important, you want to come across as an applicant with no serious drawbacks. There should be no reason for the personnel interviewer to fear criticism for sending you on to the supervisor.

The employment interview, however, is an entirely different matter. Here you are talking to the person for whom you will be working. Sometimes this will be an executive or supervisor in a large corporation. Often it will be the owner or manager of a small business. Doing well in this interview, handling the final salary negotiations and getting off to a good start on your new job are the topics discussed in this section.

A good lawyer begins by preparing the other side's case. You will similarly benefit from considering how things look to the employer. Keep in mind that employers, when hiring, are often just as uncomfortable as those they interview. Many employers have made serious hiring errors. They have hired people who stole from them, lied to them, walked out on them and generally caused the full range of difficulties of which human beings are capable.

The employer, therefore, approaches the interview with the same mixture of hope and fear that you do. The hope is that you are a talented person who works hard, and will accept a position at reasonable pay. The fear is that you will exaggerate your skills, be hard to get along with and make unreasonable demands. The employer is in the awkward position of wanting to sell you on the job, while still remaining free to reject you if necessary.

You, of course, are in a parallel bind. You want to interview well, and thus stimulate a job offer. You want to show your enthusiasm for the opportunities the position presents. At the same time, you want to be free to say no if the salary offer is inadequate, or the match begins to look like a bad one.

This is why interviews vary so much depending on how they are obtained. A referral from a trusted relative or colleague gives both sides some idea of what they are getting into. An interview obtained by a cold call or a want ad, on the other hand, puts two strangers in a room with very ambiguous feelings about the situation. It all seems rushed, as if one had to decide for or against marriage after the first or second date.

In understanding the dynamics of the employment interview, therefore, you must take seriously the degree of fear and knowledge on both sides. When both know little and fear much, there is great potential for mistrust, misjudgment and misunderstanding.

Under these conditions, employers easily say no. There is little obvious cost if a potentially good employee is not hired. There are, in today's market, many other applicants. Hiring the wrong person, on the other hand, has high and obvious costs. In the extreme case, it can ruin the business.

Employers are therefore acting rationally when they decide to reject a particular applicant, even when the negative evidence is slight. Inappropriate dress, an inconsistency between the applicant's resume and what is said in the interview or the unenthusiastic response of a reference can all suggest trouble. Why should the employer take risks when other qualified applicants are available?

You, as the person seeking employment, therefore face an interpersonal challenge during a job interview. You have to build rapport and trust. You have to do more than tell the interviewer what skills and experience you have. The way you present your strengths must convince an often skeptical employer that your accomplishments are real and not exaggerated.

The value of the self-analysis and information gathering activities outlined in the first part of this book will now become evident. You know more about yourself, and also about the needs and demands of the job, than most applicants. You are therefore in a better position to handle the employment interview. First, though, you need to add one additional ingredient: practice. You need to prepare what you are going to say, and become comfortable saying it.

A job interview is a very personal discussion. You will be talking about your goals, motivations, successes and frustrations. You will be asking questions that implicitly communicate your values. It is a serious mistake to think this will all happen spontaneously. It is not easy for most people to discuss such personal matters in a thoughtful and articulate way with someone whom they do not know well.

Preparation and practice are therefore essential. You can't learn to swim by reading a book about swimming. You have to do it. The same is true of interviewing.

You need to sit down with a friend and a tape recorder. If at all possible, find someone who hires at his or her place of work. Role-play an interview. Practice discussing your goals, why you want this job, what you have learned from past experience and the salary you expect. Be sure you are asked the most difficult interview questions the two of you can think of. Try wording your answers in different ways. Ask the other person how it sounds. When you play back the tape recording, pretend you are an employer. Would you hire yourself?

It takes effort to learn how to interview effectively. It also pays off. Many people do not interview well. In most job interviews the applicants are "playing it by ear," and hoping for the best. If you are thoroughly prepared, you will have a significant advantage.

For most positions, interviewing is really a two step process. There is a first meeting with the employer or supervisor, perhaps after a screening interview by the personnel department. Both parties usually begin this first interview with a fair amount of uncertainty about each other. After this meeting, either or both may decide to break off further discussion.

If the first interview goes well, however, and both parties think the relationship is worth pursuing, then one or more additional meetings will follow. At these sessions the emphasis will be quite different. The question is no longer whether you are a serious candidate for the job. It is now a matter of confirming good impressions, working out the details, negotiating salary and benefits and so on.

Section V reflects the change in emphasis that usually occurs during the hiring process. Chapter Twelve focuses on the employment interview, and the critical first impressions that are made there. The emphasis is on establishing rapport with the interviewer. Your goal is to build trust as you lead the employer to see you as the right person for the job you want.

Chapter Thirteen, on the other hand, discusses the matters that become more important after the first interview has been successfully concluded: obtaining a definite job offer, coming to agreement on salary and benefits, handling negotiations with more than one employer and beginning in your new position.

You have a big investment in your job search efforts, given all you have done so far. This is the time to redouble your efforts, the way a championship runner sprints for the finish line at the end of a long race.

Twelve. The Job Interview: It All Comes Together

Whether you arranged the meeting through an intermediary or on your own, you are now at the moment of truth. You have an interview: an appointment to talk to an employer about a job. If you handle this discussion well, there is a chance you will soon have a job offer. If you don't handle it well, you may lose an opportunity you really want. No wonder you have sweaty palms!

Of course, one must be realistic. There's a big chance element throughout the job search process. An applicant may come along who is even more qualified than you. The boss may have a nephew who suddenly applies. The firm may decide not to hire anyone after all. A manager may quit or be promoted, so that no positions can be filled until someone else takes over.

Keep at It

Because of these uncertainties, there is one essential rule you should follow as your job search reaches its final stages. *Never* let up your efforts until you have been offered a position, and have accepted the offer.

Realistically, you have to plan on obtaining interviews at several firms. In today's economy, many talented candidates are applying for every job. As a result, you may have five or even ten interviews before a position is yours to accept or decline.

Over and over again people have interviews that go well. They stop most of their other job search efforts and wait for the final decision. Then, for some reason, the offer doesn't come through. In the meantime they lose momentum. Other trails have grown cold, and it is harder than ever to start up again.

To combat this, make it your goal to obtain at least two job offers. That way, even when you seem close to one, you'll keep going. Of course, if the first offer is great, take it. But don't let your efforts grow slack too soon. If nothing else, that second offer may give you some leverage when negotiating salary.

The ability to interview well is separate from the ability to do the job. Some people interview beautifully but work badly. Others interview awkwardly but are great at the job itself. However, since you have to interview acceptably to get an offer, it's worth the effort to learn how to handle job interviews as well as you can.

There is something to be said for accepting any job interview that comes along. It helps you become more comfortable with the process. After all, you never know. A position may turn out to be a better match than you expected. What starts as an unacceptable job can sometimes be negotiated into something satisfying. Even if it can't, every interview gives you more experience. When you apply for a position which is an obviously good match, you want to be as polished as possible.

The Unpredictable Encounter

Almost any generalization about job interviews will not hold in some situations. First, an interview is a conversation. Like any human encounter, it is unpredictable. Any rules for interviewing, including ours, are made to be broken. If you and the interviewer hit it off well, just "go with the flow" and ignore the rest of this chapter.

Second, interviews vary a great deal depending on the job being sought. An interview for a technical job often concentrates primarily on the specific tasks the position requires. An applicant may be probed at length to determine his or her level of technical competence. An interview for an outdoor job, on the other hand, may take place in a pickup truck as the boss runs an errand. An interview for a managerial position will focus primarily on the candidate's organizational abilities, and how he or she handles people.

For some jobs you will interview with only one person and may even start work the same day. For more senior positions it is common to have a series of interviews with several people, as well as one or more group interviews. You may have to return more than once for additional meetings. Even after all this, weeks or months may pass without a decision.

Major corporations sometimes use a "structured interview." In these, every candidate for a position is asked the same questions in the same order. Since it takes some training to handle a structured interview, they are usually conducted by personnel officials rather than supervisors. If you run into one of these, just sit back and answer the questions. You probably won't be allowed to ask anything yourself until the end.

Focus on the Employer

Despite these differences, however, there are some consistent employer concerns which should be discussed at some point in all job interviews. It is on the employer's needs, and your ability to meet them, that the employment interview must focus.

Some employers, however, are not particularly good interviewers. They may interview only rarely. Most have no formal training at it. What they often really want is to hire someone good as quickly as possible, and then get back to running the business.

The employer, therefore, may not articulate his or her concerns clearly. If you are properly prepared, *you* will bring these topics up for discussion. It may seem strange to suggest that *you*, the applicant, raise issues of concern to the employer, but it is the wise thing to do. If the employer leaves the interview with detailed information about you and your ability to do the job, and does not have this information about the other candidates, you are more likely to be offered the position. We therefore suggest that you take the responsibility for being sure that the employer gets a clear idea of what you have to offer.

Knowing the Corporate Culture

One thing the employer will be wondering is why you applied to his or her firm. If you have come because of a referral from a friend or acquaintance, the answer will be obvious. In any case, be sure you find out as much as you can about the company before the interview, so you can express a knowledgeable interest. The more you know about the firm's history and special characteristics, the more you can show how well you would fit in. Corporations and agencies, like people, have their own personalities. Understanding the corporate culture is a major aim of your preparatory research.

A surprising number of people don't do this. They come to the interview with only a vague idea of the business in which the firm is involved. They know nothing of the corporation's goals and culture, or recent changes in its business strategy.

This always makes a bad impression. Even if you have only a short time before the interview, get some help from a reference librarian. Uncover whatever information you can about both the industry and the firm.

Be Ready to Talk about Yourself

A second major concern of any employer is discovering what type of person you are. An interviewer may draw you out with any number of questions. "Tell me about yourself," "What do you like to do during your free time?" "Describe some difficult decisions you've had to make, and how you made them." However the questions are phrased, what an employer actually wants to know is how you will do on the job: your attitude toward work, how you approach unexpected problems and how well you get along with others.

Some employers will be much better than others at drawing you out on these topics. You need to volunteer information even if not asked. Whether they say so or not, all employers are concerned about these issues.

When explaining your personal characteristics, always discuss your aptitudes and personality traits with the help of concrete examples. Instead of saying, "I get along well with people," point out that you were voted Miss Congeniality. Or let the interviewer know that you were asked back by a part time employer because you were so friendly and easy to get along with. Or describe how you play the peacemaker in your family when people get upset with each other. Specific examples are much better remembered than generalities. And how much is remembered plays a critical role when the employer makes a hiring decision.

Where Are You Going?

Your long-term goals are also of interest to the employer. He or she wants to know how this job fits into those goals. You will be asked questions such as, "What do you think you'll be doing five years from now?" Employers are favorably impressed with applicants who have concrete objectives. This is especially true when these objectives can be reached by being successful at their firm or agency.

Keep in mind that employee turnover is a major concern for most employers. Every time a person quits it costs the firm money. There is often a period of time when the job sits unfilled, and the work must be picked up by others. This has a negative effect on everyone else's work flow. There can be considerable effort and expense involved in recruiting and interviewing new applicants. A new employee must be trained and integrated into the organization. He or she will be slow and inexperienced at first. All of this hurts productivity. Employers therefore want to know whether, if you are hired, you are going to stay with them. Your answers must take this concern into account. The more you make it clear that your personal objectives can be met by staying with the company, the more the employer is likely to see you as a long-term employee.

Are You Good at What You Do?

Another central issue in any interview is, of course, whether you can do the job. The employer needs to know what your skills are, and what prior experience you have. Above all, he or she wants to know something about the quality of your work.

The skill analysis process is your best preparation to handle these concerns. Use the most appropriate specific examples you can to make your strengths clear and vivid. If you've had a similar job before, describe what you did best. Wherever possible, use numerical measures of your effectiveness (sales went up 25%, for example). Give details about anything you started that worked out well.

Initiative and an interest in learning always make a good impression. Mention courses you took at night, seminars you attended or anything you asked your last employer to teach you. Any circumstance where you saw a need, and took the initiative to solve a problem, will count in your favor.

Decision Time

An employer's hiring decision is based, more than anything else, on the answers to three fundamental questions. First, are you someone he or she likes and instinctively trusts? Would you fit into the team that he or she is building? Second, do you have the skill, experience and judgment to do the job? Third, do you have the commitment, drive and motivation to produce results when the going gets tough?

It will be easier for you to demonstrate these qualities if you learn as much as possible before the interview about the team you would be joining. You want to use this information to build rapport early in the interview. Having done this, you can then communicate your skills and motivation as clearly as possible, showing how they would fit the needs of this particular position.

In our society there is a strong bias against bragging. Although you don't want to exaggerate your skills and accomplishments, you do have to set this bias aside sufficiently to tell an employer your strengths, and to show how these strengths fit the demands of the job. You don't have to claim that you are perfect, or that you can do everything. You do, however, have to show that you're good at what the job requires. You also have to be comfortable using examples. These can show you're not exaggerating. They portray you as someone who can be counted on to produce results.

Immediate Preparation for the Interview

You have a job interview tomorrow. What do you do to get ready?

The first issue is how you will dress. When you were interviewing people to get the information you needed to set your career goals, you had a chance to observe how people typically dress for this job. This should be your guide. You want to dress at, or preferably slightly above, that level.

If you are applying for a clerical or manual job you should show up neatly dressed for work, so that you could begin immediately if that's what the employer wants. If interviewing for a professional job, get one of John Molloy's dress for success books. Molloy discusses color psychology and the total impression made by dress.

Do not fail to check on any dress code, formal or informal, in use at the firm where you are interviewing. We know of one company where there is a running joke about people who wear brown suits, and another where a memo was circulated suggesting that no one wear yellow ties. Silly though some of these things may seem, you have to know what the customs are. It's up to you to choose where you want to work, but if you want a job at a firm which has such rules you need to show up dressed appropriately.

Never underestimate the importance of appearance when dealing with someone you are meeting for the first time. One study of 600 managers in the life insurance industry found that over half of them were willing to make a hiring decision based only on a picture of the applicant!

It is easy to be irritated at this. In an ideal world, people should be hired because of who they really are, not because of how they look.

However, when people meet you, they don't know who you really are. The have only their first impressions. These first perceptions, for better or worse, are deeply colored (pun intended) by how you're dressed.

Employers read proper dress as a message that you know what's appropriate for a given occasion. Being well dressed signals that you take them, and the job interview, seriously. Being poorly or inappropriately dressed sends the opposite message. That alone will get the interview off to a bad start, which usually means no job offer unless you are somehow able to turn the interview around.

Our recommendation, therefore, is that you take a close look at your wardrobe, haircut and jewelry. If you are applying for a professional position, it is worth the expense to go to a store which specializes in business attire and purchase an "interview suit," complete with any needed accessories. If you are male and have a beard, you need to find out how common beards are in the field in which you are seeking employment.

In all of this, ask yourself one fundamental question: given an employer who does not know me well, but who desperately wants to know what I'm really like, what impression will my appearance give? If the frames on your glasses look out of date, an employer may take that as evidence that you are not the kind of person who keeps up with changes of all kinds. Flashy jewelry can suggest a personality which would not fit in a conservative organization. If you still use a tie clip or pen with the name of your old firm, the interviewer may wonder if the ties to your previous employer have been fully cut.

The point of this discussion is not whether an impression you give is accurate. It may not be. But an inaccurate perception will still influence the employer's behavior. What is important, therefore, is to control the impression you make as much as possible by dressing carefully and properly.

Pre-Interview Jitters

Before a job interview, review how nervous you usually get before stressful meetings. There are several things you can do to help yourself relax. While waiting for the interview, take some deep breaths. Try to think of the most calming scene you can imagine. Picture a waterfall. Imagine yourself standing on a high hill, with the ocean sparkling at the bottom of lush foliage, and a few balmy clouds in a deep blue sky. Let the peacefulness and beauty of the scene become part of you.

Avoid coffee and other drinks with caffeine on the day of the interview. This will help you stay calm. If you sweat when nervous, sit with your palms exposed. Let them dangle at your sides, or in your lap facing up, so that any sweat dries.

Another visualization exercise that can help is picturing yourself walking into a pleasant and successful job interview with someone whom you immediately like. Sometimes such a "mental movie" can become a self-fulfilling prophecy.

Finally, give yourself plenty of time so that you do not become tense and flustered if you get caught in traffic. Arrive at the building where the interview will be held early, so you have plenty of time to take a relaxed walk around the area, and still arrive at the appropriate office five to ten minutes early.

The First Few Minutes

How you will handle the first informal minutes of the interview is worth some thought. Research on job interviews suggests that interviewers establish a bias early in the exchange. A bad first impression can be overcome, of course, just as a good first impression can be ruined. Obviously, though, it's to your advantage to start out on the right foot.

The first few minutes in a job interview may often seem to be insignificant chatter. Actually, this is a much more important time than most people realize. Both parties are "breaking the ice," and trying to make each other comfortable. In addition, however, each is also sizing up the other.

The employer's first "gut reaction" to you plays a major part in determining whether you are ultimately offered the job. Employers frequently say they know within five minutes whether an applicant is the right person for a position. They may be right or wrong, but remember: they make the decision. It therefore makes sense to use these first few minutes to establish the beginnings of a good relationship.

If the interviewer has been seeing a series of candidates, for example, he or she is probably having a hard time telling one from the other. Interviewing can be a very boring process. Be sensitive to this, and let the employer talk about it. Chat a little about what it's like to interview all day. Let the interviewer see you as different from the others.

Early in the interview, look for a good time to bring up anything you have in common with the employer. Any similar experience (having attended the same college, majored in the same subject, grown up in the same city, having the same hobby or whatever) can help to generate a "we" feeling. This is the value of learning, before the interview, as much as possible about the person to whom you will be speaking.

Chris Kleinke has pulled together a variety of research findings on first impressions in a book entitled (appropriately enough) *First Impressions*. He reports that we think people like us if they look at us. Hence the importance of good eye contact during an interview. Sitting either too close or too far from people can make them feel either awkward or alienated. Sitting about four feet away seems most friendly. People tend to like us better if we lean forward a bit when talking, with body relaxed. It is also more pleasant when someone speaks without interruptions (such as stuttering, or constant "ah's" or "you know's").

There are some other findings which also have implications when interviewing. The more people are similar to us, the more likely we are to feel at home with them. Hence the value of finding something in common with an interviewer. Someone who disagrees mildly, and then agrees, is more attractive than someone who always agrees. There is therefore no need to avoid all disagreement during an interview. Just handle it smoothly. People usually like to be addressed by name, but job applicants who do it continually come across as insincere. We like those who disclose themselves to us, as long as they don't go overboard.

Into the Interview Itself

As the preliminary, informal exchanges subside, you will find yourself moving into the body of the interview. The interviewer will begin asking some questions. Your natural reaction at this point will be to sit back and do your best to answer each question as it comes. Pretty soon you will be deeply involved in a "ping pong" interview. The interviewer serves you a question, you hit it back, he or she serves another, and so on.

There is another approach which works better. It will keep the exchange positive, and focus the employer on the match between you and the job.

Make it your objective, during the first part of the interview, to discuss the demands of the position. That is, you and the interviewer should talk about the job itself, rather than about you. Aim for agreement on what needs to be done, what pitfalls must be avoided and what will constitute success or failure in the position in question.

How do you do this? Even though it takes an effort on your part, *start asking questions*. And it will take effort, because the natural psychology of the interview is to sit back and answer the interviewer's questions. You must resist that inclination. Begin questioning. And don't ask just anything. Ask, in as many ways as you can phrase it, one fundamental question: just what is it that you, the employer, want done?

There are many ways to put this. "Of course I know in general what the job requires, but you're closest to the needs of the organization. I would benefit a lot from knowing how you see the demands of the job." "I'm sure the person who had this job before me did some things better than others. Are there any aspects of the job you think need particular attention?" "In your expe-

rience with this position, what is the key skill or attitude that makes the difference?" "If you hire exactly the person you want for this job, what will happen as a result?"

You want the supervisor to stop focusing on you for now. Instead, you want to concentrate on the position for which you are applying. Even if you have a good idea of what the job demands, you want the person who will supervise your work to spell out what is desired in his or her own words.

Now Give Feedback

After several exchanges, when you have received a complete description of the job, summarize your understanding of the position's demands. "If I understand you correctly, then, what you're looking for is someone who can...."

The Positive Employment Interview
Introductory Chatting Establishing Rapport
Discussing the Demands of the Position
Summarizing What the Interviewer Said
Describing Your Skills, Experience and Personality
Expressing Enthusiasm about the Position Transitioning to an Offer or Next Meeting

There are three reasons for doing this summary, and each is important. First, if you have misunderstood something, it will be apparent. This gives the interviewer a chance to correct any misunderstanding. Second, you are communicating how seriously you take the job. You want to be sure you know what it demands. Third, you are demonstrating that you listen carefully to other people, and work at being sure you understand them.

Done properly, summarizing will generate in the interviewer a sense of having been heard. This should lead to a positive and friendly reaction toward you.

Be a Volunteer

With mutual agreement on the job's requirements, now is the time to volunteer more information about yourself.

"Well, let me tell you a few things about myself" — or words to that effect — will make the transition.

Your goal now is to tell the employer everything important about yourself that fits what you have just heard. Omitting anything irrelevant, review your job-related natural aptitudes (with examples). Summarize your prior work experience, emphasizing the quality of your work and what you learned from it. Note any extracurricular accomplishments that relate to this position. Make it clear that, point by point, you will be able to do this job unusually well. Spell out explicitly how the demands of the job match what you have to offer.

This self-presentation will work best if it has been carefully prepared. It is quite possible to give a short personal history in a minute or two. Give a few facts about your origins and education, your early job history, your most recent employment and your goals for the future. Then move on — discuss your skills, personality traits and interests, and their relevance to this job. The art of interviewing lies in your having this all well prepared, and yet adapting the presentation on the spot to what you have just learned about this particular position.

While doing this, be sensitive to non-verbal behavior. Suppose the interviewer takes a deep breath, or sits back in his or her chair. This may mean he or she is convinced that you are the person for the job. This may be the point to stop selling and begin closing (that is, asking for the job offer).

It Could Be a Bad Match

What if the match is not a good one? What if the employer's description of the position convinces you it would not be a good job for you after all?

Then say so. Your candor will allow one of two things to occur. In some cases the employer may be willing to redesign the position so that it *would* be a good fit. Alternatively, the meeting can be transformed from a job interview into a referral interview. You can point out why the demands of the job, now that they have been explained in detail, are not well matched to your skills. Indicate in a sentence or two what led you to think at first that it was a good match. Explain what you are really seeking. Ask if the interviewer can refer you to anyone, either in this organization or some other, where a position more consistent with your strengths can be found.

Don't be afraid that such candor will make you look bad. On the contrary, employers usually have great respect for those who know what they're good at. You obviously care enough about both yourself and the employer to decline a position at which you would not do your best work. At least some employers, realizing this, will go out of their way to help you find a more appropriate opening.

If the match is good, however, you should not hesitate to let the employer see your enthusiasm for the position. If you sense that he or she is convinced you are qualified for the job, you have reached an important milestone. The two of you agree on what the position requires, and you have shown you could fill it. What remains is the critical last step: the actual job offer.

The Key Is Being Positive

The approach to interviewing we have just outlined centers on a positive discussion about the job, and your fitness for it. This is important. Research on interviewing shows that negative information has far more impact on the final hiring decision than positive information. You want, therefore, to keep the entire discussion as positive as possible. If asked a question that would tend to draw a negative reply (for example, "What's your greatest weakness?") try to give a humorous or positive reply ("Well, I'm a lousy cook, so I sure hope you don't put me in charge of the company picnic"). Be particularly careful not to say anything negative about any past job or employer. This always makes a bad impression, and leaves employers wondering what you might later say about *them*.

If all has gone well up to this point, you are ready to move into the "end game." You need to wrap up the job offer, obtain the best possible salary and go to work. These topics are discussed in detail in the next chapter.

Occasionally this will all happen at the first interview. Usually, however, there will be at least a second meeting. There may be several, depending on the nature of the position and the number of people who are involved in the final hiring decision.

A considerable time may go by before you are phoned and offered the job. In the interim, final details must be worked out. Other candidates will be reviewed, references contacted if this has not been done already and higher authorities seen for approval.

Toward the Offer

What is essential at this point is to leave the interviewer with the clear understanding that you are seriously interested in the position. In addition, be sure there is an explicit agreement about when you will again be talking. The simple question, "What's the next step?" works well. If told you will be phoned next Thursday, ask if *you* can call sometime Wednesday or Thursday, and what would be the best time. Try hard to avoid a "don't call us, we'll call you" situation. Keep the initiative in your own hands if you can.

Then go home and immediately write a thank you letter. (It's a business letter, by the way, so it's perfectly appropriate to type it.) This letter serves several purposes.

First, just being polite enough to write it will set you apart from many applicants. Second, it is a perfect opportunity to repeat in writing some of the more positive exchanges you had with the interviewer. This reinforces the favorable impression you've made. Third, if you realize that something you said in the interview may have given a false impression, you can correct it.

Fourth, you'll probably think of something you should have said but didn't. Bring this up in the thank you letter.

Having done all this, mention when you will again be contacting the interviewer. Note anything you are going to do between now and then to follow up on the interview discussion. The whole letter, both in tone and content, should make it clear that you are a serious, competent and unusually strong applicant.

You will then need to do the follow-up work you promised in the interview, or mentioned in your thank you letter. With this done, you are ready for the final steps that will, all going well, take you into the job you've chosen.

The uncertainties of the process being what they are, however, you will continue seeking interviews with other firms. Don't let up until you receive an attractive offer, and accept it.

Thirteen. The End Game and After

The difference between interviewing for a job and going to work is a bit like the difference between dating and getting married. One tends to lead to the other, but not always. There is every potential for problems and misunderstandings along the way: broken dates, meetings with other suitors, sudden attacks of cold feet, offers later overruled by higher authority and even being left at the altar. It does happen that people show up for their first day at work and, because of something unexpected, find they don't have the job after all.

Experience teaches, therefore, that Yogi Berra is right. The game isn't over until it's over. No matter how promising a job possibility looks, your search efforts must continue until you receive and accept a job offer in writing.

Why Keep Going?

We know this is difficult to do. Some people even feel that it's somehow not *right* to interview seriously with more than one firm. The net result of slowing down, however, can be (and often is) that you find yourself in one of two awkward situations.

One possibility is that the job for which you waited falls through, sometimes after weeks or even months of discussion. In the meantime, other leads have gone unfollowed, and other possibilities unchecked. At this point you are likely to feel emotionally upset, and unenthusiastic about beginning again.

The other possibility is almost as bad. The job may eventually be offered, but with some negatives which were not previously mentioned. The pay is lower than expected, there is no travel budget, your office will be in an out-of-the-way and inconvenient location, the person with whom you wanted to work is leaving for another assignment or any number of other possibilities. You now have no other alternatives to turn to or use as bargaining chips. This presents you with a difficult decision. Should you accept a position that now seems much less desirable, or should you once again start up your job search activities?

There is no need to belabor the point. No matter how well an interview went, you must continue to see other employers. An employer who interviewed you will not hesitate to see a new applicant who shows up and looks interesting. Up to the point of accepting an offer and going to work, it's all just talk and possibilities, no matter how optimistic the talk or how promising the possibilities.

Checking Out the Company

We hope you do a good bit of homework on a company before going to an interview. If you leave an interview with a sense that it went well, so that a second interview is a good possibility, you will want to make additional efforts. Continue trying to learn as much as you can about the business and the people who work for it. You will need this information when deciding whether to accept a position if it's offered.

It does happen that people accept a job and then realize they've made a terrible mistake. After one week at work they know they're in the wrong place. If they're wise, they quit and immediately get back to their job search activities. The temptation, however, especially after a period of unemployment, is to make the best of things. At least now there's a paycheck coming in.

This is obviously a situation you want to avoid. Better to invest additional time and effort finding people (present or former employees, or business people who deal with the company) who can tell you what the place is really like. Tell them you interviewed there and naturally want to know as much as possible about the work environment. If the company knows what it's doing, they're carefully checking your references. You should be checking them out just as carefully.

Closing the Sale

In some interviews you will sense that the employer is almost ready to offer you a position. What should you do to get him or her over any final hesitation, so that a job offer is made?

This is the challenge which salespeople call "closing the sale." The most direct way to approach the issue is to say something like, "I've enjoyed our discussion. Frankly, after seeing what you have to offer, I want this job. What's the next step?" In many cases this will generate an immediate offer. The discussion can then turn to forms to be filled out, salary, starting date and so on.

You can also take a more subtle approach, saying something like, "I find this position very attractive. Do you have any reservations about *me* at this point?" If there are any, this question will tend to draw them out so you can deal with them. Quite often, the interviewer will realize that he or she has no reservations of any consequence, in which case the offer naturally follows.

Another way to move the employer toward a decision is to make the question hypothetical. "If you decide to offer me this position, when would you like me to start?" This moves the employer toward a discussion of concrete details. As you move toward agreement on these details, you can stick out your hand and say, "It sounds fine to me. How about it?" If the employer shakes your hand (and it's very hard *not* to under these conditions) you now have a job offer.

A final classic closing technique can work well in a situation where you believe the employer has essentially decided to offer you the job, but has not yet said so explicitly. Give him or her a choice of two options, under both of which you are hired. "Do you want me to start tomorrow, or wait until Monday?" Say it with a smile.

Final Details and All That

If an interview goes well, you may be told an offer will be coming if the final details can be worked out. At this point you want to clear up any remaining questions you have about whatever is essential to your getting the job done: the budget available for supplies or services, the extent of your authority and so on.

Let the employer know you see the job as desirable, and one you could do well. There is a fine line to walk at this point. You usually should not, as a matter of strategy, come right out and promise you will definitely accept the position. That has to be decided later. Yet you do want to show your interest and enthusiasm.

From your prior research, you should have a good idea of the typical salary range for the position you are seeking. If necessary, review these figures. The *Occupational Outlook Handbook* has salary data on most major occupations. The College Placement Council publishes average starting salaries for new college graduates. There is also information on salaries available from many professional associations. The National Telephone Cooperative Association publishes salaries in the telephone industry, for example. The National Association of Service Managers does the same for their membership. AMACOM (American Management Associations) collects salary data on groups such as middle managers and sales representatives. A reference librarian can help you find the particular figures you need.

You may be asked about your salary history. Under some conditions you will simply give the employer these figures. There are other times, however, when it will not be in your best interest to do so. Although you need to explain your position tactfully, your salary history is a private matter. No one has a right to know it. If you were paid less in the past, you do not want this to inhibit a good offer. If you were paid more, you do not want this to interfere with a job offer you want now.

Under these conditions, it is best to reply that you were paid fairly for prior jobs, given the circumstances. Now, however, you want to start fresh. Your past positions were different enough from what you are seeking that your past salary history is really not relevant. Keep the focus on the future. Negotiate your salary based on the skills you bring to the job, and what you will be doing for the company.

Negotiating Pay

In many cases, you will be asked what salary you expect. There are several ways to handle this question. Each approach has its advantages and disadvantages.

You can reply that, as a matter of principle, you prefer not to discuss salary until you have been offered the job. Until then, you would like to keep the discussion focused on the position itself, and your qualifications for it. Sometimes, "So may I consider that I've been offered the job?" may get you an explicit offer, or at least a clearer idea of how close you are to one.

Not naming a desired salary until the job is offered can work well when dealing directly with an employer who owns the business. It may not, however, be the best strategy when dealing with a major corporation. Here the person with whom you are negotiating usually needs final approval for a salary offer from one or more higher officials. It can be essential that he or she leave the interview knowing what salary it will take to get you. Otherwise it will be difficult to negotiate intelligently with the executives who must approve the offer.

You can always throw the pay question back at an employer: "I'm sure a company like yours would offer a fair salary for a position like this. What did you have in mind?" The interviewer will usually then name either a figure or a range. If a figure is given, you can indicate that something in that area would be acceptable. Or, if you think you can and should do better, you can pause for a minute, obviously surprised by an offer that is lower than expected. If you are asked for a reaction, answer that although you are enthusiastic about the position, you feel the salary is a bit modest. Then let the interviewer speak next, and negotiate from there.

If you don't feel comfortable doing it this way, try repeating the figure mentioned. Say it seems low, and you hope you haven't misunderstood the nature of the position. Then review the job's responsibilities in some detail. Point out that responsibilities at this level normally call for a salary of a certain range (high twenties to low thirties, for example). You don't understand why the employer is considering a salary which is lower than this. Notice that the focus of salary discussions is always on the appropriate pay for the work to be done. This is far more effective than discussing your personal needs or desires.

If a range is mentioned, repeat only the highest figure in the range. If the job is pegged at $18,000 to $20,000, you can say something like, "Well, $20,000 is not that far from what I had in mind. I'm sure we can work the salary out without much trouble." If you think it is too low, mention the $20,000 figure and then proceed as in the last paragraph.

Another approach is to let the salary figure pass without comment. Go on to other concerns: fringe benefits, use of a company car or any other form of compensation. You are implicitly indicating the offer is low, and seeing if it is counterbalanced by any other attractive features.

Home in on the Range

Although all these approaches to salary negotiation can work well in particular situations, one method seems appropriate in almost any. Employers usually go into the final interview with a salary range in mind. People rarely say, "We'll hire someone at $24,687." They more commonly decide, "We need someone in the $23,000-25,000 area."

From your research, you should have a good idea of what this range is. You then construct your own range, with the bottom end at the middle of the employer's range, and the top end a bit above it. If your best guess is that the employer wants to hire in the $28,000-32,000 area, indicate you are looking for something around $30,000-34,000.

The value of this approach is that it allows you to give a direct answer to the employer's question about salary. At the same time, it helps you avoid naming a figure which is too low — thus causing the employer to wonder why you don't value yourself properly — or which is too high, so that you appear unrealistic. And the fact that you answer with a range rather than a figure leaves the matter open to negotiation.

The employer will usually feel a little cheap offering the lowest figure in your range. There is a natural tendency, therefore, to offer a salary somewhere in the middle. Because the middle of your range is toward the high end of what is likely, however, you have positioned yourself for a good offer.

Do It Your Way

If none of these approaches appeals to you, simply say you assume the company will pay a fair wage, and a good job is what's really important to you.

This is a weak reply, however, because applicants are expected to negotiate for the best possible salary. You may seem undesirably passive in not doing so. And, although accepting what's offered may appear to be the easy way out if you don't like to haggle, it has important disadvantages. It is much easier to get an extra $500 or $1000 in pay when you are hired than it will be to get that same amount as a raise after you have been working for six months or a year. This is true even if you are doing a fine job. To take a lower salary when hired in the hope of making it up later is a risky strategy. The odds are against you.

On the other hand, particularly if you are seeking an entry level position, there may be little leeway anyway. By accepting a standard salary, you make sure you do not appear unrealistic, or ask for more than the employer considers reasonable.

Be certain you at least know what the salary offer is, however. Occasionally people accept a job and don't ask, which can lead to a real shock when the first paycheck is opened.

If you did the preparatory work suggested in this book, you are more suitable for the job than most candidates. You have devoted much time and effort to finding a position which matches your interests, temperament, and natural and acquired skills. You are, as a result, likely to be more productive. There is no reason, then, that you shouldn't be fully paid for your work.

A Word to Women

Women who are setting employment and salary goals need to be aware that research on women in the labor market suggests four things. First, women are concentrated in a small number of occupations. Second, as the proportion of those who have a given job title becomes increasingly female, salaries decline. Third, it is somewhat rare for men and women to share the same job title *in the same firm*. A restaurant, for example, will often have mostly waiters, or mostly waitresses, but rarely half of each. Fourth, women often stay at the same real salary (net of inflation) over their working careers, while men usually go up. This is particularly true when most of those holding a given job title are women.

The practical implication is that women who wish to earn higher salaries should seek positions where most of those with the same job title are men. They also need to learn as much as they can about the potential for women in occupations that attract them.

How does it happen that women do so poorly compared to men? There is no single answer to this question, but some important factors are clear. One government study found that women receive much less on-the-job training. This is important. It is on-the-job training that allows you to be promoted, or to leave one job and go to another with higher skill levels, and so to earn higher pay.

Another long-term study found that women are largely excluded from positions on both extremes of the occupational prestige range. Although women often start at more prestigious jobs, they do not advance, while men do. Women's earnings increase because of educational attainment, but not because of work experience, in such occupations as nursing and library work. Even here, men are overrepresented at the higher levels.

Two other factors may also be involved. A study of the "strength of weak ties" idea discussed earlier found that, although women belong to just as many voluntary organizations as men, their organizations are typically much smaller. Men are therefore exposed to more potential "weak ties," and may hear of more job possibilities. Men work more hours and more overtime. Finally, men stay longer with a given employer. Women move in and out of the labor market more often, and hence do not get the returns to seniority that men get.

Whatever the reasons, let no one doubt the power of sexual discrimination. *Business Week* once quoted a study by a Stanford psychiatrist who followed the results of 170 people involved in sex-change operations. He found that each person who changed from female to male had higher earnings after the change!

No practical implications are suggested.

Periodic Review

However you negotiate starting salary, be sure to ask for a periodic review of your work, including a salary review, during your final negotiations. Make it clear you want to be paid according to the quality of your work. Ask for feedback from your supervisor on how to improve on the job. If your work is deficient in any way, you want to be aware of the problem so you can correct it. On the other hand, if your work is excellent, then naturally you want to be paid accordingly.

This commitment to regular salary reviews is particularly important if you accept a starting salary lower than you had planned. Unless there is a definite agreement to review your work and salary regularly, you may be permanently underpaid.

The Last Few Steps

Let us assume you have been offered a job, with all details of salary and other matters settled. It is usually best, since this is an important decision, to take two or three days before you submit a written reply. This is common practice, and almost all employers expect it. Asking to delay a decision much beyond three days, however, can cause problems. The employer may begin to think you are indecisive, or not as seriously interested in the job as you claimed.

Use these two or three days to talk things through with your family, and to complete any final research you need to do on the company. In addition, go back to other employers with whom you interviewed. Let them know you have a firm offer. Ask if they can make a decision in the next day or two. It is always possible this will move them to action. You may get an even better offer.

The most difficult situation is the one where you have a strong preference for a job which has not yet been offered to you, and then receive another offer to which you must respond quickly. Sometimes you can stall for a day or two beyond the customary three days by asking that the offer be put in writing. In the meantime, you can candidly tell the company you prefer that they are your first choice, but that you need a definite answer. If you can get an answer from them quickly, you may get the position you want.

If not, though, your best bet is to take the job that's been offered. Stalling too long may leave you in the worst of all worlds: not receiving the offer you want, and so finally accepting the other offer — with a company that now has cause to doubt your commitment and loyalty.

What to Do if You Have Two Good Offers

Any negotiating with more than one employer requires you to act diplomatically. Some employers do not like being played off against one another. On the other hand, an employer who still has some doubts about the wisdom of hiring you will often feel much better knowing other employers are also after you. Changing his or her attitude from "Am I doing the right thing?" to "I'd better hurry or someone else will get this person first" is to your benefit. Even if the original salary offer is not raised in the process, and you decide to take the job anyway, you will come on board as a more esteemed new employee if you handle this stage of the negotiations carefully.

The final thing to do, when you decide which offer to accept, is to write a letter formally accepting the position. Be sure to summarize your understanding of the conditions of employment. Be specific about the authority you will have, the agreed-upon timing of work and salary reviews, any training you have been promised, future promotion possibilities and so on. Do your best to get a reply that confirms these agreements. These letters will go into your personnel file. You should, of course, keep copies.

If the passage of time dulls memory, or the person who interviewed you goes on to another assignment, there is a written record of what transpired. You might not be able to make these letters stand up in court, but at least you have documents to which you can refer at a later date.

Ending

There is something to be said for leaving your job search activities in limbo until after completing the first day on your new job. Then, and only then, get back to everyone who helped you along the way. Thank them, and let them know where you're working. And, of course, let any employers who interviewed you know you're no longer available.

Be sure these notes and phone calls are warm and friendly. Invite others to keep in touch. This is partly a matter of courtesy and gratitude. In addition, although you're employed now, who knows what your situation (or theirs) will be a year from now?

Now What?

You're at work at last. You've got a job, and one which is reasonably close to what you wanted. Now, believe it or not, is the best time to start preparing to get your next job.

There is a high probability, in today's economy, that before too many years you will be seeking a new position. An extended discussion of how to prepare yourself for future possibilities is beyond the scope of this book. There are a few particularly important things, however, which are worth mentioning.

1. *Map the organization.* Find out who the most productive people are, and get to know them. Be particularly sensitive to the possibility of finding a mentor. An older and more experienced person who will introduce you to others, and advise you on the most effective ways to handle problems, can be a great help. A study of executives mentioned in the "Who's News" column of the Wall Street Journal found that nearly two-thirds of these successful administrators reported having had a mentor or sponsor. There was a clear payoff for this group. They earned more money at an earlier age, and were more likely to follow a career plan. They also said they were happier with their career progress than did those who had no mentors.

2. *Keep careful records* of your achievements. Invest five or ten minutes each Friday afternoon jotting down what you accomplished during the past week. As they build up, these records can be a real help. When you get ready for your periodic salary and performance reviews, you will have easily available data to bring to the discussions. If you decide to leave your present position, these records will make it much easier to review your skills and re-think what you most enjoy and do best. They are the raw material for a new and updated resume. You will need them as you prepare an effective presentation of your experience and accomplishments for your next set of employment interviews.

3. *Set specific goals* and, when appropriate, share these goals with your employer. If you know what you want, and your employer does too, it will be easier for you to get it. Do not let average salaries in your field limit your salary goals. The best people in any field do much better than average. A recent government survey found, for example, that accountants earn more than technicians. The top tenth of

engineering technicians, however, earn more than four-fifths of accountants. Similarly, the top tenth of drafters earn more than half of all engineers. Average salaries can mislead. Find out the range of salaries in your field, not just the average.

4. *Keep up your contacts* and data gathering. Informational and referral interviewing have introduced you to a variety of helpful people. Now that you have an increased appreciation of the value of personal contacts when gathering information and obtaining referrals, build up your contact list. Get in the habit of recording names, addresses and phone numbers as you meet new people.

5. *Seek visibility*. It's not enough for career advancement to do a good job. Other people have to know where you excel. Writing for professional journals and newsletters is an excellent way to attain visibility. So is chairing committees or being elected to office in local and state professional associations. The next time you seek a new job you'll find the process much easier if people already know you and your work. If you do this well, you may simply be able to let word get around that you are thinking of moving. People who think well of you will then come on their own initiative to discuss job possibilities.

Keep Building on Strengths

Now that you have made the effort to think through your strengths, you are better prepared to continually seek ways to build on them. You want to acquire a wider variety of specific skills, and a greater range of experience. At the heart of the process discussed in this book is an explicit awareness of what you do best and enjoy most. What will change your life is the commitment to become highly skilled and widely experienced in these areas. Not only will this lead to the best situation for you, but to increased productivity for your employers.

The labor market, as you have learned, is just that: a market. If your new job is challenging and enjoyable, it should lead to the acquisition of additional skills and experience. It is these which will allow you to reenter that labor market with even more to offer, should you need to do so. It is experience and transferable skills, combined with your ability to find information and communicate effectively with employers, which will get you to the right place at the right time.

NOTES

NOTES

Chapter One

A more detailed discussion of the labor market changes reviewed in this section, along with specific references for each piece of information cited, can be found in Robert Wegmann, Robert Chapman and Miriam Johnson, *Looking For Work in the New Economy*. This book is available for $15.95 from Olympus Publishing Company, 1670 East Thirteenth South, Salt Lake City, UT 84105.

Throughout the book, we have used "professional" as a convenient way to describe any job requiring a college education. The more complete way to describe these jobs is "professional, technical, managerial and wholesale sales." We chose the common usage because we thought it would make easier reading.

Readers with an interest in public policy may well object that we do not argue for economic and social changes that would lower the rate of unemployment. We have not done so for two reasons. First, these topics are highly controversial. More important, the purpose of this book is to help people deal with the present situation, and few individuals are in a position to make the changes in public policy needed to lower unemployment and stimulate new job creation. We agree that much needs to be done, but that is the topic of a different book. We also worry that deploring the lack of needed social change can be an excuse for not vigorously pursuing the employment opportunities that do exist.

All statistics through 1985 are actual. The 1990 and 1995 figures are projections done by the Bureau of Labor Statistics. Most of these projections are summarized and discussed in the November 1985 issue of *Monthly Labor Review*. Results of the follow-up study of 1979-1980 college graduates were published in the Summer 1984 issue of *Occupational Outlook Quarterly*. Both of these publications of the Department of Labor are available in almost any college or university library.

The Bureau of Labor Statistics is the government agency which collects information on jobs and workers. The data they supply can be a real help in understanding why you have a hard time getting one job and a much easier time getting another. You do, though, have to understand their "lingo." As the Red Queen said to Alice in *Alice in Wonderland*, "I pay my words well, and I expect them to mean what I want them to mean."

When the Bureau of Labor Statistics talks about the "labor force," they mean both those who have jobs and those who are seeking them. In other words, the number of people in the labor force is the sum of the employed and the unemployed.

To be counted as unemployed, a person has to be actively looking for work. To meet this requirement, he or she must have contacted at least one employer in the last month to apply for a job. Persons not in the labor force are those who are not applying for jobs. This includes people who want jobs but don't believe they can find them, those who are retired, in school, working as homemakers, and so on.

It is not physically possible for any government agency to take a total count of the employed and unemployed. Instead, the Census Bureau selects a large random sample (about 60,000 households) each month and visits them in order to collect information on employment and unemployment. Data are also collected directly from a sample of employers. While these sampling techniques are imperfect, the projections and estimates generated by the Bureau of Labor Statistics are much better than many people realize. It is a very professional agency.

Chapter Two

The figures in Table 6 were published in the *Wall Street Journal* (June 4, 1986): 10. The Census Bureau, which is part of the United States Department of Commerce, regularly provides updated information on population growth and decline in both central cities and metropolitan areas.

Chapter Three

It has become common for either the corporation closing a plant or the government to offer job search assistance to workers who are losing their jobs. There is a discussion of how to run such group job search programs in *Looking for Work in the New Economy*, cited in the notes to Chapter One. Many of those who could participate in these job search groups, which are available without charge, do not bother to use them. They seem to assume that they have gotten jobs before, and will do so again. By the time many of these workers realize how things have changed, and recognize that they need assistance, the groups are often no longer available. This is a particularly serious problem in plants with many older workers who have high levels of seniority and have not sought work in many years.

Chapter Four

Bernard Haldane places a strong emphasis on the importance of building on strengths in his book, *How To Make A Habit Of Success* (Washington, DC: Acropolis, 1975). Haldane is a founder of modern career counseling, and this little paperback is a good source for his main ideas.

The quotation from Norah Lofts is from Ralph Daigh's *Maybe You Should Write A Book* (Englewood Cliffs, NJ: Prentice-Hall, 1977).

The Comments of Peter Drucker can be found in his book *The Effective Executive* (New York, NY: Harper and Row, 1967). This is an extraordinarily well written and thoughtful volume. Much of what Drucker says about managing a corporation also applies to managing one's own life.

The self-descriptions and accomplishments contained in Sections II and III are largely taken from papers done by students at the University of Houston — Clear Lake. They have been lightly edited for readability and to remove references to specific individuals.

Richard Bolles' *What Color Is Your Parachute?* (Berkeley, CA: Ten Speed Press, annual editions) has deservedly become a classic job hunter's guide. My debt to his ideas is great. Because the book is revised yearly, it continues to grow and improve. Through the work of the National Career Development Project, Bolles is in touch with thousands of people who are unemployed or considering career shifts. It is this contact that helps to keep his work fresh, up-to-date and realistic. The concept of trioing, the list of 244 verbs, and the *Quick Job Hunting Map* are also his creations, used with his permission.

Eli Djeddah's *Moving Up* (Berkeley, CA: Ten Speed Press, 1978) draws on his many years of experience doing career counseling with Haldane Associates. It is a good source of practical ideas, particularly about how corporate people go about the hiring process.

Another good discussion of the skills needed to do a job, as well as the process of deciding what job you want and how to get it, can be found in Howard Figler's *The Complete Job-Search Handbook* (New York, NY: Holt, Rinehart & Winston, 1979).

Studs Terkel has over a hundred short descriptions of what people do for a living and how they feel about it in his book *Working* (New York, NY: Avon, 1972). What people told Terkel over and over was that their jobs were too small for them. Toward the end of the book, in a section called "Second Chance," there are some good descriptions of people who have successfully changed occupations.

Offices of the Johnson O'Connor Research Foundation can be found in over a dozen major cities around the country. For more information, write the foundation at 161 East Erie Street, Chicago, IL 60611, or call them at (312) 787-9141.

Chapter Five

Tom Jackson's *Guerrilla Tactics in the Job Market* (New York, NY: Bantam Books, 1978) is an excellent summary of job choice and job search procedures. The grid combining personality traits and skills in this chapter, and that combining interests and skills in the next, is adapted from Jackson's book.

There are several books which discuss the use of visualization as a way of creatively picturing a job that's right for you. Among them are Barbara Sher's *Wishcraft* (New York, NY: Viking, 1979), Adelaide Bry's *Visualization: Directing the Movies of Your Mind* (New York, NY: Barnes & Noble, 1979) and Frances Vaughn's *Awakening Intuition* (Garden City, NY: Doubleday Anchor, 1979). *Wishcraft* is an outstanding book on life/work planning, and is particularly recommended.

The decision tree is taken from the books by John Crystal and Richard Bolles mentioned in the notes for Chapters Four and Six. If you have an Apple II computer, there is a BASIC program that will allow you to work through the decision tree process on screen, and then give you a printed list of your factors, in priority order. This is a real time saver when you have many lists to work with. The program can be found at the end of "Appendix C" in Richard Bolles' book, *What Color is Your Parachute?*

Chapter Six

There are several excellent books on adult growth and development. Their ideas have much influenced this chapter. Daniel Levinson's *The Season's of a Man's Life* was originally published by Knopf in 1978. A paperback edition is available. Roger Gould's *Transformations* also came out in 1978, from Simon and Schuster, and is available in paperback. Lillian Rubin's *Women of a Certain Age* (New York, NY: Harper Colophon, 1981) has an excellent discussion of the achievement needs of women at midlife, based on interviews with 160 women aged 35 to 54. George Vaillant's *Adaptation to Life* (Boston, MA: Little, Brown, 1977) is a follow-up study of the 1939-1944 graduates of an eastern university (presumably Harvard). These men were in their fifties at the time of the follow-up, so the book has a longitudinal perspective. Finally, a useful study based on men from a wide range of socioeconomic levels is reported in Michael Farrell and Stanley Rosenberg's *Men at Midlife* (Boston, MA: Auburn House, 1981). Their findings are much more pessimistic than the other studies, which focused more on middle and upper-middle class populations. They see more avoidance than growth during the adult years, and many casualties.

Richard Irish's books on job choice and job search make stimulating reading. In addition to *Go Hire Yourself an Employer*, revised edition (Garden City, NY: Doubleday Anchor, 1978) he has also written *If Things Don't Improve Soon I May Ask You to Fire Me* (Garden City, NY: Doubleday Anchor, 1976). Running through Irish's books is a theme: jobs must be both big enough for a person's spirit and well matched to an individual's "flair factor" (that vital skill, capacity, or orientation that the job requires). Irish believes in changing jobs and careers frequently. As he sees it, a "growth job" depends on the quality of your judgment, is fun, addresses real needs, involves risk and ends when the task is done.

A book by John Crystal and Richard Bolles, *Where Do I Go From Here With My Life?* (Berkeley, CA: Ten Speed Press, 1980) is a must for anyone professionally involved with career counseling. This volume, however, is not a "book" in the sense of a continuing narrative. It is, instead, a description of what John Crystal does in his life/work planning workshops. This sometimes makes for challenging reading. It's hard to capture the action and exchange of a good workshop in print. Nonetheless, there is a wealth of information and insight to be found here.

Barbara Sher's *Wishcraft* (New York, NY: Viking, 1979), mentioned briefly in Chapter Five, is also excellent reading. She has a solid approach to thinking through interests, personality and style. Our Style Identification Exercise is adapted from one of her ideas. She also presents an unusually effective method for goal-setting. Above all, she urges her readers to build the necessary social support system to make sure their goals are achieved. Her strong sense of the way personal accomplishments are rooted in social settings is a necessary corrective for the almost totally individualistic orientation of most books about career choice and job search.

Paula Robbins' *Successful Midlife Career Change* (New York, NY: American Management Associations, 1978) has a summary of research in the area of adult growth and development. She gives a good description of how a group of middle class men successfully accomplished major occupational changes in midlife.

The poll information on high school students' attitudes toward work and career choice is taken from Diane Hedin, Howard Wolfe, Jerry Fruetel and Sharon Bush, *Youth's Views on Work: Minnesota Youth Poll* (Minneapolis, MN: University of Minnesota, 1977).

Two other books which discuss the ideas in this chapter and are worth reading are Richard Bolles' *The Three Boxes of Life* (Berkeley, CA: Ten Speed Press, 1978) and John Wareham's *Secrets of a Corporate Headhunter* (New York, NY: Atheneum, 1980). Bolles' book has a strong emphasis on the need to avoid the "victim mentality" and take control of one's life. He also has a wealth of information and suggestions on how to do this. Wareham, on the other hand, spent many years recruiting top executives, trying to find just the right person to fill a particular corporate position. He has an excellent sense of what makes some matches work, and others fail. Wareham also has a good feel for the influence of family background on occupational choice and job performance. He notes that, although academics debate whether nature (genetic inheritance) or nurture (upbringing) plays the major part in personality formation, it is parents who provide both.

Edgar Schein's concept of career anchors is discussed in his book *Career Dynamics* (Reading, MA: Addison-Wesley, 1978), in chapters 10, 11 and 12. This is an unusually good book on the relationship between the organization and the individual. Anyone who is interested in career development in a corporate setting will find it useful reading.

A draft of the discussion of career anchors in this chapter was sent to Professor Schein for his comments. He was kind enough to send back an exercise which he had designed to help people think through their career anchors. Drawing on his experience with that exercise, he also made an important point: questionnaires and other "forced choice" instruments, used by themselves, may produce only superficial insight. There is a strong temptation to respond based on an idealized self-image instead of experience. Professor Schein has found that real growth in self-knowledge comes from the interactive process of reviewing one's career history with another person. This makes it possible to discuss the reasons why different career decisions were made.

His comments, based on wide experience, reinforce what has been emphasized throughout this section. Thinking through your skills, interests and personality traits, and how these blend together, is best done with the help of others whom you trust. If you try to do all this work alone, the danger of self-delusion is great. Another person can question you, and provide you with an opportunity to talk things out. He or she also serves as a "reality check" for you as you reflect on these issues. Professor Schein has recently published his own instrument to identify career anchors, to be used with such a partner. It is *Career Anchors: Discovering Your Real Values* (San Diego, CA: University Associates, 1985).

Arthur Miller and Ralph Mattson have written an intriguing book, *The Truth About You* (Old Tappan, NJ: Fleming H. Revell, 1977). Their concept of a motivational pattern which recurs throughout life is thoughtfully developed and illustrated. This is an important book which has not received as much attention as it deserves.

Chapter Seven

Max Gunther's *The Luck Factor* (New York, NY: Macmillan, 1977) is an interesting and enjoyable book. In addition to gregariousness, some of the other characteristics he noted in "lucky" people were: an ability to generate accurate hunches; a willingness to act boldly if a good opportunity comes along; a determination to cut losses and an unwillingness to trust luck. These people know that Murphy's Law ("If anything can go wrong, it probably will") is the only universal rule of human life!

Ben Greco has a good discussion of the importance of researching the entire industry as well as a specific firm in *How to Get the Job that's Right for You* (Homewood, IL: Dow Jones-Irwin, 1980).

Alden Todd's *Finding Facts Fast* (Berkeley, CA: Ten Speed Press, 1979) reviews a variety of practical research methods and names many useful sources of information. A researcher, Todd argues, is part reference librarian, part university scholar, part investigative reporter and part detective. There is much information available. The trick is to find it. Most people give up too quickly. When you can't find something, ask yourself: Who needs to know? Who would care enough to put it in print?

Chapter Eight

Charles Guy Moore's *The Career Game* (New York, NY: National Institute of Career Planning, 1978) is an excellent analysis of the factors to be considered when choosing an occupation. He has a thorough discussion of how to get the necessary information, not only to make an employment decision, but also to maximize the probability of successful advancement. His approach has had a major influence on the presentation in this chapter.

Ben Greco's *How to Get the Job That's Right for You* (Homewood, IL: Dow Jones-Irwin, 1980) draws on his many years of experience as Director of Career Services, Graduate School of Business Administration, University of Southern California.

Many employers think of their work forces as consisting of two parts: a core group who will be kept on the payroll no matter what; and a flexible group who are hired when business is good and let go as business declines. Obviously, when seeking employment, it is important to know which of these groups you are joining. Research on this issue is reported in Marged Sugarman's "Employer Dualism in Personnel Policies and Practices: Its Labor Turnover Implications," in Malcolm Cohen and Arthur Schwartz, eds., *Proceedings of the Employment Service Potential Conference* (Ann Arbor, MI: Institute of Labor and Industrial Relations, 1978): 117-148.

A dated but still entertaining book which communicates an irreverent sense of what you can learn by interviewing is Peter Sandman's *The Unabashed Career Guide* (New York, NY: Collier Macmillan, 1969). Reading this book will give you a good feel for what to believe, and what to take with a grain of salt, when gathering occupational information. A more recent and very useful example of the information that can be gathered to aid an occupational choice is Glenn Kaplan's *The Big Time: How Success Really Works in 14 Top Business Careers* (New York, NY: Congdon & Weed, 1984).

Management positions often begin with rapid promotions and raises, but then advancement slows and eventually stops. What happens next is discussed in Emanuel Kay's *The Crisis in Middle Management* (New York, NY: American Management Associations, 1974).

For a good sense of how varied the personalities of different organizations can be, read Rosabeth Kanter and Barry Stein, eds., *Life in Organizations* (New York, NY: Basic Books, 1979).

To interview well, you need to be comfortable acting in your own self-interest, and willing to ask others for assistance. Those who have difficulty in these areas will find it useful to read a book by Robert Alberti and Michael Emmons, *Your Perfect Right* (San Luis Obispo, CA: Impact, 1978). A certain degree of assertiveness is essential to every part of the job search process, and it can be worth the time and expense to obtain some assertiveness training if you need it. The essential thing to remember is that you always have a right to ask, others always have a right to say no, and neither party need be embarrassed to say either.

For a different perspective on interviewing, read John Brady's *The Craft of Interviewing* (New York, NY: Vintage, 1977). Brady discusses the interviewing done by reporters and writers. Their goals are the same as yours: get the interview; relax the interviewee; and then learn as much as you can from him or her.

If you want to find all of the principles discussed in this book in a novel, read Allen Dodd's *The Job Hunter* (New York, NY: McGraw-Hill, 1965). It is long since out of print, but can be found in some libraries (try interlibrary loan if your local library doesn't have a copy). What fascinates us is that this novel was written well before today's widely read books on choosing and finding employment, and yet contains all of their important ideas.

We thank Patsy Dozier for her last-minute assistance in preparing the sample resumes in Chapter Eight for publication.

Richard Lathrop's *Who's Hiring Who* (Berkeley, CA: Ten Speed Press, 1977) contains an excellent section on resumes (which he prefers to call "qualifications briefs") and cover letters, with many examples. These qualifications briefs are essentially functional resumes. Lathrop argues that a good qualifications brief, like a lawyer's brief in a court case, is totally focused on arguing your qualifications for the job. Instead of trying to list every job title you have had over the years, a qualifications brief first states your occupational objective. This goal statement contains a

description of your strongest skills. The brief then presents evidence demonstrating that you really have these skills and could do the job. Since most resumes run out of steam at the end, Lathrop argues, your last sentence or two should be particularly interesting and thoughtful. If the reader is still somewhat uncertain whether to invite you for an interview, the last section of your brief should motivate a favorable decision.

A simple form of resume for high school students is described and illustrated in Bernard Haldane, Jean Haldane and Lowell Martin, *Job Power* (Washington, DC: Acropolis, 1980). Another good source of ideas to use with high school students is Martin Kimmeldorf's *Job Search Education* (New York, NY: Educational Design, 1985).

Chapter Nine

Studies containing the data on job search behavior cited in this and the other chapters in this section are summarized and referenced in Robert Wegmann, Robert Chapman and Miriam Johnson, *Looking for Work in the New Economy* (Salt Lake City, UT: Olympus Publishing, 1985).

Much of the work on referral interviewing has been done by Bernard Haldane and those who have worked with him. Among the books which discuss his approach are: Bernard Haldane's *How to Make a Habit of Success* (Washington, DC: Acropolis, 1975); Richard Germann and Peter Arnold, *Bernard Haldane Associates' Job and Career Building* (Berkeley, CA: Ten Speed Press, 1981); and Fli Djeddah's *Moving Up* (Berkeley, CA: Ten Speed Press, 1978). An interesting discussion of how this approach can be used by high school students can be found in Bernard Haldane, Jean Haldane and Lowell Martin, *Job Power* (Washington, DC: Acropolis, 1980).

Information on the extent to which employees who are referred by other workers are more likely to remain with an employer can be found in Phillip Decker and Edwin Cornelius III, "A Note on Recruiting Sources and Job Survival Rates," *Journal of Applied Psychology*, 64 (August 1979): 463-464; Joseph Ullman, "Employee Referrals: Prime Tool for Recruiting Workers," *Personnel*, 43 (May/June 1966): 30-35; and Martin Gannon, "Sources of Referral and Employee Turnover," *Journal of Applied Psychology*, 55 (June 1971): 226-228.

Evidence on how better-paying jobs are filled by informal referrals can be found in Mark Granovetter, *Getting A Job* (Cambridge, MA: Harvard University

Press, 1974), and in Lee Dyer, "Managerial Jobseeking: Methods and Techniques," *Monthly Labor Review*, 95 (December 1972): 29-30. Granovetter's work was done as a doctoral dissertation at Harvard. It is one of the best scientific studies of the job search process available. His concept of the "strength of weak ties" (the idea that you are more likely to hear about a job opening from someone you hardly know than from a close friend or relative) has been confirmed by additional research. A study by Nan Lin and his colleagues in New York State also discovered something else: the higher the status of the person from whom information is received, the more likely this information will lead to a good job. Lin studied a modified random sample of 399 males, aged 20 to 64. The mean income of respondents using weak ties was $2500 above that of those who only asked close friends and relatives about job possibilities. This study is reported in Nan Lin, Walter Ensel and John Vaughn, "Social Resources and Strength of Ties: Structural Factors in Occupational Status Attainment," *American Sociological Review*, 46 (August 1981): 393-405.

John Kotter, in his book *The General Managers* (New York, NY: Free Press, 1982), describes how a manager's success is related to his or her ability to develop a network of cooperative relationships. The people in this network are both above and below these successful managers, and are inside as well as outside the manager's organization. In a referral interview, what you are really doing is asking to be included in this network, which implies both a willingness to contribute to it and a need to draw from it.

Chapter Ten

The "no-no-yes" chart is taken from Tom Jackson, *Guerrilla Tactics in the Job Market* (New York, NY: Bantam, 1978). Jackson's treatment of the topic is worth reading.

Some degree of initiative and assertiveness is obviously essential when approaching employer after employer during a job search. One article on this is Kathleen Wheeler, "Assertiveness and the Job Hunt," in Robert Alberti, ed., *Assertiveness: Innovations, Applications, Issues* (San Luis Obispo, CA: Impact, 1977): 261-270.

Chapter Eleven

The research findings on the want ads cited in this chapter come largely from John Walsh, Miriam John-

son and Marged Sugarman, *Help Wanted: Case Studies of Classified Ads* (Salt Lake City, UT: Olympus, 1975); and U.S. Department of Labor, *The Public Employment Service and Help Wanted Ads: A Bifocal View of the Labor Market* (R&D Monograph 59). Other research on employment agencies is reported in "The Private Employment Agency as a Labor Market Intermediary," in *Labor Market Intermediaries* (Washington, DC: National Commission for Manpower Policy, 1978): 283-307. An interesting analysis of the want ads in one small town can be found in Herbert Meyer's "Jobs and Want Ads: A Look Behind the Words," *Fortune*, 98 (November 20, 1978): 88-90, 94, 96.

A good summary of information on the operation of private employment agencies can be found in Eve Gowdey, *Job Hunting with Employment Agencies* (Woodbury, NY: Barron's Educational Series, 1978). Chapter 3, "Agencies and Their Clients," is particularly useful. It presents one day in the life of an agency counselor, as he deals with one client after another.

A breezy look at what may be behind both employment agency and want ad action can be found in David Noer, *How to Beat the Employment Game* (Radnor, PA: Chilton, 1975).

Those interested in executive search firms should read Robert Perry's *How to Answer a Head-Hunter's Call: A Complete Guide to Executive Search* (New York, NY: American Management Associations, 1985).

Chapter Twelve

Particularly good treatments of how to interview well can be found in John Crystal and Richard Bolles, *Where Do I Go from Here with My Life?* (Berkeley, CA: Ten Speed Press, 1980) and Ben Greco, *How To Get the Job That's Right for You*, revised edition (Homewood, IL: Dow Jones-Irwin, 1980). The latter discussion has had a particularly strong influence on this chapter, and I am indebted to Ben Greco for his insight.

H. Anthony Medley is a lawyer who videotapes interviews with law students and sells them to major law firms. His book, *Sweaty Palms* (Berkeley, CA: Ten Speed Press, 1984), is based on his experiences conducting these interviews.

John Molloy has summarized his work on dress, and the impressions various forms of dress make on different types of people, in two books: *Dress for Success* (New York, NY: Warner, 1975) and *The Woman's Dress for Success Book* (New York, NY: Warner, 1978).

The psychology of first meetings is discussed in Leonard Zunin and Natalie Zunin, *Contact: The First*

Four Minutes (New York, NY: Ballantine, 1972). The Zunin's discovered that four minutes is the average time strangers who are introduced, or who strike up a conversation, spend with each other before deciding to go their separate ways. To meet someone and leave much before four minutes seems abrupt and impolite, so most people will chat for that period of time. To stay beyond four minutes, however, requires that a deeper contact be made. The key, suggest the Zunin's, is whether you can communicate a healthy self-confidence while creatively tuning in on the feelings of the other person. You need to show you are a caring and considerate individual who can listen sympathetically. If you can do this, they suggest, you can break through the "four minute barrier." Something similar may be happening in many employment interviews.

Chris Kleinke's book, *First Impressions* (Englewood Cliffs, NJ: Prentice-Hall, 1975) has a wealth of information that can be applied to the interview setting.

Another book with helpful ideas on interviewing is Robert Traxel, *Manager's Guide to Successful Job Hunting* (New York, NY: McGraw-Hill, 1978).

The place of assertiveness in the interviewing process is discussed in Thomas McGovern, "Assertion Training for Job Interviewing and Management/Staff Development," in Arthur Lange and Patricia Jakubowski, eds., *Responsible Assertive Behavior: Cognitive/ Behavioral Procedures for Trainers* (Champaign, IL: Research Press, 1976).

The research literature on job interviewing is quite extensive. Half a century's work, however, can be summed up in one phrase: keep it positive. For a discussion of this research, with citations, see Robert Wegmann, Robert Chapman and Miriam Johnson, *Looking for Work in the New Economy* (Salt Lake City, UT: Olympus, 1985).

Chapter Thirteen

David Noer has an interesting discussion of salary negotiations in *How to Beat the Employment Game* (Radnor, PA: Chilton, 1975). His other book, *Jobkeeping* (Radnor, PA: Chilton, 1976), has some equally useful thoughts on keeping the job once you've got it.

Several of Richard Germann's ideas on negotiating salary are used in this chapter. His book, *Bernard Haldane Associates' Job and Career Building* (Berkeley, CA: Ten Speed Press, 1981), is definitely worth reading.

John Crystal and Richard Bolles are convinced

that the "construct a high range" approach to negotiating salary is the wisest way to approach this problem. My discussion of that topic is heavily influenced by their ideas. See *What Color Is Your Parachute?* (Berkeley, CA: Ten Speed Press, annual editions).

A good discussion of the "reality shock" which is typically part of adjusting to a new employer, particularly in one's first full time job, can be found in Edgar Schein, *Career Dynamics* (Reading, MA: Addison-Wesley, 1978).

For an idea of how differently various interviewers approach the salary question, see Ann Marshall, "The Salary Subject: When Students Should Speak Up," *Journal of College Placement*, 42 (Summer 1982): 19-20. One point she makes is important. Although it is usually better to put salary questions off until a job is offered, this may not be wise when time and money must be spent traveling to another area of the country for interviews. An illustration will make the point. A colleague of one of us (Wegmann) was twice flown to a distant state to interview for an administrative position. When he asked about salary he was told not to be concerned about it. After investing much time and effort in the interviewing process, he was finally offered the job — at $15,000 below his present salary. He turned it down, and both he and the person making the offer ended up quite irritated because of the time and money that had been expended. This was one of those cases where both sides would have been better off discussing the range of possibilities earlier in the employment process.

Government data showing how misleading it can be to look only at average salaries can be found in "Average Salaries...And Why They're Not So Average," *Occupational Outlook Quarterly*, 25 (Fall 1981): 24-25.

Gerard Rouche's article on the value of mentors is "Much Ado About Mentors," *Harvard Business Review*, 57 (January/February 1979): 14-16, 20, 24, 26-28. The subject of mentors is also a major topic of discussion in most of the books on adult growth and development mentioned in the notes at the end of Chapter Six.

There are several good books on time management. They can be particularly helpful to someone who is starting in a new job (or trying to be more productive in an old one). Among them are Alan Lakein, *How To Get Control Of Your Time And Your Life* (NY: New American Library, 1973) and Edwin Bliss, *Getting Things Done* (NY: Bantam, 1978).

For data on how the earnings of both sexes decline

as the percentage of females in an occupation increases, see Aline Quester and Janice Olson, "Sex, Schooling and Hours of Work," *Social Science Quarterly*, 58 (March 1979): 566-582.

For data on the lower level of on-the-job training given women (and blacks), see Saul Hoffman, "On-the-Job Training: Differences by Race and Sex," *Monthly Labor Review*, 104 (July 1981): 34-36.

Long-term data on the changing status of men and women in the labor force can be found in William Sewell and Robert Hauser, "Sex, Schooling, and Occupational Status," *American Journal of Sociology*, 86 (November 1980): 551-83.

Information on the nature of the voluntary organizations which women join, and their smaller sizes, can be found in J. Miller McPherson and Lynn Smith-Lovin, "Women and Weak Ties: Differences by Sex in the Size of Voluntary Organizations," *American Journal of Sociology*, 87 (January 1982): 883-904.

Betty Harragan, a management consultant, gives her ideas on why women often fail to understand the "corporate game" in *Games Mother Never Taught You* (New York, NY: Rawson Associates, 1977). She is also the author of a follow-up book, generated by the many letters she received in response to her first volume, entitled *Knowing the Score* (New York, NY: St. Martin's Press, 1983).

The study on what happened to those involved in sex-change operations was quoted in *Business Week* (January 25, 1982): 12-13.

Two other books which can be helpful to those interested in a better understanding of the role of women in the labor market are Louise Howe, *Pink Collar Workers* (New York, NY: Avon Books, 1977) and a volume by the staff of Catalyst, an organization dedicated to the full participation of women in business and professional life, entitled *Upward Mobility* (New York, NY: Holt, Rinehart & Winston, 1981).

For a discussion specifically aimed at women and the way they should approach salary negotiations, see Sherry Chastain, *Winning the Salary Game* (New York, NY: John Wiley, 1980).

INDEX

INDEX